C0-AYI-746

Changing Health Care Systems and Rheumatic Disease

Committee on Changing Health Care Systems
and Rheumatic Disease

Division of Health Care Services

INSTITUTE OF MEDICINE

Frederick J. Manning and Jeremiah A. Barondess, *Editors*

NATIONAL ACADEMY PRESS
Washington, D.C. 1996

National Academy Press • 2101 Constitution Avenue, NW • Washington, DC 20418

NOTICE: The project that is the subject of this report was approved by the Governing Board of the National Research Council, whose members are drawn from the councils of the National Academy of Sciences, the National Academy of Engineering, and the Institute of Medicine. The members of the forum responsible for this report were chosen for their special competencies and with regard for appropriate balance.

This report has been reviewed by a group other than the authors according to the procedures approved by a Report Review Committee consisting of members of the National Academy of Sciences, the National Academy of Engineering, and the Institute of Medicine.

The Institute of Medicine was chartered in 1970 by the National Academy of Sciences to enlist distinguished members of the appropriate professions in the examination of policy matters pertaining to the health of the public. In this, the Institute acts under both the Academy's 1863 congressional charter responsibility to be an adviser to the federal government and its own initiative in identifying issues of medical care, research, and education. Dr. Kenneth I. Shine is president of the Institute of Medicine.

Support for this project was provided by the National Institute of Arthritis and Musculoskeletal and Skin Diseases (Contract No. N01-OD-4-2139, Task Order #15). This support does not constitute an endorsement of the views expressed in the report.

International Standard Book No. 0-309-05683-7

Additional copies of this report are available from: National Academy Press, Lock Box 285, 2101 Constitution Avenue, N.W., Washington, DC 20055.

Call (800) 624-6242 or (202) 334-3313 (in the Washington metropolitan area), or visit the NAP on-line bookstore at **http://www.nap.edu**.

Call (202) 334-2352 for more information on the other activities of the Institute of Medicine, or visit the IOM home page at **http://www.nas.edu/iom**.

Printed in the United States of America

The serpent has been a symbol of long life, healing, and knowledge among almost all cultures and religions since the beginning of recorded history. The image adopted as a logotype by the Institute of Medicine is based on a relief carving from ancient Greece, now held by the Staatlichemuseen in Berlin.

COMMITTEE ON CHANGING HEALTH CARE SYSTEMS AND RHEUMATIC DISEASE

JEREMIAH BARONDESS, *Chair*, President, New York Academy of Medicine, New York, New York
JORDAN J. COHEN, President, Association of American Medical Colleges, Washington, D.C.
DEBORAH A. FREUND, Vice Chancellor, Academic Affairs and Dean of Faculties, Indiana University, Bloomington, Indiana
BEVRA HAHN, Professor of Medicine and Chief, Division of Rheumatology, School of Medicine, University of California, Los Angeles
WILLIAM R. HAZZARD, Professor and Chairman, Department of Internal Medicine, The Bowman Gray School of Medicine, Wake Forest University, Winston-Salem, North Carolina
DEBRA R. LAPPIN, Senior Vice Chair, Arthritis Foundation, Englewood, Colorado
MICHAEL R. MCGARVEY, Senior Vice President, Health Industries Services, Blue Cross and Blue Shield of New Jersey, Inc., Newark, New Jersey
ROBERT NEWCOMER, Professor and Vice Chair, Department of Social and Behavioral Sciences, School of Nursing, University of California, San Francisco
NAOMI ROTHFIELD, Professor of Medicine and Chief, Division of Rheumatic Diseases, School of Medicine, University of Connecticut, Farmington

Project Staff

CLYDE BEHNEY, Director, Health Care Services Division
FREDERICK J. MANNING, Project Director
ANITA ZIMBRICK, Project Assistant
ANNICE HIRT, Administrative Assistant
NINA SPRUILL, Financial Associate

Preface

Despite the failure of the Clinton administration's efforts to establish a comprehensive national health care plan, market forces are today driving a radical restructuring of health care delivery in the United States. At the same time, the epidemiology and demography of health care conditions is changing and greater numbers of individuals live comparatively long lives with a variety of severe chronic diseases. Moreover, the needs of these populations are continually changing, as they experience the daily challenges imposed by their disorders as well as facing the need for access to effective primary and preventive care and hospitalization during acute illnesses.

Efforts to control accelerating health care costs were a major goal of the proposed health care reform, and are in large measure responsible for the rapid growth of "managed care" throughout the 1990s. Control of health care costs will be an empty victory, however, if it is achieved by sacrificing the quality of care. In 1994 the Institute of Medicine (IOM) released a White Paper, *America's Health in Transition: Protecting and Improving Quality*, announcing its intention to promote the development and application of quality assessment tools and to inform consumers, policymakers, and providers of opportunities for and obstacles to achieving high-quality health care.

As part of its quality initiative, the IOM proposed an invitational workshop examining the relationship, if any, between the mode of health care delivery and the outcomes of care for populations with serious chronic illness. The National Institute of Arthritis and Musculoskeletal and Skin Diseases (NIAMS) agreed to fund the project, understandably suggesting systemic lupus erythematosus (SLE) and rheumatoid arthritis (RA) as focal points representative of chronic diseases characterized by major disability, periodic acute flares, and complex clinical care needs involving generalists, subspecialists, and other care givers as well as requiring major involvement of the patient. The IOM appointed a small oversight committee for this activity and charged it with planning and conducting the workshop and producing a short consensus report for dissemination with the workshop proceedings. Not unexpectedly, recommendations for future research were a particular concern for NIAMS.

It quickly became apparent that there was little in the way of empirical data in the published literature that specifically addressed the effects of variations in the organization and financing of care on the treatment and health status of persons with RA or SLE. The committee thus chose to focus the workshop on recommendations for research to remedy this situation, and structured the workshop around a number of questions likely to be central to that research: What would ideal care look like? What are the best measures of outcomes? How is the subspecialist/generalist interface best managed? What are the current barriers to care, both patient-related and system-related? How easily do various care systems adopt new knowledge (and what kinds of new knowledge are imminent)? What kinds of systems make the best use of resources? What are the long-term implications of various delivery models for research, education, and training? Experts in chronic disease were invited to address these topics, using RA and SLE as their terms of reference wherever possible. Designated "reactors" insured that the committee heard a variety of views, and a small audience of invited guests added still more variety to the discussion engendered by each talk. Subsequent to the workshop, the committee reassembled in private to draw the conclusions and make the recommendations specified in the contract with NIAMS.

As committee chair I am acutely aware of the contributions that the Institute of Medicine staff have made to the success of the study. Special thanks are due to Project Assistants Annice Hirt and Anita Zimbrick, who made our travel and meetings as comfortable and convenient as possible and provided outstanding administrative support both at the meetings and in the painstaking production of the final report. We are particularly grateful to Study Director Rick Manning for his skilled and professional support through all phases of the committee's task.

Finally, I would like to acknowledge the individual and collective efforts of the committee members. It was a pleasure to have worked with this group of busy but unselfish professionals who volunteered their valuable time to share their knowledge and experience with their fellow scientists.

Jeremiah A. Barondess
Chair

Contents

1 **Introduction** 1
Changing Health Care Systems, 2
Chronic Disease, 5
Rheumatic Disease, 6
Practices and Achievements of Managed Care Systems, 7
Work Force Issues, 14
Research, Education, and Training, 15
The Workshop, 16

2 **Opening Remarks,** *Jeremiah A. Barondess,* 17

3 **Keynote Address,** *John M. Eisenberg* 21
Changing Health Care, 21
Hospitals, 22
Managed Care, 23
Physician Payment, 24
Specialist–Generalist Interaction, 25
Policy Issues, 28

4 **What Would Ideal Care Look Like?** 31
Introduction, *Jordan J. Cohen,* 33
Invited Address, *Halsted Holman,* 35
Invited Reaction, *Saralynn Allaire,* 47
Invited Reaction, *Teresa Brady,* 51
Invited Reaction, *Debra R. Lappin,* 55
Discussion, 67

5 **Managed Care and Rheumatoid Arthritis: Utilization and Outcomes Over 11 Years** 73
Introduction, *Bevra Hahn,* 75
Invited Address, *Edward Yelin,* 77
Invited Reaction, *Elizabeth Badley*, 85
Invited Reaction, *Bradford H. Gray*, 87
Discussion, 91

6 **Measuring Medical Outcomes: Longitudinal Data on the Differential Impact of Health Care Systems on Chronic Diseases** 95
Introduction, *Robert Newcomer*, 97
Invited Address, *Alvin R. Tarlov*, 99
Invited Reaction, *Carolyn Clancy,* 107
Invited Reaction, *Matthew H. Liang,* 109
Discussion, 111

7 **Changing Health Care Systems and Access to Care for the Chronically Ill** 115
Introduction, *Naomi Rothfield,* 117
Invited Address, *Karen Davis and Cathy Schoen,* 119
Invited Reaction, *Leigh F. Callahan,* 135
Invited Reaction, *Norman G. Levinsky,* 137
Discussion, 141

8 **Training and Utilization of Generalists and Subspecialists at the University of California, Los Angeles** 147
Introduction, *William R. Hazzard*, 149
Invited Address, *Alan M. Fogelman,* 151
Invited Reaction, *Jerome H. Grossman,* 159
Invited Reaction, *William Arnold,* 161
Discussion, 165

9 **How Easily Do Health Care Systems Adopt New Knowledge, and What Are the Likely Future Developments?** 169
Introduction, *Michael R. McGarvey,* 171
Invited Address, *Larry M. Manheim,* 173
Invited Reaction, *Mark L. Robbins,* 177
Invited Reaction, *Michael R. McGarvey,* 181
Discussion, 185

10 Issues and Insights Regarding Research, Education, and Training **189**
Introduction, *Deborah A. Freund,* 191
Invited Address, *Robert F. Meenan,* 193
Invited Reaction, *Robert Mechanic,* 201
Discussion, 203

11 Commentary on the Day's Papers, *John W. Rowe,* **209**

12 Conclusions and Recommendations **213**

Appendixes **223**
A Biographies of Committee Members and Speakers, 223
B Workshop Guests, 239

Changing Health Care Systems and Rheumatic Disease

1

Introduction

Many individuals with chronic conditions are concerned about the trend toward the creation of managed care systems. On the one hand, managed care systems seem ideal for integrating the financing and delivery of primary, acute, and chronic care of the types that such patients require; on the other hand, a major stimulus to the growth of managed care has been the hope that they will halt the spiraling costs of health care. Individuals with serious chronic conditions are likely to be frequent users of medical services (often complex sets of services requiring specialist attention) and to need assistance with daily living tasks. Consequently, a concern is growing that persons with serious chronic disorders will be excluded from, be underserved by, or receive inappropriate care from the kinds of integrated delivery networks now emerging.

Little information exists on the number of adults under age 65 with significant chronic conditions who are enrolled in managed care plans. Even less is known about differences in outcomes of care of individuals with chronic conditions across the array of managed care models. The present study grew out of the desire of the National Institute of Arthritis and Musculoskeletal and Skin Diseases (NIAMS) to convene significant stakeholders and researchers to determine what information can be gleaned from existing data and delineate the key research questions needed to address concerns regarding the effect of the changing health care system on the quality of care for individuals with chronic conditions, particularly chronic rheumatic diseases. Specifically, the Institute of Medicine (IOM) was charged with planning and conducting a workshop focused on the following questions:

1. Does the model of managed care or integrated delivery system (e.g.,

fully capitated managed care, gatekeeper-only model of managed care, discounted fee for service) influence (a) the types of interventions provided to patients with chronic conditions and (b) the clinical and health status outcomes of those interventions?

2. If so, are these effects quantitatively and clinically significant, as compared to the effects that other variables (such as income, education, or ethnicity) have on patient outcomes?

3. If the mode of health care delivery system appears to be related to patient care and outcomes, can specific organizational, financial, or other variables be identified to account for the relationships?

4. If not, what research agenda should be pursued to provide critical information about the relationship between types of health care systems and the processes and outcomes of care delivered to populations with serious chronic conditions?

NIAMS further suggested, in the interest of coherence, focusing the workshop on two autoimmune diseases with characteristics that would make them, as a set, case studies representative of other rheumatic diseases and chronic diseases in general. Systemic lupus erythematosus (SLE) is an intermittent, relapsing illness with effects that involve multiple organ systems. The main organs affected are joints, skin, kidney, brain, heart, and lungs. There is a relatively high probability of death at a young age, but the illness itself has the characteristics of an intermittent illness with peaks and valleys of severity and remission. In contrast, rheumatoid arthritis (RA) is an ailment that can range from very minor symptoms over a long time to an extremely crippling disorder with physical deformity of the joints—that is, it is a model of chronic, progressive, and severely disabling disease. Although persons with RA also have a reduced life expectancy, RA does not generally pose the same threat to life as SLE does. A considerable amount of information is already available about these two diseases; they represent quite different clinical, epidemiological, and social problems; and both diseases are significant contributors to morbidity and health care costs in the United States.

CHANGING HEALTH CARE SYSTEMS

In the early decades of this century the purchase and delivery of health care in the United States resembled typical transactions in other fields: patients directly purchased all or nearly all services from a general practitioner in solo practice. Rapidly accelerating growth in new medical knowledge and technology improved medical care, but increased both the number of specialists and the costs of treatment. Health insurance, most often subsidized by employers, assumed an increasingly important role after World War II. It helped consumers predict and control out-of-pocket expenses but, in the opinion of many, contributed to unsustainable rates of increase in medical costs by reducing patient concerns about price. The public policy and the payer response to these costs have been "managed care."

Managed care has many meanings. The most fundamental feature of managed health care is the "management" of physician practice. This occurs in the form of the selection and retention of physicians into eligible provider networks, utilization and practice pattern profiling and feedback, limits on provider reimbursement, financial risk sharing or other financial incentives to reduce costs, and most recently, practice guidelines specifying appropriate care for specific diagnoses. Varying combinations of these procedures are used within any one managed care plan or organization. As characterized by Miller and Luft[1] managed care plans include health maintenance organizations or HMOs, preferred provider organizations (PPOs), and point-of-service (POS) plans. HMOs themselves come in a variety of forms. Staff model HMOs (e.g., Group Health Cooperative) are characterized by directly employing physicians. Another type of HMO is the prepaid group practice (or group model HMO) in which an administrative entity (e.g., Kaiser Foundation Health Plan) has an exclusive relationship with one or more large medical groups (e.g., the Permanente Medical Group). This contrasts with a network HMO (e.g., Pacificare Health Systems) in which the medical group relationship is not exclusive. Finally, there is a mixed model HMO (e.g., Prudential Health Care Plans Inc.) in which the administrative intermediary may contract exclusively with medical groups and nonexclusively with solo practice physicians in the same area.

Preferred provider organization refers to the combination of financial intermediary organization and the network of providers with which it contracts to provide care. Providers in these organizations offer care to PPO enrollees on a fee-for-service (FFS) basis, generally at a discounted unit price from the community's "usual, customary, and a reasonable" price. Often there may be a preset fee schedule. PPO enrollees come from employer groups, unions, and other groups with which the PPO has negotiated the opportunity to recruit such members. Providers (e.g., solo and group practice physicians, hospitals, mental health and other providers) participating in a PPO usually have nonexclusive relationships (i.e., they may participate in more than one PPO and/or see patients independently). Providers participate in PPOs to gain ready access to patients. The absence of risk sharing by providers in a PPO places the incentives for utilization control on the PPO rather than the provider. PPOs have historically covered services from providers outside the plan's network

---

[1]Miller, R, and H Luft (1994). Managed care plans: characteristics, growth, and premium performance. *Annual Review of Public Health, 15:* 437–459.

at a lower rate and with higher copayments by the patient.

Point-of-service plans are variations on the provider "lock-in" provisions of both HMO and PPO coverage. The distinguishing characteristic of a POS plan is that enrollees can be covered for services obtained outside of the HMO or PPO network providers. When this is done, service copayments and deductibles usually are higher than they would be from a network provider. This type of coverage within an HMO is also called an "open-ended HMO plan." Both HMOs and PPOs are increasingly offering a point-of- service option for their enrollees.

This typology emphasizes the variations in the relationship between health care providers and the managed care organization. An alternative typology might instead emphasize the manner in which the consumer (the patient) pays for health care. Many of the earliest managed care plans were staff model HMOs that paid their providers a fixed salary and in turn charged their members (patients) a fixed annual fee independent of services required or received. Later variations, which did not actually employ providers, extended their members a similar fixed annual fee plan by paying their contracted providers a fixed amount per member (capitation). As noted above, many of the PPOs and POS plans that have flourished most recently have returned to an FFS payment system and have cut costs instead by using their large membership to negotiate reduced fees with participating providers.

Managed care plans began to become more widespread during the 1980s as employers reacted to high rates of increase for indemnity health care insurance premiums. By 1993, all types of HMO plans covered 26 percent of the employees of mid-and large-size employers. Other forms of managed care (e.g., PPO and POS) had enrolled 36 percent of those insured, while those covered by indemnity insurance had declined to 42 percent.[2] The movement from indemnity toward managed care coverage has varied greatly by region of the country and local market area, but the trend toward capitation as the dominant payment method seems established. Although no consensus has developed concerning the ideal managed care strategy, some now estimate that indemnity products will represent only about 10 percent of the insurance market by the turn of the century.[3] As a recent IOM report noted,[4] medical practices and plans across the country are devising a variety of ways to provide affordable health care within the limits of this country's preferences

---

[2]McMillan, A (1993). Trends in Medicare health maintenance organization enrollment: 1986–1993. *Health Care Financing Review*, 15: 135–46.

[3]Armstead, R, P Elstein, and J Gorman (1995). Toward a 21st century quality-measurement system for managed-care organizations. *Health Care Financing Review, 16:* 25–37.

[4]Institute of Medicine (1994). *Defining Primary Care: An Interim Report.* Washington, DC: National Academy Press.

for high technology, a wide choice of providers, and particular methods of financing and organization.

CHRONIC DISEASE

Today's health care system has emerged from an era during which acute and dramatic illness resulted in one of two possible outcomes: either the patient died or the patient recovered fully within a relatively short, defined period. Delivery mechanisms were designed to respond effectively to such acute episodes of illness. This system is predicated on the assumptions that disease onset is abrupt, often caused by a single agent, limited in duration, and subject to a relatively accurate diagnosis and prognosis. The aim of intervention is return to normal health (cure). The professional often relies heavily on technology and assumes the role of a knowledgeable expert who controls a traditional doctor-patient relationship. The patient, in turn, endures the disease process as a passive recipient of medical intervention struggling with surprise, ignorance, confusion, and fear.

Ironically, the success of the traditional system in reducing mortality, along with improved public health programs, better nutrition, and the aging of those born in the post-World War II "baby boom" has created a vastly different patient population from the one faced by physicians in the first half of this century. Life expectancy in Europe and the United States has risen from less than 50 years at the end of the last century to more than 75 years in the 1990s, but chronic diseases now account for 80 percent of all deaths and 80 percent of all morbidity, and the rate of increase in chronic disease continues to surpass the growth of acute illness.

Chronic disease demands a markedly different paradigm. By its nature, chronic disease is complex and continuing, and it must be understood as illness that penetrates and compromises, deeply and widely, all aspects of a patient's life. The aim of therapy is most often management of these impacts rather than cure; illness must be understood as an undulating, longitudinal process; maintenance of function and pain reduction may be as important or more important to the patient than modification of disease activity per se. Therapeutic interventions involve weighing the tolerability of the current level of illness against the risk of a proposed new therapy. Psychological responses and social support can play a significant role in coping with chronic illness, so the patient with a chronic disease becomes a uniquely involved participant in the system of care, and the system cannot hope to divest itself of this patient at the end of a single event of ill health.

RHEUMATIC DISEASE

More than 100 discrete disorders, with a wide variety of clinical manifestations, fall under the classification of rheumatic disease, but arthritis in its many forms is the most common disease evaluated in ambulatory care settings, accounting for an estimated 1.2 million physician visits annually.[5] It is more prevalent and limits activity more frequently than heart disease, cancer, or diabetes.[6] In fact, arthritis is the most prevalent cause of chronic physical disability and a leading cause of work disability and activity limitation in the United States.[7]

Rheumatoid arthritis, one of several types of arthritis, is an autoimmune disease that afflicts 1–3 percent of Americans. It is an inflammatory disorder affecting primarily joints, where it causes pain, swelling, and stiffness. The disease, which is two to three times more common in women than in men, usually strikes between the ages of 30 and 40. Ten to twenty percent of victims have an acute onset over a period of days, but symptoms are usually intermittent at first, with more problems emerging over time; clinical illness is greatest among those aged 40–60. Even with appropriate drug therapy, up to 7 percent of patients are disabled to some extent 5 years after disease onset, and 50 percent are too disabled to work 10 years after disease onset. Treatment includes physical therapy to maintain mobility, drugs to slow or halt the disease and/or ameliorate its effects, and occasionally, orthopedic surgery to repair damage or replace nonfunctional or painful joints. Nonsteroidal antiinflammatory drugs (NSAIDs) such as ibuprofen have supplanted aspirin as the most common initial drug treatment, but most RA patients eventually receive disease-modifying arthritis drugs (DMARDs). These include methotrexate, gold compounds, penicillamine, and antimalarial drugs such as hydroxychloroquine, which are thought to go beyond symptom relief. Up to 20 percent of patients may experience complete remission, and roughly half of the remaining patients will experience stabilization of the disease while under treatment. DMARDs are not always effective, however, and often prove too toxic for chronic use. Unfortunately, RA almost always recurs when DMARDs are discontinued.

---

[5]Yelin, EH, and WR Felts (1990). A summary of the impact of musculoskeletal conditions in the United States. *Arthritis and Rheumatism, 33:* 750–755.

[6]Lawrence, RC, MC Hochberg, JL Kelsey, FC McDuffie, TA Medsger, WR Felts and LE Shulman (1989). Estimates of the prevalence of selected arthritic and musculoskeletal diseases in the United States. *Journal of Rheumatology, 16:* 427–441.

[7]Reynolds, MD (1978). Prevalence of rheumatic diseases as causes of disability and complaints by ambulatory patients. *Arthritis and Rheumatism, 21:* 377–382. Yelin, EH, and WR Felts (1990). op. cit. Centers for Disease Control and Prevention (1994). Arthritis prevalence and activity limitations—United States, 1990. *Morbidity and Mortality Weekly Report, 43:* 433–438.

Systemic lupus erythematosus is also an autoimmune disease characterized by chronic inflammation. Although joints are often affected, SLE is far more general in its effects. Skin rashes and lesions, often on the face and highly sensitive to sunlight, are characteristic, but inflammation of the tissues surrounding the heart may occur in up to 30 percent of cases; half of all cases may involve the kidneys, and 40–50 percent of cases may affect the lungs at some point in the course of the disease. Involvement of the central nervous system, particularly with cognitive impairment, is common. Involvement of the gastrointestinal tract is less frequent but not uncommon. Overall prevalence of SLE is 15 to 51 cases per 100,000. Ninety percent of the cases are women, and black women have three times the incidence and mortality of white women. As many as 1 in 250 black women will get SLE. Onset of the disease is usually between the ages of 15 and 40; onset during childhood is associated with a more severe course, and onset after age 50 with a milder course. The actual course of SLE varies widely depending on the pattern of organ system involvement but, in general, is one of relatively asymptomatic intervals punctuated by exacerbations of varying severity. Individuals with severe kidney disease, hypertension, anemia, hypoalbuminemia, or hypercomplementemia have mortality rates that approach 50 percent over 10 years, but some individuals have mild disease that produces disability but does not shorten lifespan. As in the case of RA, medication usually begins with NSAIDs, often in combination with corticosteroids. Antimalarial drugs are commonly used for cutaneous, musculoskeletal, and mild systemic symptoms, although the mechanism of action is unknown. Immunosuppressive agents are reserved for patients for whom conventional therapy has failed. The toxic effects of all of these drugs must be monitored closely, and relapse is frequent with discontinuation.

PRACTICES AND ACHIEVEMENTS OF MANAGED CARE SYSTEMS

Published studies directly comparing the treatments received and/or outcomes achieved by persons with RA or SLE under various models of medical care organization and financing are practically nonexistent. Two studies comparing RA patients in FFS arrangements with RA patients in prepaid group practice HMOs were published by Yelin and colleagues in the mid-1980s.[8] They are not discussed in detail here, since Yelin provides an

---

[8]Yelin, EH, CJ Henke, JS Kramer, MC Nevitt, M Shearn, WV Epstein (1985). A comparison of the treatment of rheumatoid arthritis in health maintenance organizations and fee for service practices. *New England Journal of Medicine, 312:* 962-967. Yelin, EH, M Shearn, and WV Epstein

update on this longitudinal study in a subsequent section of this volume. In a sentence, Yelin and his colleagues reported that RA patients in prepaid systems received similar kinds and amounts of health care and achieved similar outcomes as their FFS counterparts. Similar findings were reported by Ward, et al.[9] at the 1995 meeting of the American College of Rheumatology. The remainder of this section briefly reviews some of the many comparisons of FFS health care with HMOs, most often of the prepaid staff or group practice type, that have not specifically focused on RA or SLE, or even chronic disease.

Hospital Use

One of the principal ways HMOs have reduced their costs relative to FFS systems is by controlling hospital admissions and lengths of stay. Prior to the advent of widespread managed care systems and diagnosis-related hospital reimbursement,[10] HMOs serving the non-Medicare population showed reductions of 10–40 percent in hospital days over FFS indemnity reimbursed care.[11] During the 1980s and early 1990s, studies have been less consistent in this finding. The Medical Outcomes Study found that HMO hospital utilization was 26–37 percent below FFS.[12] Other studies, including the Medicare risk contract evaluation, have shown small and statistically insignificant differences in admissions.[13] This latter finding likely reflects the

---

(1986). Health outcomes for a chronic disease in prepaid group practice and fee for service settings. *Medical Care, 24:* 236–247.

[9]Ward, MM, JP Leigh, and D Lubeck (1995). Long-term health outcomes of patients with rheumatoid arthritis treated in managed care and fee-for-service practice settings (abstract 437) *Arthritis and Rheumatism, 38 (suppl.):* S225

[10]Beginning in 1985, the Medicare program began a prospective payment system for hospitals based on a patient's diagnosis. This program reimburses the hospital a set amount for each of a set of diagnoses, regardless of the length of stay and thus provides an incentive for hospitals to reduce lengths of stay. The RAND Corporation and others have shown that unnecessarily lengthy stays diminished and the proportion of patients judged to be receiving "poor" or "very poor" care decreased from 25 to 12 percent. On the other hand, there was approximately a doubling in the proportion of patients (i.e., 7 percent versus 4 percent) discharged too soon or in an unstable condition. [Kosecoff, J, K Kahn, W Rogers, et al. (1990). Prospective payment system and impairment at discharge: the quicker-and-sicker story revisited. *Journal of the American Medical Association, 264:* 1980–1983.]

[11]Luft, H (1987). *Health Maintenance Organizations: Dimensions of Performance*. New Brunswick, CT: Transition Books.

[12]Greenfield, S, E Nelson, and M Zubkoff (1992). Variations in resource utilization among medical specialties and systems of care: Results from the Medical Outcomes Study. *Journal of the American Medical Association, 267:* 1624–1630.

[13]Miller, M, and H Luft, op. cit.

decline in FFS hospital admissions per Medicare beneficiary by 25 percent between 1985 and 1989. These differences extend to hospital days per enrollee. Among Medicare risk plans, hospital days per enrollee were 6–9 percent fewer than the fee for service comparison group, although group and staff model plans had longer lengths of stay than Independent Providers Association (IPA)–network model plans.[14] In an analysis of the 12 (out of 30) most rigorously conducted evaluations of the impact of Medicaid managed care programs, Hurley et al.[15] found that four MCOs decreased in patient use, one increased use and the other five had no impact. Other studies of enrolling Medicaid eligibles are similar and do not uniformly find reductions in either admissions or lengths of stay.[16]

Physician Use

The relative reduction in inpatient services within HMOs and managed care systems carries an implied assumption that physician or other services expand to accommodate a shift in care to an outpatient setting. There is no consistent empirical support for this. Of 14 studies reviewed by Miller and Luft,[17] 7 showed lower physician use (3 were statistically significant) and 7 higher use (5 were statistically significant). Complicating such comparisons are the parallel decline in inpatient days within the FFS sector and differences among the various managed care models. For example, in the Medicare risk contract evaluation by Brown and Hill, staff and group models had substantially higher physician visit rates (19–25 percent more visits than FFS) than network–IPA plans (3 percent fewer visits than FFS).[18]

Though it often has been hypothesized that managed care for Medicaid would mean greater use of physician services, this has not been shown to be the case. In the evaluation of 12 programs by Hurley and colleagues, three programs were found to experience an increase in physician visits, 5

---

[14]Brown, R, and J Hill (1993). *Does Model Type Play a Role in the Extent of HMO Effectiveness in Controlling the Utilization of Services?* Princeton, NJ: Mathematica Policy Research Inc.

[15]Hurley, R, D Freund and J Paul (1993). *Managed Care in Medicaid, Lessons for Policy and Program Design*. Ann Arbor, Michigan: Health Administration Press.

[16]Miller, M, and M Gengler (1993). Medicaid case management: Kentucky's patient access and care program. *Health Care Financing Review, 15:* 55–69. Buchanan, J, A Leibowitz, and J Keesey (1996). Medicaid health maintenance organizations: Can they reduce spending? *Medical Care, 34:* 249–263. Leibowitz, A, J Buchanan, and J Mann (1992). A randomized trial to evaluate the effectiveness of a Medicaid M/HMO. *Journal of Health Economics, 11:* 235–257.

[17]Op. cit.

[18]Op. cit.

experienced a decrease, and the remainder had no change.[19] A study of the first Medicaid Competition Demonstration found an overall decline in primary care physician use and a decrease in the total number of physicians seen.[20] Such "concentration of care" in the hands of fewer doctors, however, is what one expects from medical plans that require enrollment with a primary care gatekeeper. Rates of referrals to specialists in Medicaid managed care programs appear to be uniformly lower than in fee-for-service Medicaid. Studies of the Medicaid Competition Demonstrations[21] found that the probability of seeing a specialist at least once during the year declined by at least 30 percent in all sites studied but one.

Tests and Procedures

Another presumed means of HMO savings is to use fewer services or to substitute less costly services when possible. Access to appropriate tests and procedures is both an important example of such cost controls and a presumed indicator of the quality of care within health plans. There is some evidence that HMOs are economical in the use of tests and procedures, while still being attentive to prevention and health promotion. Findings from 14 studies reviewed by Miller and Luft[22] showed either better or equivalent access to tests and procedures. This was interpreted as indicative of quality of care. These studies generally showed that enrollees, whether Medicare beneficiaries or from group enrollment, were likely to receive the same or more frequent levels of routine and preventive care (such as cancer and hypertension screening tests; breast, pelvic, rectal, and general physical examinations) and to receive care similar to that received by nonenrollees for a variety of specific conditions. For example, analyses from the Medicare Competition Demonstration found that enrollees generally received tests and treatment comparable to nonenrollees for congestive heart failure, colorectal cancer, diabetes, and hypertension.[23] Similar findings were also found in the

---

[19]Op cit.

[20]Freund, DA, L Rossiter, et al. (1989). Evaluation of the Medicaid Competition Demonstration. *Health Care Financing Review, 11:* 81–97.

[21]Ibid. Freund, D, and E Lewit (1993). Managed care for children and pregnant women: Promises and pitfalls. *The Future of Children, 3:* 92–122.

[22]Op. cit.

[23]Preston, J, and S Retchin (1991). The management of geriatric hypertension in health maintenance organizations. *Journal of the American Geriatric Society, 39:* 683–690. Retchin, S, and B Brown (1990). Quality of ambulatory care in Medicare health maintenance organizations. *American Journal of Public Health, 80:* 411–415. Retchin, S, and B Brown (1990). Management

treatment of stroke among Medicare risk contract plans,[24] rates of cancer screening with the National Health Interview Survey,[25] and an analysis of myocardial infarction within the HMO Quality of Care Consortium. This latter study found greater compliance with process of care criteria among HMO physicians and nurses compared to a sample of fee-for-service providers. Only in the area of diagnostic testing (e.g., electrocardiograms and chest radiographs) did FFS compliance with guidelines exceed that of HMOs.[26]

A review of the published literature on Medicaid and managed care[27] reported recent studies showing a higher percentage of 3-year-olds with up-to-date immunizations for managed care[28] and a higher percentage of breast examinations and Pap smears for women in Medicaid managed care programs[29] but it concluded that, overall, the use of preventive care services does not appear to either improve or decline under most Medicaid managed care arrangements.

One demonstration evaluation approached the quality of care issue from a different perspective: the comparison of changes in health status, life expectancy, and active life expectancy among prepaid plan members and those with FFS indemnity coverage. These results suggest generally comparable performance between the prepaid and indemnity systems among most health status groups. Prepaid health plan performance slightly trailed that of FFS in the case of female members, but performance of the two types of coverage was

---

of colorectal cancer in Medicare health maintenance organizations. *Journal of General Internal Medicine, 5:* 110–114. Retchin, S, and B Brown (1991). Elderly patients with congestive heart failure under prepaid care. *American Journal of Medicine, 90:* 236–242. Retchin, S, and J Preston (1991). The effects of cost containment on the care of elderly diabetics. *Archives of Internal Medicine, 151:* 2244–2248.

[24]Retchin, S, D Clement, and B Brown (1994). Care of patients hospitalized with strokes under the Medicare risk program. Pp. 167–194, in H Luft, Ed., *HMOs and the Elderly.* Ann Arbor, MI: Health Administration Press.

[25]Bernstein, A, G Thompson, and L Harlan (1991). Differences in rates of cancer screening by usual source of medical care: Data from the 1987 National Health Interview Survey. *Medical Care, 29:* 196–209.

[26]Carlisle, D, A Siu, E Keeler, K Kahn, L Rubenstein, and R Brook (1994). Do HMOs provide better care for older patients with acute myocardial infarction? Pp. 195–214, in H. Luft, Ed., *HMOs and the Elderly.* Ann Arbor, MI: Health Administration Press.

[27]Rowland, D, S Rosenbaum, L Simon, and E Chait (1995). *A Report of the Kaiser Commission on the Future of Medicaid.* Menlo Park, CA: The Henry J. Kaiser Family Foundation.

[28]Balaban, D, N McCall, and EJ Bauer (1994). *Quality of Medicaid Managed Care: An Evaluation of the Arizona Health Care Cost Containment System (AHCCCS).* San Francisco: Laguna Research Associates.

[29]Carey, T, K Weis, and C Homer (1990). Prepaid versus traditional Medicaid plans: Effects on preventive health care. *Journal of Clinical Epidemiology, 43:* 1213–1220.

comparable among males.[30]

Home Health and Skilled Nursing Care

Reductions in hospital admissions and days within managed care or other systems might be expected to increase nursing home and home health care use. However, Medicare patients in managed care, after adjustment for case mix, tend to use about 15 percent fewer days of skilled nursing home care, 21 percent fewer nurse or therapist visits, and 28 percent fewer home health aid visits.[31] These results do not directly connect the use of such services to post-hospital care; so it is possible that some reduction in hospital care is balanced by increased nursing home and home health care, but that this increase is offset by reductions in admissions to these services for other cases. Another study specifically examining the effects of post-hospital care for Medicare patients found that membership in an HMO had no significant effect on the likelihood of receiving various types of post-hospital care.[32] Results from both of these studies should be interpreted in the context that managed care plans are financially at risk for nursing home and home health care services as well as hospital stays. Within the FFS sector, hospitals are at risk for days of care and thus have a greater incentive to shift patient care (and its associated financial risk) to other settings and providers.

Outcomes of home health care have been examined in terms of improvement and stabilization in functional status, mortality, discharge to independent living, and hospital utilization. The most extensive of these studies looked at rehabilitation and cardiac patients and their home health service utilization. Fee-for-service patients received about one-third more total home health visits and at least twice the number of home health aide visits and social service visits. There were, however, no significant differences in the number of skilled nursing, physical therapy, or occupational therapy visits for these conditions. After adjustment for case mix, Medicare fee-for-service patients had better outcomes, relative to those in HMOs, on measures of

---

[30]Manton, K, R Newcomer, G Lowrimore, J Vertrees, and C Harrington (1993). Social/health maintenance organization and fee for service health outcomes over time. *Health Care Financing Review, 15:* 173–202.

[31]Brown, R, and J Hill (1994). The effects of Medicare risk HMOs on Medicare costs and service utilization. Pp. 13–49, in H Luft, Ed., *HMOs and the Elderly*. Ann Arbor, MI: Health Administration Press.

[32]Kane, RL, M Finch, L Blewett, Q Chen, R Burns, and M Moskowitz (1996). Use of post-hospital care by Medicare patients. *Journal of the American Geriatric Society, 44:* 242–250.

functionality.[33] Among those with mild or moderate levels of impairment on "admission" to home health care, between 6 and 16 percent more FFS patients improved status than did their HMO counterparts over 12 weeks. There were no differences among those beginning with severe levels of disability. Importantly, however, there were no differences in the proportion discharged to independent living within 12 weeks or in hospitalization within 12 weeks of the start of care.

Social/Health Maintenance Organizations

The first generation of this Medicare demonstration, known as the S/HMO, was implemented in 1985 with the objective of adding a package of chronic care benefits to the acute services and operational structure of the Medicare HMO model. These chronic care benefits included unskilled nursing home stays (usually a maximum of 30 days) and personal care, homemaker, and case management services. S/HMOs also offered expanded care benefits to all members, such as prescription drugs, eyeglasses, transportation, and preventive dental care. The liability of the plan for chronic care of any individual member was initially limited to $6,000–$12,000 per year depending on the plan, and did not extend to long-term care.

The lessons learned in the first generation S/HMO program were that (1) merely placing a case management program into a health plan, even if charged with coordinating access to chronic care benefits, did not change the plan's usual approach to primary care or hospital care: (2) in part because of the absence of such structural changes, the plans realized no real savings in hospital and other medical costs from the provision of the added community care benefits; (3) limiting the target population to patients sufficiently impaired to qualify for nursing home placement may also have limited potential cost savings.[34] Overall, S/HMOs would have to be judged a promising approach which has yet to be properly tested. A second generation S/HMO demonstration begins in late 1996, retaining the chronic care benefit package implemented in the first generation plans but adding several refinements, including a reimbursement formula directly tied to health care risk factors.

---

[33]Shaughnessy, P, R Schlenker, and D Hittle (1994). Home health care outcomes under capitated and fee-for-service payment. *Health Care Financing Review, 16:* 187–221.

[34]Harrington, C, M Lynch, and R Newcomer (1993). Medical services in social health maintenance organizations. *The Gerontologist, 33:* 790–800.

WORK FORCE ISSUES

A near-universal target of cost saving measures proposed by health policy experts and implemented by health care plans of all varieties is specialty and subspecialty care. Although hard data are scarce, seldom involve measured outcomes, and most often address only one or two subspecialties, it is widely believed that specialist and subspecialist care is too expensive, less controllable, and sometimes unnecessary. The United States does in fact have a disproportionately high percentage of specialists compared to the rest of the world,[35] and Wennberg and his colleagues[36] reported that in 1989, successful HMOs were employing specialist and subspecialist physicians at per capita rates far lower than their prevalence in the United States would suggest. Managed care systems of all varieties now rely heavily on "primary care physicians" as gatekeepers, that is, a mandatory starting place for all patient–plan interactions and one that takes the decision to utilize a specialist out of the hands of the patient. Like the term *managed care* itself, primary care means many things to many people. Some understand primary in its sense of first in time or order, which leads to a narrow concept of primary care as simply first contact or entry point and connotes only a triage function. Others, *including this committee,* understand primary in its sense of chief, main, or principal, which leads to the definition of primary care recently promulgated by another IOM committee:

> Primary care is the provision of integrated, accessible health care services by clinicians who are accountable for addressing a large majority of personal health care needs, developing a sustained partnership with patients, and practicing in the context of family and community.[37]

This definition, involved as it may be, does not specify the medical training required by physicians delivering primary care other than to require that they be able to address a large majority of their patients' health care needs. Context makes it clear that the authors are ruling out mere triage to subspecialists, although they recognize that part of managing a patient's problem may well require involving other practitioners. Nevertheless, the

---

[35]Barondess, JA (1993). The future of generalism. *Annals of Internal Medicine, 119:* 153–160.

[36]Wennberg, JE, DC Goodman, RF Nease, and RB Keller (1993). Finding equilibrium in U.S. physician supply. *Health Affairs (Millwood), 12:* 89–103.

[37]Institute of Medicine (1996). *Primary Care: America's Health in a New Era.* Washington, DC: National Academy Press.

question of who should deliver primary care remains a topic of lively debate. Rheumatologists, for example, argue that they should be the primary care providers for persons with rheumatic diseases pointing to data suggesting that RA patients do better with regular care by a rheumatologist.[38] Proponents of a less specialized primary care physician, on the other hand, would argue that persons with rheumatic disease remain subject to all the other health problems with which the rest of the population must cope, and that these problems may be diagnosed and treated less well by a necessarily highly focused rheumatologist. Recognizing that the training and experience of the providers will be an important variable in any comparison of health care delivery models, the committee made generalist–subspecialist issues one of the major segments of its workshop.

RESEARCH, EDUCATION, AND TRAINING

The charge to this committee focuses very explicitly on clinical practice and how it may differ as a function of the organization and financing of the health care plan in which it is delivered. The committee nevertheless believes that it would be short-sighted to ignore the possibility that the longer-term well-being of persons with RA and SLE might be differentially affected by changes in the care system that have had no measurable short-term impact. The current emphasis on cost containment and market competition has already raised alarms in academic medical centers, where teaching and research functions are partially funded by clinical income. Any change in the numbers or types of physicians or other health care providers will take many years to accomplish, given the status quo and the length of the educational pipeline, and it will take just as long to reverse should the change prove maladaptive.

As Robert Meenan points out later in this report, there is no reason to think that research into rheumatic diseases will be affected differently from research on other diseases as managed care and managed competition evolve or that rheumatology will fare any differently than other medical subspecialties. The remarkable improvements in the mortality and morbidity of RA and SLE patients over the last 20 years, however, suggest that any comparison of health care models ought to extend beyond cost-effective delivery of today's best practices and include the likely effects on the discovery and implementation of tomorrow's best practices.

---

[38]Ad hoc Committee on Costs and Outcomes of Rheumatologic Care (1995). *Specialty Care for Chronic Disease in Integrated Health Care: The Role of the Rheumatologist in Arthritis, Rheumatic, and Musculoskeletal Disease Management.* Atlanta: American College of Rheumatology.

THE WORKSHOP

The remainder of this report, with the exception of Conclusions and Recommendations, consists of edited proceedings of the workshop conducted by the committee on May 16, 1996, in Washington, D.C. The report is divided into sections, the central features of which are prepared addresses by invited experts selected by the committee at a planning meeting in February. Each invited talk is preceded by a brief introduction written by a committee member and followed by one or more brief commentaries from predesignated "reactors" and by excerpts from the lively discussion that ensued among speakers, reactors, committee members, and a small number of other invited participants. Brief biographies of the committee members and speakers, and a list of other participants, are included in the appendix material. The invited speakers and reactors were all asked to check the text for accuracy, and the opinions expressed are solely those to whom they are attributed. The final section is the work of the committee alone and brings together the committee's conclusions and recommendations.

2

Opening Remarks

Jeremiah A. Barondess

Traditionally, medicine and the health care system have been oriented around the management of acute disease. For a variety of reasons, notably the enhanced management of infections and a variety of other clinical advances, and preventive activities largely effected by changes in individual behaviors—the average age of the population has been increasing. Further, we are increasingly able to treat a number of disorders to the point of chronicity. The result of all this, of course, is that the system is now required to care for chronic disorders to a vastly greater degree than previously obtained. The corollaries of that fact include an important shift from cure to care as the paradigm in which we operate and new emphases in the direction of the maintenance of function and on patient values as they relate to treatment priorities, research, and outcomes assessment.

In addition, focusing on chronic disease brings special prominence to the critically important distinction between disease and illness. It is a distinction that has substantial pertinence to the issues to be considered in this conference. Disease, in this construct, is a biological phenomenon, to be understood ultimately in structural, physiological, or biochemical terms, increasingly at the molecular level. Much of the clinically relevant output of research in recent decades and a great deal of clinical practice, as a result, have focused on the aberrant biology of disease processes. Illness, on the other hand, is not a biological process but a subjective one. It is a term that encompasses the variety of discomforts, dysfunctions, limitations, and interferences with social as well as symptom-determined physical functioning and also involves the various fears, concerns, and emotional dislocations produced by ill health. The illness needs of patients are sometimes lost in the shuffle in our focus on addressing the biological abnormalities that characterize disease. For patients with chronic disorders, attention to management of the illness phenomena becomes even more important than in the case of acute disease.

Of course, both disease and illness should be attended to, not only by the physician and other care givers, but by the care system as well. I would add that disease and illness are not congruent. That is, it is possible to have a disease without being ill, for example, in the case of an asymptomatic pulmonary atherosclerotic plaque or a presymptomatic neoplasm. By the same token, it is possible to be ill without having a disease. Clinical practices have traditionally contained large numbers of people who are ill, that is, symptomatic, without having an underlying disease. In the case of the disorders that we are focused on today, systemic lupus and rheumatoid arthritis, all of these features come importantly into play and help to describe the needs of these patients in a more comprehensive way. For example, at various points in the course of either disease, it is possible to have biologically active disease without necessarily being ill from that activity. Further, it is possible for patients to be ill, that is, symptomatic and limited, without necessarily being in a phase of biological activity of the disease. Important management decisions flow from that divergence.

This workshop is focused at the confluence of chronic disease and an evolving care system, using systemic lupus and rheumatoid arthritis as exemplars. The remarkable shifts taking place in the care system resemble in some ways the grinding of tectonic plates: there is a fair amount of energy being released, there is a fair amount of noise, a lot of furniture is being shifted, and a lot of dishes are being broken. Traditional features of clinical management are being challenged; the challenge is generated primarily by fiscal considerations. Major shifts in the power structure of health care have emerged: for example, in clinical care arrangements, shifts away from physicians toward nurses and other non physician providers; within medicine, a very substantial shift from subspecialist to generalist care; within the organizational system, shifts from providers to payers and from physicians to administrative professionals, trustees, or stockholders. The traditional fiduciary responsibilities of physicians and of hospitals and other health care institutions are under substantial pressures as the focus on the bottom line increases in intensity. The impacts of those pressures on chronic care institutions or other chronic care arrangements are less clearly defined but no less important. In general, I think it is fair to say that from the point of view of the physician there is a perception of perverse incentives in the system, away from a primary focus on fiduciary responsibilities and in the direction of payment incentives, care giver selection that may be based on characteristics that are sometimes perverse, gag rules, issues of patient eligibility in care systems, and so on. From the point of view of some care givers, corporate priorities and the issues they brings in their wake amount to an unsought second opinion. Threats to confidentiality, ethical considerations in patient care, and gaming the system are looming risks. From the sector of the patient, new vulnerabilities are produced by the shift to managed care arrangements. At the same time, managed care structures have the potential to bring some advantages, including a clearer focus on costs; the assembly of cohorts; of defined populations, perhaps allowing easier evaluation of interventions and outcomes; and the potential for greater accountability in the system.

From the point of view of this workshop, focused as it is at the intersection of the patient and the care system, with particular reference to chronic disease, we should focus ultimately on patient welfare, patient outcomes, and the things that need to be done to enhance both; then we should know with some confidence whether we are in fact doing so. The central issues for us to consider are what is needed from care system arrangements, the system characteristics that are most likely to yield enhanced patient outcomes, the nature of the evidence we have in hand bearing on that issue, and very importantly, the additional things we need to know.

3

Keynote Address

John M. Eisenberg

This workshop addresses one of the fundamental issues of medical care in the future. As health care systems change, as we improve our ability to avert death from acute diseases, and as the population ages, the care of individuals with chronic disease becomes more central to the mission of health care worldwide.

As requested, today I will address "changes in the system of health care organization and finance as they relate to management of persons with chronic disease." I will explore what our best leading indicators predict the effects of these changes to be. I will discuss some broad trends in medical care today, comment on the payment of physicians, and reflect on the overall system of care. I will also discuss managed care, the training of physicians, both the tension and the collaboration between primary care physicians and rheumatologists, and what these forces mean for the rheumatology work force. I will conclude with comments on issues related to the intersection between health policy and clinical practice.

CHANGING HEALTH CARE

In preparing this talk, I looked into the crystal ball that sits on my desk. Reflected there I saw trends in the future for which we should be planning today.

First, it is clear that hospitals will downsize and close or, as an intermediate step between downsizing and closing, merge. Whichever scenario occurs, a significant decrease in the number of hospital beds will take place.

This decrease in hospital beds will continue the trend of moving the focus of medical care, especially for chronic diseases, away from the inpatient setting.

Second, managed care organizations will compete on price. What is not so clear yet is whether they will be able to compete on quality as well. This is a fundamental issue for health care delivery and certainly for the future of chronic disease care.

Third, technical services, which have long been sources of revenue, are becoming sources of cost. This changes the way we look at services such as endoscopy, cardiac catheterization, and surgery. We can no longer use them to comfortably cross-subsidize specialist care for chronic conditions.

Fourth, physicians' rewards and relationships will continue to change. We are moving away from traditional fee-for-service payment and higher payment for more technical procedures. Our professional relationships no longer will be determined solely by our personal preferences, but will be determined by new payment systems and re-engineered systems of care.

Fifth, gatekeepers will manage patient care, primary care will become primary, specialists will specialize, and consultants will consult.

Finally, physicians will redefine their relationships to organizations and third-party payers. More physicians will be employees; fewer will be self-employed.

HOSPITALS

The decreasing use of hospitals is an important element in the changing face of medical care. Medicare-reimbursed hospital stays are already shorter and admissions fewer. The national average hospital use for Medicare is about 2,800 hospital days per 1,000 people annually. The California health maintenance organizations (HMO) rate is about half that, and for California integrated systems of care, the rate is only 960 days per 1,000 people per year. Soon, we will likely experience as few as 800–900 hospital days per 1,000 Medicare beneficiaries per year. That is about one-third of the days of hospitalization currently used.

Commercially reimbursed hospital stays are shortening as well, and admissions are fewer. As a result, the national average is about 500 hospital days per 1,000 people annually; for California HMOs, 250; and for California integrated systems of care, 200. Many will remember Kerr White's description, a generation ago, of the health care system being like a pyramid. For every 1,000 people there were 1,000 days of hospitalization per year. No more. We will soon be experiencing 200 days per year per 1,000, at least for relatively young populations.

MANAGED CARE

As different types of managed care plans emerge, it becomes increasingly difficult to consider managed care as a monolithic form of health care delivery. They are as different from each other as they are from traditional fee-for-service medicine. The heterogeneity is remarkable!

- Staff model HMOs hire their doctors directly. There are few of these plans—Group Health of Puget Sound and the Harvard Community Health Plan, for example.
- Group model HMOs such as Kaiser Permanente contract exclusively with a single physician group.
- Network model HMOs differ from staff and group in that they contract with several physician groups, usually on a non exclusive basis.
- Independent practice associations (IPAs)—in an IPA model, doctors generally practice in community-based offices. They may have individual practices or share a practice with a group of physicians. They contract with the IPA on a non exclusive basis, sometimes, but not always, taking capitation.
- Preferred provider organizations (PPOs) are organizations that contract with individual doctors for fee discounts to list the doctor as a "preferred provider" for their enrollees. This is not really a new model. In fact, in the mid-1980s, Blue Shield of Pennsylvania contracted with almost every doctor in Pennsylvania, set fee limits, had a vigorous utilization program, and could drop doctors from the plan. PPOs are basically a way of finding a group of doctors willing to accept a discount and putting them on a list of physicians eligible for a negotiated or previously established fee-for-service payment.
- Point-of-service (POS) plans are still called "managed care" plans, but they are really open-ended plans with a list of participating doctors. If subscribers go to the listed doctors, they can get covered services for either no co-payment or a lower co-payment than from doctors who are not plan participants. Sometimes in these plans, patients have an even lower copayment if they are referred by their gatekeeper than if they seek service from consultants on their own. Thus, there may be three levels of fees in some point-of-service plans—referral in-plan, nonreferral in-plan, and out of plan.

What can we conclude from this brief survey? Managed care is not any one of these particular models. When we talk about managed care we should avoid getting trapped in the notion that there is a single model of managed care synonymous with Kaiser Permanente. In fact, a substantial amount of managed care is paid fee for service, albeit at a discount.

Enrollment in group and staff model HMOs has been relatively flat for some time. In fact, in some areas they have lost market share and numbers of patients. PPO and POS plans, however, have been growing rapidly. They do not alter the nature of medical practice as much, change relationships among physicians, or change the organization of care. The more restrictive plans may alter referral patterns or, at least, redirect referral patterns. However, in most instances all they do is force physicians to sign with a plan and accept a lower fee. They also may not save as much money as group and staff model HMOs do.

Much of the change in health care systems stems from buyers, and now sellers of care having organized in response to the need to negotiate fees. As a result, more physicians are moving toward larger multispecialty group practices, such as physician networks, to gain negotiating power. If the buyer of services has market power and the seller does not, there is an inequity. The sellers of service, in this case doctors, have now begun to consolidate in order to gain market power that matches that of the purchasers.

How much of this can occur before doctors are in restraint of trade? If consolidation reaches the point of one organization (or a very few) negotiating on behalf of all doctors, the market advantage swings from buyers to sellers, from health care plans to doctors. In that case, medical practice will border on monopoly or oligopoly and will be subject to intensive antitrust scrutiny.

Many believe that there will be both vertical and horizontal integration of medical practice. Vertical integration is coordination, sometimes but not always common ownership, of all the various levels of care from hospitals to specialty care, primary care, nursing home care, and home care. Horizontal integration means that multiple hospitals and multiple groups of physicians come together at the same level of care—be it hospital, specialist, or primary care—to consolidate their activities in a particular geographic area. We are moving from a model of physicians in solo practice to one of physicians enmeshed in different modes of consolidation as the market propels us toward both vertical and horizontal integration.

PHYSICIAN PAYMENT

Physician payment will change dramatically. There are three major questions about payment: What are we going to be paid for; who is going to be paid; and what controls will there be on the way we are paid? Traditionally, in the United States, we have been paid on a fee-for-service basis according to a market price structure—whatever the doctor could get. These market-driven fees were soon locked into place by a customary, prevailing, and reasonable payment system used by Medicare and many third-party payers. The market had stopped influencing physicians' fee levels; third-party payer fee schedules, based on historical data, were now determining fees.

With the 1989 Omnibus Budget Reconciliation Act, we moved to the resource-based fee-for-service system for Medicare, built on the premise that in a free market, what one is paid is determined by the cost of producing a product as well as the demand for that product. Doctors are now paid by Medicare based on the resources consumed in taking care of patients.

A major payment change is the increasing popularity of payment not for actual services rendered but for taking responsibility for the care of a patient. This could be capitation payment—taking responsibility for subscriber's care for a year—or it could be global payment—taking responsibility for a disease or disorder (e.g., diabetes) or a procedure (e.g., bone marrow transplantation). Hospital payment may or may not be included. Another form of payment that we may see in the future is bundled payment for an episode of illness. However, these forms of payment are not really a new concept. Obstetricians have long accepted fixed payment for prenatal care and delivery. In any case, the physician is clearly being paid for accepting responsibility for care rather than for providing a particular service on a particular day.

Traditionally, doctors have been paid individually for their services. However, increasingly we are practicing in teams and in organizations. Of course, this is a an important cultural change for our profession. We will need to develop payment mechanisms that recognize the contributions of individuals practicing in teams or organizations.

What controls will govern our payment systems? Capitation, of course, is the ultimate control. It tells physicians, "Here is what you get; live within this budget." Short of capitation, four other payment controls are popular.

First, under the gatekeeper system, a medical arbiter (usually a primary care physician) decides what care will be given, sometimes with incentives for that gatekeeper. The gatekeeper controls the flow of services that the system provides.

Second, copayment puts some responsibility on patients. If they have to pay more, they will be more concerned about the cost of care and its appropriateness.

Third, utilization control represents the classic American approach. Let everybody do what they want, but slap them on the hand if they do too much of it. This approach invokes monitoring medical practice and auditing doctors for aberrant practice patterns, then penalizing them for inappropriate utilization.

Fourth is the use of supply constraints. That is, limit the number of physicians, limit the number of hospitals, and do it either through certificates of need (which don't work very well), regional planning (which didn't work very well), or the market, which does seem to be working—although causing major perturbations and dislocations as it decreases our capacity to provide medical care.

SPECIALIST–GENERALIST INTERACTION

Who will provide chronic care services in the future? Will we have a work force of health professionals capable of providing needed services?

About a decade ago, the American Board of Internal Medicine (ABIM) established a Task Force on the Future Internist to propose the kind of training internists will need in the future. Although there might be more agreement on this list today than 10 years ago, not much has changed in medical education in response to the changing nature of practice—the emerging dominance of chronic disease, the need for more attention to the healthy patient, and the changing organization of health care.

About the same time, that the ABIM task force was studying changes in physician education, I wrote an article in which I addressed the need to train primary care physicians, especially general internists, for their role as gatekeepers. This training should prepare physicians to

- Evaluate risks, benefits, and costs of potential treatments;
- deal with a wide variety of clinical problems and settings;
- maintain strong primary care skills;
- develop skills in working with consultants; and
- teach primary care physicians and specialists how to collaborate.

Each training area needs more attention, but in my opinion, none is greater than the need to train specialists to collaborate with primary care physicians. Medical residents still ask subspecialists, "Why don't you send patients back to me when I refer them to you? Why don't you write me a note? Why don't you learn to be a consultant instead of stealing all my patients away from me?" The subspecialty fellows respond, "How come you never send me any consults? You are managing all these patients with rheumatoid arthritis and lupus, and you never send me a patient?"

This debate between specialists and generalists can end up as a war over patients. It is not only the patients who will suffer but also future specialists who now so rarely learn how to be consultants and how to collaborate with primary care physicians.

What does this mean for rheumatology and other specialties? What will rheumatologists do in the future? What will their practices look like? Unfortunately, rheumatologists have not clearly defined for themselves how they are likely to practice in the future. They may consult on referred patients with severe or unusual diseases of the musculoskeletal system and immunologic disorders. They may be primary care doctors for patients with rheumatic diseases. They may be primary care doctors and also provide rheumatologic care for selected patients.

To what extent do rheumatologists function as primary care doctors now? There are no adequate, unbiased data on the quality of care they already provide. The best data available, although somewhat dated, suggest that rheumatologists spend about half of their time as principal physicians. Whether they are truly serving as primary care physicians is not clear. Consultation comprises only about one-sixth of the activities of rheumatologists. Thus, even though it is a consulting specialty, consulting is a relatively small percentage of rheumatology practice.

Can rheumatologists be effective general internists? I believe that a two-year rheumatology fellowship should not nullify prior board certification in internal medicine. As well-trained clinicians, rheumatologists should maintain and update their skills in general medicine (e.g., rheumatologists should be familiar and comfortable with performing pap tests themselves rather then sending patients to a gynecologist). Equally important, they should enjoy providing primary care in addition to specialty care.

William Winkenwerder has written that the functions of primary care and specialty physicians clearly differ. Primary care doctors navigate, negotiate, evaluate, educate, and make decisions, he writes. Consultants consult, providing diagnostic and rehabilitation expertise, which is underemphasized in most of our training programs. Consultants also periodically review patients and educate both patients and their primary care physicians.

I believe it is time that we consider an alternative to such clearly demarcated boundaries between primary care and specialty medicine. Perhaps some doctors will be generalists with an area of expertise. For example, is there is a role for a generalist who has completed six months or a year of rheumatology training? Is there a role for the fully trained subspecialist who maintains his skills as a generalist?

The American Board of Internal Medicine has taken the position that specialists not only can, but should, maintain their skills as generalists. The upcoming recertification exam encourages physicians to become recertified in internal medicine as well as in their subspecialty.

Do specialists provide better care? There is evidence that receiving care from a rheumatologist seems to slow disease progression and to be associated with higher functioning levels for rheumatoid arthritis (RA) patients. However, there are also data showing that specialists do not provide better care and that, when they do, it is because of systems of care, especially the involvement of non physician health professionals.

Even if we could agree on the proper role of rheumatologists, work force issues would likely remain fuzzy. Data of the Graduate Medical Education National Advisory Committee from the early 1980s demonstrated that the supply of rheumatologists totaled about 3,000, whereas we needed only 1,900 (i.e., we had about 1.5 times the number of rheumatologists needed).

Jonathan Weiner[39] also concluded that an oversupply exists, suggesting that we have 0.9 rheumatologist per 100,000 in the United States but need between 0.4 and 0.7. Another study also suggested that we have about twice as many rheumatologists as we need. In Europe, the need for rheumatologists is perceived to range from 0.3 to 0.5 per 100,000, and that is actually close to the European supply today. Meenan and colleagues suggested that if the methodology of the Committee on Graduate Medical Education is used, the supply of rheumatologists is actually less than the need.

I think there are some problems with using specialty as a proxy for capacity. Specifically, there is overlapping capability of providers. Providers may be capable but unwilling to perform some necessary services. We assume that a rheumatologist trained 30 years ago provides comparable services to a rheumatologist trained today.

Another reason for the uncertainty about the number of rheumatologists needed is that estimates of rheumatologic populations vary substantially. These work force studies also make assumptions about referral patterns that are likely to change in the future. As we think about the need for rheumatologists to care for chronic disease patients, we also must consider whether there will be alternative providers for any of these chronic diseases.

POLICY ISSUES

How will the contributions of this conference affect the care of individuals with chronic rheumatologic disease? I believe there are three levels of policy that may be influenced by a conference such as this.

The first level is that of public policy. Is there a set of recommendations that can be made at the public policy level, for example, approval of a new service by the Food and Drug Administration (FDA) or new coverage by Health Care Financing Agency (HCFA)? The second level is clinical systems policy. In emerging systems of care, policies are being instituted not by individual physicians, but by managed care organizations, hospitals, and health care systems. Often these policies are aimed at saving costs, but often they are also aimed at improving clinical outcomes or patient satisfaction. The third level is clinical policy, for example, the institution of guidelines, audits, or criteria. These may come from professional societies or expert groups.

New research can inform policy. The Agency for Health Care Policy and Research is a beleaguered agency, but it is the only one that has accepted

---

[39]Weiner, JP (1994). Forecasting the effects of health reform on U.S. physician workforce requirements: Evidence from HMO staffing patterns. *Journal of the American Medical Association, 272:* 222–230.

primary responsibility for linking health services research to policy. This responsibility for linking research to policy, as well as for linking policy to politics, is essential to improving systems of care. As medicine and rheumatology enter a new practice era, we need to address these key issues. With careful thought about innovative payment schemes, appropriate numbers of trainees, and responsiveness to the need for outcomes assessment, the future of rheumatology and—more fundamentally—the care of patients with chronic disease will be brighter.

4

What Would Ideal Care Look Like?

Introduction

Jordan J. Cohen

Halsted Holman's contribution was solicited to help the committee focus on the optimal characteristics of any future health care system. He begins with the observation that our present system is the byproduct of an era dominated by acute disease. In such an era the prevailing paradigm centers on accurate diagnosis and specific treatment to effect cure or control of a limited episode of disease. Physicians practicing within this paradigm possess the bulk of the knowledge, and patients tend to be passive recipients of medical care. This system, in Holman's view, is ill-suited to deal with the rapidly changing realities of health care. In his words, "the system is no longer confronted primarily with the problems it was created to solve."

Holman reminds us that we are entering an entirely different era, one dominated not by acute disease but by chronic disease, an era in which the prevailing paradigm is management of an unpredictably undulating course of illness. In this context he offers us a useful conceptual distinction between "disease" (the biologic entity) and "illness" (the disease coupled with all of its morbid, emotional, social, and economic consequences).

In an era dominated by chronic diseases such as the rheumatic conditions under consideration in this study, physicians do not possess definitive knowledge. Indeed, patients who are forced to live day by day with their chronic *illness* bring to the therapeutic relationship as much if not more knowledge of the problems at hand than does the physician. As a consequence, effective partnerships between doctor and patient become the linchpins of quality care.

In the later portions of his paper, Holman delineates the distinct but interdependent roles of the patient, the physician delivering primary care, the specialist, and what he refers to as the health care service. He notes with vivid examples the value that each brings to the management of chronic illness. All play crucial parts in dealing with chronic illness, and together will constitute the system of the future for delivering high quality care, no matter what version of "managed care" or other delivery system provides the organizing or financing infrastructure.

Invited Address

Halsted Holman

If one looks at data from the early part of this century through the 1940s, the prevalence of acute disease, as measured at least by death rates, is declining. When the patterns from about the 1940s onward are viewed, death rates from chronic disease begin to rise.

Chronic disease is now the largest cause of disability, visits to physicians, hospital utilization, and expense in the health care system. After the age of 45, arthritis is the leading cause of disability. Our health care system is thus confronted with a set of problems that is overwhelmingly characterized by chronic illness.

My central argument today is that the health care system is attempting to deal with a set of problems for which it was not created. Our current system was created, in terms of its conceptual notions, its practices, and its institutions, to deal with acute disease. There is now a real discordance, because the system no longer is confronted primarily with the problems it was created to solve. That discordance is one of the major contributors to the health care crisis today. It follows, obviously, that solutions to the health problems that we are facing today will require us to accomplish a transformation from a system designed for acute care to one that is hospitable to, as well as efficient and effective in, the management of chronic disease.

Before getting into the substance of my argument, a pair of definitions is in order. We are considering the disease problem—for purposes of this discussion, it is the biological entity—and the illness, which is the disease plus its consequences. These are not perfect definitions in dictionary terms, but they make a great deal of sense when thinking about what the health care system must address.

To see the differences between what the system was constructed for and what it must deal with, we need to consider some of the differences between acute and chronic disease. Generally speaking, the onset of acute disease is abrupt, its duration is relatively limited, there is usually a single cause, and diagnosis and prognosis are accurate. It is usually self-limited, or a specific therapy is available. Technological intervention (laboratory tests, imaging, medications, surgery) usually is effective. The most important point is that cure is reasonably certain, or transition into chronic illness may occur. There is not a great deal of uncertainty involved, and although the patients are usually unfamiliar with the experience, the profession is quite knowledgeable. Consequently, we have a situation in which professional dominance is a characteristic of the way we treat acute disease.

With chronic disease we are confronted with something quite different. Gradual onset is common; the problem unfolds over time. The consequences of the disease, which may be physical symptoms, emotional difficulties, social inadequacies, or economic handicap, can interact with one another, and sometimes even with the biology of the disease, to create a changing illness pattern and an undulating course over time.

As we know in rheumatology, a substantial segment of patients cannot be classified. The diagnosis, although we think they have a rheumatic disease with reasonable certainty, is uncertain, and the prognosis is clearly obscure. Our technologies are not decisive. Our diagnostic modes have turned out not to give us very good information on which we can base our monitoring of the patients, much less our predictions of their outcomes. For example, joint fluid examination is useful basically only when there is an infection or a crystal-induced disease. Our serologic tests are not precise in distinguishing among rheumatic diseases. X-ray is notoriously useless in making an early and precise diagnosis, or in telling whether the symptoms themselves are a consequence of the abnormality you see. It has recently been shown, for example, that with low back pain and lumbar spine disease the correlation between symptoms and abnormality is poor, even for a sophisticated technology such as magnetic resonance imaging (MRI). We are not dealing with cures, but with management over a long period. That management is aimed, if not at cure, at maintaining the comfort and independent function of the patient. When that is the goal, clearly the consequences of the disease become targets of our attention just as much as the disease process. By consequence I am talking about discomfort, physical inabilities, emotional problems, social and economic deprivations, et cetera.

Throughout the management of chronic disease, uncertainty is pervasive. The patient lives with the disease and basically becomes more knowledgeable about both the consequences of the disease and the consequences of our indecisive therapies. We have a situation in which we know about the biology and about the array of available therapies. It is the patients, however, who know about their effects. In a sense, both of us are partially knowledgeable and reciprocally knowledgeable, so an ideal system requires a partnership between the patient and the physician or among the patient, the family, and the array of health professionals who are playing a role in the care of the patient.

These points can be illustrated in rheumatic disease by considering that we classify one cluster of rheumatic diseases with at least five names: rheumatoid arthritis (RA), systemic lupus erythematosus (SLE), vasculitis, progressive systemic sclerosis (PSS), and dermato/polymyositis (D/PM). In reality, when you watch patients over time, it turns out that the boundaries separating diagnoses are very vague and patients will pass from one category into another.

A more appropriate representation would be depicted by a three-dimensional Venn diagram in which these diagnoses all overlap with one another and, in some patients, elements of all five can be found. An individual patient can start at any point in this Venn representation and, with differing speeds, wander through it, changing and the basic classification as the disease unfolds, either spontaneously without therapy or as a consequence of therapy.

In the area of rheumatic diseases certain specific elements must be taken into account if the biology of the diseases is to be understood. The first of these elements is that, in any of these diseases, the target organ of the disease process may be different in people with the same diagnosis and can even change in a single patient over time. For example, a patient with SLE who presents in the classical pattern with rash, fever, pleurisy, and arthritis may go into either a spontaneous or, more likely, a therapeutic remission and reappear later with a seizure disorder, a nephropathy, thrombocytopenia, or many other versions of the disease. Over time, the target organs shift. Furthermore, the severity of the illness changes over time. Everybody knows that, but the ebb and flow of severity within the patient has never been understood in biological terms. We haven't a real clue as to why the disease begins or what modulates the ups and downs in its biological activity and, obviously, the illness that results.

As mentioned earlier, there is a significant discordance between clinical and laboratory abnormalities. Thus, one begins to wonder how many of the laboratory abnormalities, at least the serologic ones, might represent a response or an adaptation to the disease, as opposed to a pathogenic abnormality that must be addressed. In this setting, you do not want to treat a patient who has an adaptive or a neutral abnormality. We had a very vivid example of that type of error at Stanford in earlier days. We thought that the appearance of antinuclear autoantibodies or their rise in titer was automatically a harbinger of a flare-up of the disease. As a result, when we noted such a rise, we began to treat the patients with corticosteroids. We found over time, much to our chagrin, that half of our patients' deaths were due to treatment. At that point, we were beginning to understand that the serologies were not reliable indicators of what was happening to patients. We backed off on the frequency, intensity, and duration of therapy, and our death rate plunged. Now we respond only rarely in any therapeutic way to a change in the serologies, even though we deeply believe that those serologies are telling us that there is an immunological origin to the illness and, conceivably, that the abnormal autoantibodies are, themselves, pathogenic agents.

There is also substantial variation in therapeutic response. Some people who seem extremely ill will respond well to therapy, and others who seem minimally disadvantaged will not respond well at all. One could recite these same differences for rheumatoid arthritis.

How can we make this practical in clinical terms? Assume for a moment that these conceptual notions are correct. I want to suggest to you that there is a way that makes sense. It can be depicted very simply. Figure 4-1 presents a typical patient's symptom course, with time on the x-axis and severity on the vertical axis. Notice that points A, B, and C have the same severity, but each in a different setting. In one case the intensity of the disease is increasing, in another case it is declining, in another case it is on a plateau. A physician seeing the patient with this severity must make a judgement. What is the disease direction? What does it mean for therapy? The crucial ingredients for interpreting the patient's course involve two entities—the trend and the tempo of that trend.

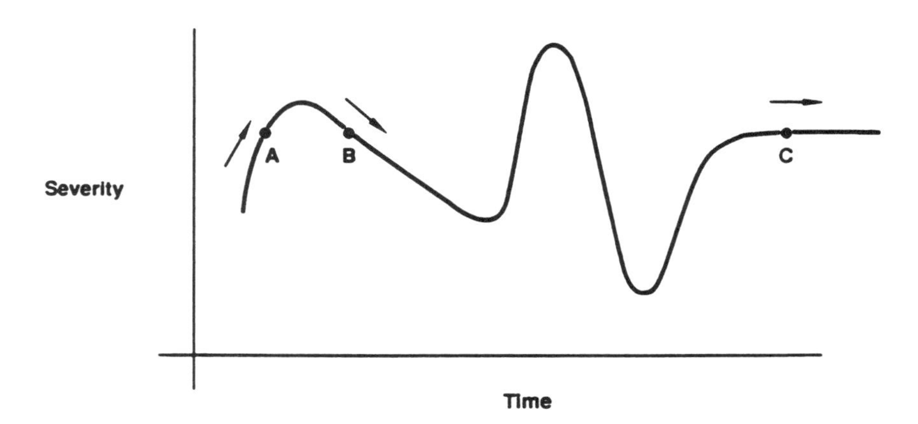

FIGURE 4-1 Idealized course of illness for a typical chronic disease.

We need to know whether the information that the patient presents is representative of a deterioration in the patient's state, an improvement that could be spontaneous or therapeutic, or a plateau. How are we going to know what the trend and its tempo are? Clearly, the crucial tool we have is time, observation time. The judgement we must make is how much time we have. This is not so unusual. Acute disease physicians in an emergency room make their decisions based on changes in minutes and hours. However, we are now talking about using much larger blocks of time as the tool to establish the trends and tempos of chronic disease. In addition, what I said earlier about the characteristics of chronic disease is correct: we are going to have to involve the patient in that process.

An ideal disease course curve is presented in Figure 4-1. A more realistic curve shows substantial oscillation around the true disease trend because of the changing symptoms and changing circumstances of the patient. Figure 4-2 illustrates how difficult this makes the problem. We have to be able to interpret whether any given observation represents a clear change in the true trend or a momentary aberration that a patient experiences as a result of the disease or of an emotional problem (e.g., something happening in the family, such as a child getting bad grades or an illness). The only way in which the distinction can be made between a change in the true trend pattern and this oscillation is through observation of the patient. The doctor and patient are engaged in a partnership to determine the reality of the events they observe.

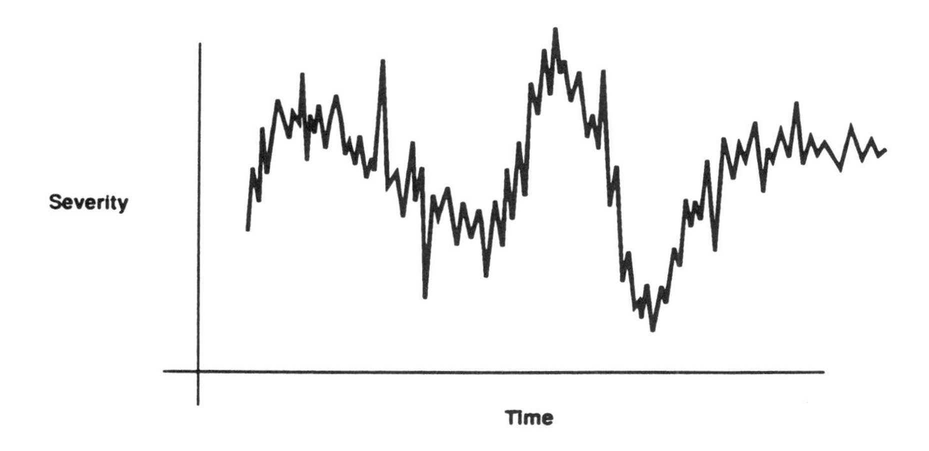

FIGURE 4-2 Realistic simulation of the course of a typical chronic disease.

Another element in making the distinction between true trend and oscillation due to a nondisease factor is continuity of care. As all clinicians know, individual patients have their own patterns to an illness. When there is continuity of care over time, we begin to recognize these patterns. We learn to say to Mr. Smith that the change in pattern is the same as he experienced the last time he ran into difficulties at work or the last time he had an intercurrent infection. He will usually recognize that this is the case and useless escalation of therapies for the specific disease can be avoided. These observations are old hat to clinicians; the point is that they are most effective in a system where the patient and the doctor can work as partners.

The rest of this paper has to do with the role of the patient, the role of the primary care doctor, the role of the specialist, and the role of the health organization or service in a system structured to manage chronic disease well. If we can define these roles, we can define the system that will be required, irrespective of whether it is a version of strict managed care or one of the variations that John Eisenberg identified for us. Tables 4-1 through 4-4 define the necessary roles of patients, physicians and the health service. The definitions are neither exhaustive nor precise, but serve to identify the activities and responsibilities that are essential for effective and efficient management of chronic disease. Patients become knowledgeable, active contributors and partners in decisions. Physicians become teachers, providers of professional information, and builders of a partnership relation. The health system creates the services and facilities necessary for sound patient and health professional functions. My view of the appropriate division of labor is contained in the four tables. Time will not allow explication of every line, so I will focus on a few issues and responsibilities.

First, I want to stress the issue of self-management practices. The patient with chronic disease is clearly his or her most important health care provider (Table 4-1). The patient must manage the medications and engage in whatever behavior changes are needed, such as exercise for reconditioning and the use of cognitive strategies like relaxation and distraction to deal with pain. How well does self-management work? An example of ways in which it appears to work quite well in the rheumatic diseases has to do with our Arthritis Self-Management Program. This program consisted of six two-hour sessions, led by trained lay leaders, to educate patients on what we knew about chronic arthritis, what we knew and did not know about its therapy, what they could do for themselves, ways to use medical and community resources, how they could interpret their symptoms, and self-management practices such as relaxation, exercise, and compensation for handicaps.

TABLE 4-1 Responsibilities of the Patient with Chronic Disease

1. Learn about:

- The disease and its treatment
- Self-management practices
- Prevention of disability
- Monitoring the course of the illness and its treatment in collaboration with the physician
- Ways to use the health system effectively

2. Take responsibility for:

- Participating in health risk appraisals
- Using appropriate prevention and self-management practices
- Participating with health professionals in joint decisions about health care by describing the personal meaning and impact of the disease, evaluating the disease/illness course, stating preferences for management directions, and choosing among treatment options

3. Evaluate the health care experience by:

- Expressing needs and desires for medical and health care
- Rating the character of care received
- Identifying the importance of changes resulting from health care and the satisfaction given by those changes
- Participating in outcome assessments, in the work of patient councils, and in other related activities aimed at improving health services.

We measured the health outcomes over time, along with patient behaviors, and found that patients changed their behaviors as suggested in the learning experience.[40] They also had reduced pain and depression, increased physical and social activity, and decreased use of medical services. Four years later, they still reported a 20 percent reduction in pain, an increase in their activities, and a 40 percent decline in visits to physicians, even though their mean disability score increased 9 percent. We were so surprised by this result that we got another group together and found very similar results: maintenance of pain reduction and physician visit reduction, despite the fact that disability continued to increase over those four years.

---

[40]Lorig, KR, PD Mazonson, HR Holman (1993). Evidence suggesting that health education for self-management in patients with chronic arthritis has sustained health benefits while reducing health costs. *Arthritis and Rheumatism, 36:* 439–446.

I do not want to go into the details here, but when we asked ourselves whether practicing what we taught was responsible for the beneficial outcomes, the answer was essentially no. The correlations between practice of what we taught and health outcomes were never better than 0.20. After focus groups with participants, we took the results to psychologists and hit upon the notion that their perceived self-efficacy to deal with the consequences of arthritis might be playing a role. We constructed instruments to measure self-efficacy and found correlations in the range of 0.6 to 0.7 between patients' self-efficacy at baseline, before the program began, or their growth in perceived self-efficacy over the four years following the program, on one hand, and decline in pain or in the use of physician services on the other. Thus, in this aspect of self-management, one can see fairly significant improvement in patients that appears to arise from attitudinal change and is additive to medicinal therapy.

There are other aspects of self-management that are very important. A crucial one is that the patients take certain responsibilities, but they would be unwilling to do so unless they were satisfied with their experience, feeling that it was benefiting them. We now have good evidence that the way in which physicians behave determines the degree of patient satisfaction. In the setting of chronic disease, the physician becomes a person who is an educator, who encourages, and who provides continuous partnership-type care. It is known that the more participatory the attitude and behavior of the physician toward the patient during encounters, the greater are the patient satisfaction, the patient's compliance, and the willingness of the patient to remain in the care of that physician. Physician support is important for effective self-management by patients.

As Tables 4-2 and 4-3 illustrate, the responsibilities of primary care physicians and specialists in managing patients with chronic disease are complementary but often quite different from the roles they play in the case of acute disease.

In the presence of chronic disease, the role of the specialist changes. The specialist usually does not provide continuous care. Therefore, the specialist is not the right principal physician for the individual with chronic disease, particularly an older individual; the average person over age 65 has more than 1.5 identifiable chronic diseases and many have three or four. So, the role of the specialist is one of advising the patient and the primary care physician. How well is that done today?

In multispecialty groups it is sometimes done very well, but in many settings no appropriate role integration exists between specialists and primary care physicians, with the specialist advising, doing certain things, occasionally taking full responsibility, and then passing that responsibility back to the primary care physician. We are not trained or structured for that kind of role.

TABLE 4-2 Responsibilities of Primary Care Physicians in Managing Patients with Chronic Disease

1. Provide and/or coordinate comprehensive, continuous medical and health care as needed.

2. Learn the consequences and meanings of disease and illness to the patient.

3. Assess the trends and tempos of the disease clinically through collaboration with the patient and family.

4. Involve specialists as partners in initial evaluations and outcome monitoring over time while remaining the principal physician in most cases.

5. Educate patients concerning both the disease and its treatment and the value of and ways to develop a partnership method of managing the disease/illness.

6. Conduct joint decision processes with the patients, in which the physician explains disease consequences, prognosis, and treatment options while the patient assumes responsibility for assessing disease and treatment effects and choosing among treatment options.

7. Locate health care in the most appropriate site—be it office, home, hospital—employing the most efficient methods to determine disease tempos and trends, such as proactive and reactive telephone contact, remote monitoring, mobile services, and visits to any site of care.

8. Elicit assessments from patients and families concerning the quality of their health care, its efficiency, and their satisfaction with it.

Table 4-3 also makes two points that I think are very critical in this setting. One is how we use diagnostic technologies, and the other is how we use treatments. Ideally, in acute disease, diagnostic tests identify a specific cause, and treatments cure. With chronic disease, such opportunities are rare; instead, diagnostics usually reveal only cross-sectional information on a lengthy trend while indecisive therapies have both beneficial and adverse effects. Trends can often be identified by other, simpler observations such as monitoring symptoms or physical state. Potential adverse effects may make a therapy undesirable to a patient. Therefore, diagnostic tests should be used only when an action will predictably be determined by the outcome. A treatment should be used only when the patient and the principal physician agree.

TABLE 4-3 Responsibilities of Specialists in Management of Patients with Chronic Disease

1. Participate in a team with the primary care physician and the patient to design and conduct the most effective, efficient, and satisfying diagnostic and management plan.

2. Employ diagnostic technologies only when they predictably provide a specific answer that leads to an action.

3. Through a "firm arrangement," participate, wherever appropriate to the disease or the problem, at all levels and sites of care. In particular, use rapid contact, remote monitoring, mobile services, and visits to the community or the home to ensure appropriate involvement in health care.

4. Initiate treatment only when the expected outcomes are understood and agreed upon by the patient and the primary care physician.

5. Accept primary responsibility for care whenever appropriate for the disease or the problem, keeping the primary care physician involved and returning responsibility to the primary care physician when reasonable.

6. Function as a primary care physician when accepting primary responsibility beyond the specific disease or problem (i.e., when accepting the role of physician of first contact).

Table 4-4 addresses the responsibilities of the health care organization or service in managing patients with chronic diseases. I am going to elaborate on only one point. This has to do with the way the system establishes communication between the patient and the physician. I don't know how many of you are familiar with John Wasson's study[41] on the use of the telephone, but it is a beautiful study done in the White River Junction Veterans Medical Center at Dartmouth. Elderly patients with chronic disease were randomly assigned to one of two groups. Patients in one group received their usual return appointment on their initial clinic visit. Patients in the second group also received the return appointment, but before the return visit, they were called by a health professional who asked how they were and responded to questions about their medical situation. Then, if the patient was doing well, the visit was cancelled.

[41]Wasson, J, C Gaudette, F Whaley, A Sauvigne, P Baribeau, H Welch (1991). Telephone care as a substitute for routine clinic follow-up. *Journal of the American Medical Association, 267:* 1788–1829.

TABLE 4-4 Responsibility of the Health Care Service in Managing Patients with Chronic Disease

1. Readily accessible ambulatory health care, both primary and specialty, preferably in the community.

2. Health care in all other appropriate sites such as the emergency room, hospital, or the home, including hospice care, and diverse institutions for recovery or long-term care, including respite care.

3. Technologies that facilitate or enhance noninstitutional care such as rapid telephone contact, remote monitoring, mobile services (e.g., food, laboratory and x-ray, homemaker), and visits by health professionals.

4. Subscriber and patient education programs concerned with health risk assessment, disease and disability prevention, disease characteristics and therapies, and self-management practices.

5. Electronic information systems for the medical record, communication among health professionals, and remote monitoring of patients.

6. Facilities for rapid and efficient cooperation between primary care physicians and specialists (e.g., information systems, telephone, joint conferences).

7. Expeditious hospital care, including ambulatory preoperative evaluations and integration of discharge planning with home care services.

8. Evaluations of quality of service and health outcomes conducted with both health professionals and patients.

9. Subscriber and patient voice in service management.

10. Organized, integrated health care "firms" across the full spectrum of medical need extending from ambulatory care through quaternary care, and continuous working relationships between designated specialists and groups of primary care physicians.

Wasson and his colleagues studied the effect of this system over two years. The result was that the number of visits to physicians was reduced by 30 percent for members of the telephone group. Surprisingly, their health status at the end of the two years was better than those who made all their appointments without the telephone calls. Also, their hospitalization rates were considerably lower, and the savings in costs were quite substantial. Telephone care can be a central component of managing chronic disease.

In summary, by recognizing the differences between acute and chronic disease, a number of requirements essential for effectiveness and efficiency in health care become evident. The first is development of appropriate clinical practices. The second is achieving the necessary roles for patients, families, physicians, and other health professionals. The third is creating health services that are consonant with the new responsibilities. By meeting these requirements, we will come much closer to an ideal system.

Invited Reaction

Saralynn Allaire

I want to comment on three components of what I see as an ideal care system for persons with rheumatoid arthritis (RA) or lupus erythematosus (SLE). To begin, I will follow up Dr. Holman's comments on partnership between the patient and the physician, because I think this is extremely important. At least in some cases, this partnership can go one step further, so that the patient actually becomes the director of care, particularly in terms of making care decisions. This making of care decisions helps in coping with the long-term effects of chronic disease, because it facilitates a sense of control. Individuals with RA or SLE often cannot control the progression of their disease. For them a sense of control needs to come about through the ability to control decisions made about their care and their lives.

Now the question is whether different care systems affect whether or not a patient can make decisions about care. I'm not sure if they do or not. Perhaps, as Dr. Holman has suggested, it is the knowledge and attitudes of providers that are most important. However, it seems to me that fee-for-service and point-of-service care systems offer more choices and interfere little with the patient-physician relationship. Thus, they promote patient decision making more than systems that emphasize cost reduction, thereby restricting the types of care covered as well as the choices. In systems with capitation, physicians become partners with the insurer in making care decisions, and the patient is left out. Because of this and the relative lack of regulation in the health insurance business, I believe there is a need for consumer-controlled organizations to which patients can turn for advocacy and also for provision of some types of services, home care services in particular. Independent living centers are examples of such organizations. People with rheumatic diseases have never made much use of these centers or been involved in the independent living movement, but there is a need for greater involvement on their part. To summarize my comments about this component, the ideal care system facilitates care decision making by patients.

The second component I wish to address is the role of specialty versus primary care providers in caring for patients with RA or SLE, and my overall comment is that such a system recognizes that one size does not fit all. For patients like me for whom RA is the only, or major, health problem, it is more efficient for the rheumatologist to be the lead provider. I did belong at one time to a health maintenance organization in which primary care physicians were the lead providers, with the rheumatologist playing a consultant role. In this situation I found that getting the rheumatic disease care I needed was invariably a two-step process. The primary care providers simply couldn't answer the questions I had or handle my rheumatic disease problems. So, either they or I then always had to call the rheumatologist. In addition, because primary care was what they knew and wanted to do, and perhaps because I saw them more often than patients without ongoing health problems, I ended up getting a lot of primary care I didn't want or need.

I would like to say also that I believe there will be a continuing need for specialty care centers, because some providers—physicians and allied health professionals as well—need to have the experience of seeing many patients with one type of disorder. This is beneficial in helping them learn about the disorder and its treatment. These providers are the ones who will be able to develop improvements in clinical care. To summarize the second component, the ideal care system supports ongoing access to specialized care, especially for the treatment of less common disorders.

The last component I will address is support for exercise programs. I asked several friends who have RA what they wanted from their health care system that they didn't have now, and they all said access to and funding of exercise programs. The programs desired are not the traditional range-of-motion exercises. Some of you are probably aware that research is showing that aerobic exercise and programs that build lean body mass are particularly beneficial for persons with RA. Insurers have been loathe to fund ongoing physical therapy exercise programs. Such programs follow a rehabilitation or recovery model, which doesn't really fit aerobic and lean body mass building programs. The latter types of programs are more preventive in nature and thus follow more of a health and fitness model.

Some insurers, interestingly enough, are funding fitness programs, albeit to a small degree. In the Boston area, for example, some try to attract new members by offering discounts on initiation fees to health and fitness centers. Some of these centers employ physical therapists, so perhaps patients with RA or SLE ought to try to get their exercise needs met through health and fitness centers rather than through traditional rehabilitation centers. The question is whether there will be any interest or willingness on the part of insurers to fund involvement in exercise programs at fitness centers on an ongoing basis. It would be interesting to see if models with different levels of copayment, based in part perhaps on income, could be tested for cost-effectiveness. Another benefit of offering "rehabilitation" services through health and fitness centers is that the centers are a more normal setting and so might enhance compliance. The ideal care system would financially support the ongoing exercise and fitness needs of patients with RA or SLE.

Invited Reaction

Teresa Brady

I am speaking from two different perspectives. One is that, like Saralynn, I have rheumatoid arthritis. The second is that I work in a care system in the Minneapolis area that is in the process of transforming itself from a hospital holding company into an integrated health network.

As many of you know, Minneapolis is one of the more advanced managed care environments, deeply into fourth-generation managed care. The care principles that the Fairview Health System developed have become the drivers of our care model. Hal talked about several concepts in our model, so I am going to emphasize just a few of them. I have three main points: the importance of self-management, the need for changing roles, and the possibility of alternative delivery mechanisms.

Hal Holman did a very nice job of laying out the case for self-management as a crucial element of the ideal care system. We need to come to terms with the concept that in actuality the patient is the provider. As health care professionals, we have traditionally thought of ourselves as the providers, but in chronic disease we are not. Hal highlighted that it is the patients who have the opportunity (and responsibility) to take the medicines or not, to do the exercises or not, and to pace themselves or not. Thus, regardless of our recommendations, it is the patient who provides his or her own care on a day-to-day basis. Our opportunity to provide care is limited by the small amount of time we are in contact with the patient. We need to change the way we engage patients in that self-management opportunity, and the way we train professionals to help patients self-manage.

I was struck by the fact that John Eisenberg did not refer to self-management at all when he outlined the training changes he believes are needed for the future. Clearly, if patients with chronic disease are to successfully manage their disease, we need to teach them to become active partners rather than passive recipients of care. In the Chronic Disease Management Project at Fairview we have seen that many of our patients mirror their physicians' attitudes toward self-management. Participatory physicians have many patients who are active self-managers; more directive physicians have more passive patients who do minimal self-care activities and are less likely to comply with treatment recommendations. We do not know whether the self-management attitude is contagious (i.e., patients adopt the same attitude as their physicians), whether patients seek out physicians who match their own attitudes toward self management, or whether physicians alter their attitudes based on what they think patients want. However, if patients match their physicians' attitudes, we need to train professionals to engage patients in the self-management process.

One of my favorite arthritis self-managers, who has a superb relationship with her physician, recently engaged in a debate with that rheumatologist. Speaking of their partnership, they debated who had the majority share, or 51 percent, of the control and who had 49 percent. The fact that they could even have this debate showed how remarkable their partnership is. As she talked more about it—and they did differ on who held the 51 percent share—she realized that in reality she held 90 percent. Although her rheumatologist thought he held 51 percent, he really only had 10 percent.

I maintain that rather than being providers, in chronic disease the professionals are really coaches. We can motivate, we can encourage, we can run skill development drills, but the person doing the day-to-day management of the disease is the person who gets out of bed each day with arthritis. We clearly need to set up our systems so that appropriate self-management is inherent in them.

Facilitating self-management is one of the role changes necessary in the ideal care system. Other role changes are necessary, and prepaid health plans may help facilitate these changes. Rather than asking whether the specialist or primary care physician should be the lead provider, I think the question is more elemental than that. We need to step back and ask who sees the patient, when and where, and for what purpose.

We need to expand our roles to look at the patient more longitudinally over time, to be aware of the trend and tempo of the disease as Hal discussed, and also to look more multidimensionally at the patient to address not only the biological disease but the entire illness experience Hal described. John Eisenberg talked about some of the blurring of professional responsibilities. Certainly there are models in which care is delegated to other providers such as nurse practitioners and physician assistants. I maintain that some of the time the appropriate provider is not a substitute physician, but another type of provider such as a rehabilitation therapist or social worker. The Fairview Care is the delivery and/or arrangement of a broad range of care management services in a manner that is accessible, comprehensive, and coordinated over time. That function may sometimes be delivered by a rheumatologist, a primary care provider, or another type of professional.

As we change some of our roles, we also need to change our delivery mechanisms. I think prepaid medicine gives us the opportunity to explore alternative delivery mechanisms. Health care delivery is currently based on what is reimbursable. Telephone calls are not reimbursable, direct admissions to nursing homes are not reimbursable, some exercise programs or self-management classes are not reimbursable. Perhaps we would be wiser to throw away the concept of what is reimbursable and organize our care around what is going to provide the best benefit for this patient over the course of the disease. Hal mentioned telephone interventions. A study by Weinberger et al[42] found that they increased functional status with monthly telephone support. I think the support came from a lay person, not even a health professional. Who would have thought that was possible?

Like Saralynn, I have 22 years' experience living with rheumatoid arthritis. For 15 of those years I have been on methotrexate, with the exception of a one-year drug holiday after pneumonitis. Throughout most of my disease course I have made bimonthly visits to my rheumatologist. I have had several episodes of frequent medication manipulation in response to disease activity, and I have also had numerous periods of a stable treatment regimen. Presently I see my rheumatologist every two months. He does a joint exam, and we laugh together about whether or not I should get more rest. Of course, he can't rest for me; I have to figure out how to do that for myself. In the last two to three years of bimonthly visits, we made one modest increase of my sulfasalazine. I like seeing my rheumatologist, but as I was preparing for this meeting I began to question these routine bimonthly visits. Is this a good use of the health care dollar when my treatment program is stable?

I know I need a rheumatologist. I have aggressive disease and a complex situation. I need someone skilled at monitoring and adjusting these medications. I need regular monitoring of side effects, but do I need bimonthly rheumatologist visits? Could some of this monitoring be done by phone, by another professional, by self-assessment?

Perhaps we could pay for some of these alternative delivery mechanisms in place of existing (and currently reimbursable) care patterns. Kaiser of Colorado is experimenting with group visits to a physician. Similar chronic disease or elderly patients come in together for an extended session with their physician and another professional. Individual needs are taken care of during

---

[42]Weinberger, M, SL Hines, WM Tierney, (1986). Improving functional status in arthritis: The effects of social support. *Social Science and Medicine, 9:* 899–904.

the breaks. Brief individual sessions are held following the group meeting if necessary, but they are rarely necessary. This seems to be a clinically and financially effective alternative delivery mode.

In summary, my key points, which reflect some of the National Chronic Care Consortium's criteria for chronic care networks, are that self-management is essential and we need to organize our care system around it, that we need to integrate changing roles by all of our care providers into our care management, and that we need to explore alternative care delivery mechanisms. Finally, pooled or shared risk financing may provide the financial incentives to incorporate these necessary changes in the ideal care system.

Invited Reaction

Debra R. Lappin

Like Saralynn Allaire and Teresa Brady, I have had a rheumatic disease for nearly two decades. I have been asked to look at the question of ideal treatment from this perspective. I would like to examine the three critical components of an ideal care system, as defined by Hal Holman: the patient, the physician, and essential elements of the system itself. To these I would add two further components: (1) how outcomes of an ideal system will be measured, and (2) who must be assured access in order for the system to be viewed as ideal. I hope my remarks regarding these components, while redundant at times, will shed additional light on today's discussion.[43]

THE PATIENT

First, the way the patient is perceived within the system of care may drive many aspects of the model. As an example, Teresa Brady's organization, the Fairview Health System, recognizes in its internal training materials that a person is a "patient" at the point in time when he or she interacts with the delivery system. However, the label is not meant to suggest "subservience or lack of autonomy—concepts that have been prevalent in present or past uses of the word patient. . . . [P]atients should be raised up, elevating them beyond

[43]The author wishes to express her appreciation for the assistance of T.J. Brady, Ph.D., and L. Callahan, Ph.D., in preparing these comments.

member, customer or client."[44]

Patient self-management has been viewed as central to the design of any care system for any chronic disease.[45] A fortiori, this concept should serve as the keystone for a system designed to address rheumatic disease. As Holman has stated, "The patient, in the presence of chronic disease, is clearly the single most important care provider." Indeed, David Sobel, Regional Director, Patient Education and Health Promotion, Kaiser Permanente of Northern California, describes the patient as the "true primary care provider."[46] According to Brady, other members of the health care team serve as "coaches." As she has written, "In day to day life with a rheumatic or connective tissue disease, health professionals can only teach, motivate, and run skill development drills; the patient him or herself is the one that needs to actually run the plays or provide the care."[47] If this active, managerial role of the patient is widely embraced by evolving systems of care, it necessarily follows that professional training must be reoriented to prepare the physician for this very different role of, and relationship with, the patient.[48]

The importance of self-efficacy and self-management not only is something to which those of us with rheumatic disease can bear anecdotal witness; it is also supported by widely recognized clinical studies conducted at Stanford. Hal Holman, in his important work with Kate Lorig, has demonstrated that health education for self-management in patients with chronic arthritis, over a four-year period following intervention, can lead to a 20 percent reduction in pain and a 40 percent decrease in physician visits, even though physical disability may have increased as much as 9 percent.[49] Leigh Callahan has shown in her studies that socioeconomic status and a sense of learned

---

[44]Alexander, Gl, T Brady, M Brunnette, T Burmaster, B Dickie, A Ellison, R Gibson, J Lally, L McNamara, R Meiches, B Milavitz, D Walsh, (1995). *The Fairview Care Model: A Work in Progress.* Minneapolis: Fairview Health System.

[45]Zitter, M. (1995). Disease management: A new approach to health care. *Medical Interface, 7:* 71–76. Zablocki, E (1995). Using disease state management to coordinate care across the continuum. *The Quality Letter*, November, 2–10.

[46]Sobel, D. (1996). Clients/patients as partners in prevention and care management. Presented at the National Chronic Care Consortium Workshop, San Francisco, May 5-8.

[47]Brady, TJ (in press). Managed care in the care of rheumatic disease patients: Opportunity or oppression? In J Melvin and G Jensen, (Eds.), *Assessment and Management of Arthritis in Rehabilitation.*

[48]Pincus, T (1993). Arthritis and rheumatic diseases: What doctors can learn from their patients. Pp 177–192 in D Goleman and J Gurin (Eds.), *Mind/Body Medicine.* Yonkers, NY: Consumer Reports Books. Pawlson, LG (1994). Chronic illness: Implications of a new paradigm for health care. *Journal of Quality Improvement, 20:* 33–39.

[49]Lorig, KR, PD Masonson, HR Holman (1993). Evidence suggesting that health education for self-management in patients with chronic arthritis has sustained health benefits while reducing health care costs. *Arthritis and Rheumatism, 36:* 439–446.

helplessness are associated with increased mortality rates in rheumatoid arthritis.[50] In other studies, a higher sense of self-efficacy has been associated with greater psychological well-being, and psychoeducational interventions have demonstrated significant reduction in pain, depression, and disability over and above the effects produced by medications.[51]

THE ROLE OF THE PHYSICIAN AND THE RELATIONSHIP BETWEEN THE PRIMARY CARE PROVIDER AND THE SPECIALIST

An ideal care model must address the optimum terms for a "handoff" between the primary care provider (PCP) and the specialist, in most instances the rheumatologist, but also in others—to name only a few—the orthopedist, gastroenterologist, nephrologist, podiatrist, pulmonologist, or ophthalmologist.

With reference to this hand-off, John Eisenberg, who spoke earlier, stated that "primary care doctors navigate, negotiate, evaluate, educate patients and make decisions, and consultants consult." This perspective raises an obvious question not only for the system of care, but more particularly for the consumer with complex rheumatic disease who, like those of us commenting today, has come to place a high value on his or her ability to maintain a direct and continuing interchange with a specialist in rheumatology.

Simply posed, the question is, What should the role of the rheumatologist be in any ideal care system? Should the rheumatologist serve as the *primary care* physician; as the *principal* physician, who sees the patient regularly, while other less frequent primary care needs are handled by a primary care physician; or as the *consultant*? One study mentioned by Eisenberg confirmed that much of what a rheumatologist does, at least in 1979, is to see patients regularly for their arthritis. Indeed, 59 percent of rheumatologists surveyed at that time were acting as the "principal physician" for their rheumatic disease

---

[50]Callahan, LF, DS Cordray, G Wells, T Pincus (1996). Helplessness as a mediator of the association between formal education and mortality in patients with rheumatoid arthritis. *Arthritis Care and Research, 9:* 463–472.

[51]Taal, E, JJ Rasker, O Wiegman (1996). Patient education and self-management in rheumatic diseases: A self-efficacy approach. *Arthritis Care and Research, 9:* 229–238. Buckelew, SP, B Hywser, J Hewett, JC Parker, JC Johnson, R Conway and DR Kay (1996). Self-efficacy predicting outcomes among fibromyaligia subjects. *Arthritis Care and Research, 9:* 97–104. Mullen, PD, EA Laville, AK Biddle and K Lorig (1987). Efficacy of psychoeducational interventions on pain, depression and disability in people with arthritis: A meta-analysis. *Journal of Rheumatology, 14 (Suppl. 15):* 33–39.

patients, whereas "consults" were only 17 percent of their activities.[52]

The targeted use of a rheumatology consult within a model care system may contribute to direct economic savings. Preliminary findings summarized in an abstract and presented at the 1995 Scientific Meeting of the American College of Rheumatology (ACR) indicated that in a Medicare risk plan that required a rheumatology consult before other orthopedic, radiology, or therapy referrals could be made, orthopedic procedures dropped from 14.9 to 6.7 joint replacements per 1000 enrollees; payments to orthopedists dropped over $3.30 per member per month; and there was an accompanying reduction in hospital costs, which were five times those of the physicians' costs.[53] Specialist referral may also have the potential to confer other benefits on both the system and the patient. Again, in preliminary findings, rheumatologists treating complicated rheumatoid arthritis patients were shown to have achieved better outcomes with fewer physician visits than primary care physicians with similar patients.[54] Still another paper presented at the 1995 Scientific Meeting of the ACR suggested that patients sent for rheumatologic care had lower average annual costs, although comparison and control data are unclear.[55]

The future role of and need for rheumatologists remain the subject of differing opinion. On one hand, active intervention by a rheumatologist in the care of the patient with rheumatic disease is believed to benefit both the system and the patient.[56] My own case stands as a stunning example of successful intervention more than a decade ago with early and aggressive immunosuppressive therapies—therapies that, at the time, would have been used and managed only by a specialist. However, others opine that rheumatologists tend to maintain a "serious disease" orientation often characteristic of a consultant that may lead them to undertake substantial

---

[52]Aiken, LH, CE Lewis, HJ Craig, RC Mendenhall, RJ Blenden, DE Rogers (1979). The contributions of specialists to the delivery of primary care. *New England Journal of Medicine, 300:* 1363–1370.

[53]Overman, S, L Rayburn, D Kent, D Uslan, (1995). Rheumatologists and musculoskeletal managers in a Medicare risk program (Abstract). American College of Rheumatology 59th Annual Scientific Meeting, San Francisco, October 21–26.

[54]Yelin, E, C Such, L Criswell, W Epstein (1995). Outcomes for persons with RA treated by rheumatologists and non-rheumatologists (Abstract). American College of Rheumatology, 59th Annual Scientific Meeting, San Francisco, October 21–26.

[55]Singh, G, D Ramey, J McGuire (1995). Costs of medical care for patients with rheumatoid arthritis: An 11-year study (Abstract). American College of Rheumatology, 59th Annual Scientific Meeting, San Francisco, October 21–26.

[56]Epstein, S, LM Sherwood (1996). From outcomes research to disease management: A guide for the perplexed. *Annals of Internal Medicine, 124:* 832–837.

testing to rule out unusual diagnoses,[57] or may cause them to overlook the patient's nonrheumatological health care needs.

In an era when the measurement of quality of delivery of care by health systems will include increasing emphasis on outcomes—among them, patient satisfaction—it is my opinion that timely and appropriate specialist referral will be shown to correlate directly with greater patient satisfaction. In turn, preliminary data summarized above may suggest an accompanying savings to the system. Obviously, more studies in this area are required, and, indeed, this need may be met by managed care organizations as they invest in the study of specialist referrals, as a function both of their bottom line and of consumers' perceptions of quality care.

To summarize, an ideal care system must address these tensions in the relationship between the PCP and the specialist and must consider the most effective use of the specialist, here the rheumatologist, in treating systemic rheumatic disease. This can be as a *consultant,* early on for selected musculoskeletal cases, or in one of three roles later on in the face of diagnostic uncertainty, uncontrolled symptoms, or complications from the disease or medications.[58] In these latter instances, the choice must then be made whether the rheumatologist will best serve the patient and the system by continuing in the role of a consultant or by assuming an expanded role, as the *principal* physician for the patient or as a *designated primary care* provider who maintains a special expertise in rheumatology.[59] These choices, about which consumers are certain to express their opinions, will impact how specialists are trained in the future and, as Eisenberg and others have noted, will drive work force demands in the specialty in the years ahead.[60]

OTHER ELEMENTS IN AN IDEAL SYSTEM OF CARE

Elements of an ideal care system thus include, first, the changing role of the patient: this encompasses engaging the patient in his or her own self-management and rethinking the physician-patient relationship in order to vest in the patient a sense of control, self-efficacy, and ability to manage the daily physical, psychological, and social impacts of chronic illness. Second, the system must address the role of the specialist in the management of this

---

[57]Meenan, RF (1996). Managed care and the rheumatologist. *Current Opinion in Rheumatology, 8:* 91–95.

[58]Dorr, R (1996). *Guidelines to Rheumatology Referral.* Atlanta: American College of Rheumatology.

[59]Pawlson, op. cit.; Meenan, op. cit.

[60]Epstein, Sherwood, op. cit.; Meenan, op. cit.

population of patients. Finally, the system itself must recognize and integrate into treatment protocols numerous other methods of care that are critical to successful management of the rheumatic disease patient. Each of these is discussed here briefly.

Rehabilitation

As Saralynn Allaire emphasized in her comments, rehabilitation in rheumatic disease has been underappreciated, underutilized, and thus underfinanced, and must be a considered a critical component of an ideal system of care.[61] According to our keynote speaker, John Eisenberg, primary care doctors are experts at rehabilitating patients, something that is underemphasized in most of our rheumatology training programs. Whether the failure of the current system, in this regard, is rooted in the limitations and biases of specialty training programs or in the narrow focus of rehabilitation that characterizes much of medical training, most care systems today continue to view (and thus reimburse) rehabilitation as a finite event. However—and I agree with our other responders again here—the patient with acute or advanced rheumatic disease cannot function successfully without timely, and often periodically repeated, specialized rehabilitation through physical, occupational, and psychological modes of therapy.

Exercise

An ideal care system for rheumatic disease must consider the impact of exercise on patient outcomes and support patient involvement in a serious exercise program, not as part of a rehabilitation program but as part of a long-term personal commitment to health maintenance. As Allaire has noted, emphasis should be placed on "normalizing" and "mainstreaming" the patient's routine and experience.

Exercise programs for people with rheumatic disease that emphasize not only range of motion, but endurance, aerobic fitness, and strength conditioning have been shown in various contexts to produce improvements in physical and psychological function, cardiovascular health, and fitness without aggravation of disease activity and symptoms.[62] Resistance training has been considered

---

[61] Sobel, op. cit.; Epstein, Sherwood, op. cit.

[62] Minor, MA (1991). Physical activity and management of arthritis. *Annuals of Behavioral Medicine, 13:* 117–124. Stenstrom, CH (1994). Therapeutic exercise in rheumatoid arthritis. *Arthritis Care Research, 7:* 190–197. Semble, EL, RF Loeser, CM Wise (1990). Therapeutic exercise for rheumatoid arthritis and osteoarthritis. *Arthritis and Rheumatism, 20:* 32–40.

a possible means of counteracting metabolic and body composition changes that accompany advanced rheumatic disease.[63] Inclusion and reimbursement of exercise modalities within a system of care, however, represent a likely departure from today's delivery mechanisms. Certainly the experience of those of us responding, which has been confirmed by at least one study relating to osteoarthritis patients, has been that the majority of patients with rheumatic disease are not consistently advised by their physician to engage in modest range-of-motion exercises or, if so advised, are not then given specific exercise instructions.[64]

Nonrestrictive Drug Formularies

An ideal care system must consider the value of widely varying and rapidly advancing pharmacological approaches to the treatment of rheumatoid arthritis and lupus. The value of any single pharmacological intervention varies from patient to patient and fluctuates over time with each individual. Suitability of a particular intervention or of a delicate combination of drug therapies changes in response to the ebb and flow of the disease, to the patient's tolerance of the treatment, and to the continued efficacy of a particular prescribed course. Restrictive drug formularies, while especially problematical in the treatment of rheumatic disease,[65] have been shown in other contexts to result in increased physician visits, mental health visits, and nursing home admissions.[66]

---

[63] Rall, L, C Roubenoff (1996). Body composition, metabolism and resistance exercise in patients with rheumatoid arthritis. *Arthritis Care and Research, 9:* 151–158.

[64] Dexter, P (1992). Joint exercises in elderly persons with symptomatic OA of the hip and knee. *Arthritis Care and Research, 5:* 36–41.

[65] Pincus, T, LF Callahan (1989). Clinical use of multiple nonsteroidal anti-inflammatory drug preparations within individual rheumatology private practices. *Journal of Rheumatology, 16:* 1253–1258.

[66] Zitter, op. cit. Soumerai, S, D Ross-Degnan, J Avorn, TJ McLaughlin, I Choodnovskiy (1991). Effects of Medicaid drug-payment limits on admission to hospitals and nursing homes. *New England Journal of Medicine, 325:* 1072–1077. Moore, WJ, RJ Newman (1992). U.S. Medicaid drug formularies: Do they work? *PharmacoEconomics, 1 (Suppl. 1):* 28–31.

Alternative Delivery Mechanisms

Alternative mechanisms for the delivery of care to people with rheumatic disease have the potential not only for influencing positively patient satisfaction and functional status, but also for effecting economic savings within the system. In one study, the use of rheumatology nurse practitioners resulted in positive health status changes that were not found in the rheumatologist-managed patient group.[67] Telephone support provided by lay persons has been shown to improve functional status in people with osteoarthritis.[68] Person-centered, nondirective, telephone-based counseling intervention significantly improved the psychological status of patients with lupus, in comparison to usual mechanisms of care. However, in the same study, similar improvements did not occur in patients with rheumatoid arthritis.[69]

Kaiser Permanente's Group Cooperative Health Care Clinic, Wheatridge, Colorado, in a pilot study now receiving ongoing funding by the Robert Wood Johnson Foundation, has noted positive patient and system responses to consultation sessions involving groups of geriatric patients. Such preliminary responses have included reduced hospital and emergency room visits, decreased mortality, and increased physician and patient satisfaction, as well as more timely and cost-effective use of preventive care (Scott et al., unpublished manuscript). Kaiser is considering expanding this successful alternative delivery mechanism to include certain disease-specific groups. I have been advised by a member of the Kaiser Study Group that rheumatology is viewed as the likely first area for such expansion.

Further, multiple studies have demonstrated a linkage between the availability of social support and the patient's psychological well-being and decreased depressive symptoms.[70] The psychological benefits of social support, which appear to hold up even when disease severity and physical

---

[67]Hill, J, HA Bird, R Harmer, V Wright, C Lawton (1994). An evaluation of the effectiveness, safety and acceptability of a nurse practitioner in a rheumatology outpatient clinic. *British Journal of Rheumatology, 33:* 283–288.

[68]Weinberger et al., op cit.

[69]Maisiak, R, JS Austin, AG West, L Heck (1996). The effect of person-centered counseling on the psychological status of persons with systemic lupus erythematosus or rheumatoid arthritis. *Arthritis Care and Research, 9:* 60–66.

[70]Affleck, G, H Tennen, C Pfeiffer and J Fifield (1988). Social support and psychological adjustment to rheumatoid arthritis. *Arthritis Care and Research, 1:* 71–77.

dysfunction are controlled,[71] must then be considered in the design of any ideal care system.

Structured Care

To ensure that the needs of populations of patients are addressed consistently and competently, a rheumatic disease care system must rely on structured care tools. Clinical care pathways, management guidelines for specific rheumatic diseases, and sophisticated algorithmic clinical decision-clarifying tools have all begun to pervade the marketplace. Today, professional organizations, newly incorporated clinical management subsidiaries of major pharmaceutical companies, and even voluntary health organizations are all bringing their particular experience and interest to bear on this area of disease management. Although the varied and often parochial agendas of these groups may present conflicting messages, managed care organizations are nonetheless moving rapidly toward adoption and implementation of structured mechanisms for delivering care that will best reflect the idiosyncrasies, corporate philosophies, and financial capabilities of the organization.

What is clear is that the various forms of rheumatic disease, in particular lupus and rheumatoid arthritis, although fraught with uncertainty and demanding care that reflects not only a competent grasp of the prevailing "science" of medicine but an equally important appreciation for the illusive "art" of wise care, must and do lend themselves to standardized, considered, all-encompassing clinical treatment protocols. The depth of expertise resting within the established specialty community must be tapped in an effort to bring this essential balance of *art and science*—critical to the treatment of any chronic illness—into an ideal and workable disease management model for rheumatic disease.

Relationship Between Financing and Care

Essential to the success, first, of any single element of an ideal care system

---

[71]Goodenow, C, ST Reisine and KE Grady (1990). Quality of social support and associated social and psychological functioning in women with rheumatoid arthritis. *Health Psychology, 9:* 266–284. Reisine, S (1993). Marital status and support in rheumatoid arthritis. *Arthritis and Rheumatism, 36:* 589–592.

for people with rheumatic disease and second, of the overarching delivery system itself will be the long-term ability of the health care system to metamorphose in ways that support the interrelationship of financing and delivery of care around chronic healthcare needs.

The evolved system will recognize that the needs of people with chronic disease must necessarily cross provider settings and extend over long periods of time.[72] Care will emphasize disability prevention, delay, or minimization and will address patients' multidimensional needs. Financing a patients' long-term health care needs will be undertaken within a fixed-dollar capitation that is limited by the financial capabilities of the system itself, is increasingly scrutinized by the public, and is risk-adjusted for the presence of chronic disease. Further, the risk of providing care within these limitations, will be understood, accepted, and shared by all providers in a coordinated delivery system that allows for communication, innovation, and accountability.[73]

MEASUREMENT OF OUTCOMES IN AN IDEAL CARE SYSTEM

Outcomes of an ideal care system for rheumatic disease must be measured broadly. Disease management systems will be judged by clinical, economic, and humanistic outcomes.[74] Significant clinical events in a rheumatology model should include not only the traditional measurements of clinical trials (e.g., joint involvement and erosion, and physiologic and metabolic measures) but, more importantly, changes in health status outcomes. Economic outcomes must consider not only obvious short-term impacts on the system, such as patient visits and hospitalizations, but also long-term analyses of reduced disability and enhanced productivity. In turn, employers will express increasing interest in systems that address openly and effectively a decrease in work loss and restricted activity days. Humanistic outcomes will measure reduction in symptoms and enhanced quality of life, functional status, and patient satisfaction. Measurements of functional status for all outcomes must incorporate physical and psychosocial outcomes and must place values on slowing the rate of decline of functional levels, as opposed to maintaining a given functional status.

Further, outcomes must incorporate new definitions of quality care. Pawlson, for example, says:

---

[72]Bringewatt, R (1996). National Chronic Care Consortium Statement on Medicare Managed Care Programs. Testimony before the U.S. Congress, House of Representatives, Subcommittee on health of the Ways and Means Committee. Washington, D.C.

[73]Alexander et al., op. cit.; Bringewatt, op. cit.

[74]Epstein and Sherwood, op. cit.

> The patient's perceptions and his or her long-term outcome, in relationship to how well the interventions are applied, become central elements in [the] consideration of quality. Our ability to understand the interrelationship between patient satisfaction, patient compliance, and the amelioration or exacerbation of illness becomes an important focus of our efforts to measure quality.[75]

Indeed, new measures of quality of delivery will again reflect public input—from consumers, from employers, from government—and will evolve from consensus-building conferences such as that scheduled by the Health Care Quality Alliance (HCQA) for February, 1997. At this time, HCQA has committed itself to developing a white paper that can be presented to health plans, purchasers, accreditors, and other entities that will examine "where measures are lacking, what consumers want, and how existing measures can be improved."[76]

> These evolving perspectives on the success of a model care system will take place in the context of a framework of automated information, evidenced-based medicine and defined protocols of care, with explicit collection of outcomes information. . . .
>
> In the future, patient health will be improved by maximizing functionality; minimizing disease, disability, and death; and improving the efficiency and cost-effectiveness of health care. This improvement involves the use of effective outcomes tools, including linked databases and collaborative research efforts.[77]

ACCESS TO AN IDEAL CARE SYSTEM

A care system—no matter how utopian in design—will never approach "ideal" if there remain those who are in need of its services but are barred from access. The casualties of today's system of managed care increasingly appear to be those who are disenfranchised due to preexisting conditions or economic misfortune. Perhaps, then, the ideal system can only be one that incorporates measures to address the cost of today's uncompensated care, which in the past essentially has been underwritten by academic medical centers or publicly supported hospitals and clinics. Additionally, federal and state legislation, such as the recently passed Kennedy–Kassebaum bill addressing portability and preexisting conditions, must continue to expand the

---

[75]Pawlson, op. cit.

[76]Health Care Quality Allaince (1996). *The HCQA Quality Forum, 3.*

[77]Epstein, op. cit.

rights of those with chronic rheumatic disease to obtain and maintain health coverage within any "ideal" delivery system.

CONCLUSION

The resources inherent in today's emerging health care system offer great hope for the development and measurement of effective disease management systems. An ideal care system for rheumatic disease, the single most prevalent chronic condition in the United States today, should emerge within this framework and serve as a working template for numerous other chronic conditions. Systems will emerge that embrace clinical, economic, and humanistic outcomes. Systems will succeed if they are designed to retain the essential physician–patient partnership; to involve all caregivers, including the patient, in decisions geared toward successful long term outcomes; to distribute the shared financial risk and reward resulting from such treatment choices, and to recognize and address the multidimensional, longitudinal needs of, and preserve access by, the person whose life will be irreversibly molded by the presence of chronic disease.

Discussion

ALAN FOGELMAN: One term that has not been mentioned by anyone is the medical loss ratio. The fact that it has not been mentioned is almost like talking about heart disease or cancer without mentioning smoking. In terms of providing quality care, the medical loss ratio, from a practical standpoint, is one of the most important factors that we need to focus on and get the public to understand. The term implies that third-party payers feel that all premiums collected should be profit, and what is spent on care is loss from profit. Point-of-service plans in Southern California now have a medical loss ratio of 69.5. That means that 30.5 cents is taken out of every health care dollar for profit and administration, and only 69.5 cents goes toward medical services. I think Bill Kelley is right on target when he argues that in a steady state it will be impossible to provide high-quality care without a medical loss ratio that has a minimum of 85 cents on the dollar. Kaiser, which is a mature system, claims it has a medical loss ratio of 95 percent. I think it is probably closer, when you add in everything, to 90 percent. Still, that is very different from the national average of about 72 cents on the dollar.

I think that no matter what we do, no matter how we try to design systems, until the public demands that a significant portion, at least 85 cents on the dollar, is spent for taking care of patients and organizing all the programs that we heard about that are needed today, we are not going to be able to provide quality care in a steady state for our population.

JOHN EISENBERG: Alan, I am sympathetic to your concern, but I have to give the M.B.A. response to that, which is that the market will shake it all out. According to Adam Smith, if we are willing to pay a certain amount of premiums for our care and a plan is able to provide the quality of care we demand and make a profit, all the more power to it. A plan may transfer the profits from hospitals and doctors to investors, and the customer ends up the same basically. You cannot show me that the quality of care they are getting is worse than in the previous system. All you can tell me is that there are profits and that doctors aren't getting them.

What will happen over time, Adam Smith would say, is that if the profit is so large, some other investor will say, "I can provide the same quality service for lower price," or "I can provide higher quality service for the same price," and that investor will attract all the patients to its plan. Adam Smith would say that, in the long term, whatever Bill Kelley's solution is won't be necessary because the market will shake it all out and the price and the cost of providing services will come together in an equilibrium state.

Having said this, I am not at all sure that it is a perfect market, which is what is required. In an imperfect market, when there is a monopoly, there is a responsibility to have public regulation. This is the public utility model. Thus, the question that we ought to be addressing is not whether these profits are bad or not, but whether the market is going to solve the problem. Otherwise, we need a public utility model that says this is a monopoly and price regulation is required.

BEVRA HAHN: We have to be careful in planning about one size fits all in terms of patient self-management. We don't want to come up with a strictly Caucasian paradigm. A lot of ethnic groups that we deal with in Los Angeles are not interested in self-management and are much more interested in being directed. You achieve a better outcome, in my opinion, if you go with what a particular group wants.

HALSTED HOLMAN: Kate Lorig, my colleague and a designer of the Arthritis Self-Management Course, is just completing a Spanish arthritis self-management course, which has been successful. We don't have all the outcome results, but we know already that the people who volunteered for it were very, very pleased. There was some question about whether it would fit well, based on certain cultural differences. I think the jury is still out on how we approach other cultures and other ethnic groups. We will have to be sensitive and explore ways to do this.

TERESA BRADY: I agree that different cultures have different beliefs about self-management, but I don't believe a chronic disease can be managed without self-management. On fact, chronic disease is *always* self-managed by what the patient chooses to do or not do. We must find ways of engaging these populations so that they choose appropriate self-care behaviors. A physician cannot direct care 24 hours per day, 365 days per year, so patients need to assume some of that responsibility.

LAURA ROBBINS: In regard to culture and access, I think the work that has been done with lupus patients in the parallel self-management programs has opened up a Pandora's box in terms of access and utilization of services. We really must look at access to services, putting aside the socioeconomic barriers of course, and ask what we need to know to have patients come into our HMOs and managed care, whatever it may be.

JOHN ROWE: I am particularly attracted to the concepts and the comments about the patient being the provider and the need for a partnership that is a collaboration. I wondered whether the panelists have had any experience with the completion of that thought. That is, do the patients get report cards? Do we feed back to the patient-provider the data on how the patient's functional status is changing and what the utilization of health care resources is? Does the patient as well as the provider get the practice care guideline, and is that guideline developed by both the patient and the provider? I wonder how serious we are about the fact that the patient is the provider?

TERESA BRADY: I don't know of anybody who has done it. Certainly in our system we have talked about it, but this would be a nightmare to administer. Just as insurance rates vary depending on whether you smoke or not, perhaps there could be different rates for health insurance based on your self-management behavior?

HALSTED HOLMAN: As far as I know, there are no studies on that subject, but I would certainly say that the patient gets a report card every day. This report card is his or her own experience with disease consequences. In a good doctor–patient relationship, to my way of thinking, what you talk about is whether there are possibilities of improvement and what those entail. The diabetes control study showed that if patients do certain things rigorously, they will get several measurable advantages. However, patients often say, "I don't want to do those things. They are too much of a bother to my life." My own experience is that each patient presents different considerations. Patients' report cards from their own disease differ, and I try to respond to that.

JOHN ROWE: I am quite serious about my question. I was envisioning instances in which the patient might, on seeing the data, say, "You know, I am not calling enough. Look at that." Or the patient may say, "You know, maybe you are right. I am calling you too much. It seems normal to me that I should call every morning, but I see now that is not the case. I also see that the relationship between these calls and how I am doing is actually not so good." Perhaps he or she would say, "Now I see, as I look at this over time, that my disease really does fluctuate sort of independently of these other things." I am quite serious about providing feedback. The data are available. There is no extra cost to collect them. It is just a matter of sharing them with the patient.

HALSTED HOLMAN: One of the necessities is a readily available medical record. When that is available, the patient can carry it so that when you converse, you are conversing from the same database.

NORMAN LEVINSKY: I have a comment about the role of specialists and primary care physicians, but I will take one second, as Chief of Medicine at Boston City Hospital, to reinforce and emphasize the comments of a couple of speakers on the questionable utility of what I think is a middle-class model of patient involvement for some of the populations with which we deal.

It is not just African American versus white. At Boston City Hospital, we need no less than 14 different translators to deal with our patient population. In terms of telephone contact, not all of our patients have telephones. Thus, I really wonder about the generalizability of the model to the underserved. In particular, who is going to pay for the additional cost of serving such patients?

My comment concerns the specialist as primary care physician. It is true that in chronic diseases, specialists may assume responsibility as overall care giver, but that doesn't make them primary care physicians. I am thinking about some experience and information, albeit anecdotal, that we obtained in an Institute of Medicine study on nephrologists involved in the management of patients with chronic end stage renal disease, particularly patients on dialysis. Because of the technology, those patients almost always become the property, so to speak, of the nephrologist. This doesn't mean that even though they are board certified in internal medicine, nephrologists remember to do mammograms and Pap smears, and so forth. In fact, our anecdotal information is to the contrary.

ELIZABETH BADLEY: I'm from Toronto, Canada and also, as you can tell from my accent, from the United Kingdom. One of the most striking differences in moving from Canada or Britain or Australia, or for that matter, the rest of the English-speaking Western world to America is how little rehabilitation professionals are involved in rheumatology here. I know that within the American College of Rheumatology rehabilitation professionals are alive and well, and multipurpose arthritis centers do have rehabilitation professionals involved. However, the striking thing is that if you go to a rehabilitation meeting in America, a physical therapy meeting, an occupational therapy meeting, rheumatology just isn't on the program. In fact, when my colleagues organized a special session at the American Congress of Physical

Therapy that involved the care of an arthritis patient and the scenario was circulated to the organizing committee in America, the response was, "Oh, we don't deal with that kind of patient."

This is one of the challenges for rheumatologists—to include the other health professionals through their professional organizations and through their normal practice, as opposed to the special practice in rheumatology centers, in the care of patients with arthritis.

STEPHEN KATZ: I know that the focus here is on the management and care of individual patients, but it seems to me that part of good management and care is also the development of new knowledge. I would like to ask how you think that the changing health care system will be involved in the generation of new knowledge in terms of diagnosis, treatment, prevention, rehabilitation?

SARALYNN ALLAIRE: That is one of the concerns that I was trying to express: if care systems require that people with rheumatic diseases be cared for by primary care physicians, each physician will see a few people with RA, an occasional person with lupus, and so on. This will really hinder the learning that can occur about diseases. This is not only true with physicians; it is also true of allied health professionals and the rest of the team. I think there is a continuing need for specialty medical centers that focus on a particular disease, so that people gain experience with it.

JOHN EISENBERG: I would divide research into three different kinds. I am not terribly optimistic that those who are looking for big loss ratios, as Alan would put it, will want to sink their money into research whose payoff is as far away and as publicly available as fundamental research, so I think this is going to have to remain a public responsibility.

I suspect that if you get to the level of clinical research, there is good news and bad news. Managed care systems have an opportunity, because of the databases, their defined populations, and their organized systems of care, to do better clinical research than we have ever been able to do before. However, most of the companies who are trying to look out for their bottom line, non-profit institutions as well as for-profit companies, don't feel they have enough money to spend on this kind of clinical research unless it is of immediate value to the organization. Therefore, there is a disconnect between the capacity to do good clinical research in these integrated system and the willingness or resources to support it. I think the unfunded clinical research that has existed in hospitals, for better or worse, will be gone soon. Our ability to do clinical research with surplus clinical dollars is diminishing rapidly.

The situation in health services research is much like it is in clinical research. The capacity to do good health services research in integrated systems of care is truly remarkable: the databases, the organized systems, and so on. Again, however, their willingness to do research that is in the public domain and research in which the agenda is set by what is in the public interest rather than solely in the interest of a specific organization is often questionable.

JEREMIAH BARONDESS: John Eisenberg said that HMO is a grab bag term that is no longer useful. I would submit that the same is true of primary care physician, a nonhomogeneous term that embraces sophisticated generalists as well as people in various specialties and subspecialties and at various levels of training and expertise. It is not merely not useful but is counter-productive to refer to all of them with a single label.

5

Managed Care and Rheumatoid Arthritis: Utilization and Outcomes Over 11 Years

Introduction

Bevra Hahn

This portion of the discussion focuses on data from Dr. Edward Yelin and colleagues comparing the outcomes of individuals with rheumatoid arthritis (RA) who received care (1) in a fee-for-service system compared to a prepaid group HMO (predominantly Kaiser Permanente), and (2) from non-rheumatologist physicians compared to rheumatologists. It is important to note that the approximately 1,200 individuals enrolled in the study *were identified by rheumatologists*. Thus, all the persons with RA had at least one visit with a specialist. Outcomes might be expected to differ from those of individuals who never received advice or care from a specialist.

Results of these studies may be summarized as follows:

1. With regard to outcomes of individuals whose care providers at some time were rheumatologists, there were no significant differences in outcomes whether care was delivered in a fee-for-service or an HMO setting.
2. With regard to the impact of rheumatologists as the main physician care giver, persons with a rheumatologist were significantly more likely to receive treatment with a disease modifying arthritis drug (DMARD), including methotrexate; furthermore their functional outcomes (measured by the Health Assessment Questionnaire [HAQ]) and their perception of improvement were significantly better than those of patients having a nonrheumatologist as their main physician care giver. Additional measures of improvement favored the rheumatologist, although they did not reach statistical significance. These included number of swollen joints, number of painful joints, and duration of morning stiffness. Surgical interventions and use of nonsteroidal anti-inflammatory drugs (NSAIDS) were nearly identical in the two groups.

These data indicate that a person with RA may have a better outcome if she or he can interact with a physician with experience and knowledge relevant to rheumatic diseases—in this case, a rheumatologist. The health care structure by which this access is provided probably has less impact on outcome than does the ability of the care giver. Such a statement presumes that the interventions recommended by the expert are available to the consumer/patient/client with the chronic disease.

This conclusion is further supported by the preliminary survey conducted by MacLean and colleagues,[78] which showed that among some 12,000 persons with RA in a large health care database (1.7 million covered lives per year), the majority did not receive regular therapy with antiinflammatory drugs or DMARDS, and only a minority ever consulted with a rheumatologist. It is clear that knowledgeable health care providers impact positively on disease outcome in a chronic condition such as RA. Educators and managed care plans must produce knowledgeable physicians and ensure patient access to these skilled care givers.

---

[78]MacLean, CH, KK Knight, PG Shekelle, HE Paulus, and RE Brook (1996). Drug use in rheumatoid arthritis (abstract) *Arthritis and Rheumatism, 39:* R5.

Invited Address

Edward Yelin

This paper presents the results of a study designed to assess the health care used and medical outcomes experienced over an 11-year period by persons with rheumatoid arthritis receiving care in fee for service (FFS) and one form of managed care, the prepaid group practice (PGP) form of HMO.[79] Because these two sectors of care differ in their propensity to use subspecialists in the treatment of conditions such as RA, I will also present some data on whether in fact subspecialists and generalists differ in outcomes.

In order to place these results in a proper context, I will summarize what studies in the literature say about how fee for service and managed care differ in the process of care and in outcomes. Subsequently, I will describe the design of the University of California, San Francisco (UCSF) RA panel, the data set used in the analyses reported on here, and will present the study findings. Finally, because the PGP form of HMO is the slowest-growing form of managed care and because the structure of the faster-growing forms is not conducive to the conduct of research, I will close by advocating that we graft outcomes studies onto currently mandated quality assurance mechanisms in order to assess the impact of managed care on persons with chronic disease in general and rheumatoid arthritis in particular.

---

[79]For a more complete report of this work see Yelin E, L Criswell, and P Feigenbaum (1996). Health care utilization and outcomes among persons with rheumatoid arthritis in fee-for-service and pre-paid group practices. *Journal of the American Medical Association, 276:* 1048–1053. The study was supported by NIAMS Grant AR-20684 and the Arthritis Foundation.

LITERATURE ON HEALTH CARE UTILIZATION AND OUTCOMES IN FFS AND HMOs

Most of the literature on managed care concerns the PGP form of HMO, and most of these studies—including one randomized trial, the RAND Health Insurance Experiment—concern healthy populations. Results of these studies indicate that the PGP form of HMO and fee for service use similar amounts of ambulatory care. However, PGPs use the hospital 25 percent less often on average, and this results in about 25 percent savings in total medical care costs. Studies of other forms of HMO, such as the independent practice association, are less numerous, and their results in terms of health care utilization, costs, and outcomes are inconclusive.

Results from the general literature indicate that PGPs save costs by treating the healthy and acutely ill less intensively. However, there are few studies of persons with discrete chronic conditions, and their results show no consistent difference in the process or outcome of care. The largest such endeavor, Medical Outcomes Study (MOS), found no meaningful difference in outcome between fee for service and managed care for persons with hypertension or non-insulin dependent diabetes.[80]

With respect to rheumatic diseases, we published results from the first two waves of the UCSF panel and reported that utilization and outcomes did not differ for persons with RA in the FFS and PGP sectors.[81] Similarly, Holman and his colleagues from Stanford studied utilization and costs for osteoarthritis and found that persons with this condition receiving care in the FFS and HMO sectors did not differ in these parameters. Interestingly, they reported that both systems were more expensive than an experimental plan designed expressly to provide low-cost care by engaging the patient as an active partner in care.[82]

STUDY DESIGN

Data for this report derive from the UCSF Rheumatoid Arthritis Panel. The RA panel was begun in 1982 and 1983 when we drew a random sample

---

[80]Greenfield, S, W Rogers, M Mangotich, MF Carney, and AR Tarlov (1995). Outcomes of patients with hypertension and non-insulin dependent diabetes mellitus treated by different systems and specialties: Results from the Medical Outcomes Study. *Journal of the American Medical Association, 274:* 1436–1444.

[81]Yelin, EH, MA Shearn, and WV Epstein (1985). Health outcomes for a chronic disease in prepaid group practice and fee-for-service settings. *New England Journal of Medicine, 312:* 962–967.

[82]Lubeck, D, B Brown, and H Holman (1985). Chronic disease and health system performance: Care of osteoarthritis across three health services. *Medical Care, 23:* 266–277.

of 40 rheumatologists from among all then practicing in Northern California. In 1989, we replenished the panel by adding a smaller random sample of another 10 rheumatologists. Participating rheumatologists maintained logs of all persons meeting strict criteria for RA presenting to their offices over a one-month period and provided standardized measures of severity. We successfully enrolled 97 percent of all the persons with RA listed in the physician logs, 1,025 in all. Each year, a trained interviewer conducts an hour-long survey covering demographic characteristics; signs and symptoms of RA; number and kind of comorbid conditions; a complete inventory of all health care used for RA and other purposes, including the content of ambulatory encounters and hospital admissions; and generic and disease-specific measures of health and functional status. The survey also collects information about the kind and amount of health insurance. We categorize persons with RA into those receiving care in HMOs or FFS on the basis of their responses to these items.

Overall, 227 of the 1,025 patients in the panel reported that an HMO was their principal health insurer. Of these, 196 (86 percent) reported receiving care in Kaiser Permanente. Accordingly, the results of this study are especially germane to the pre paid group practice form of HMO. As of the end of 1994, we had accumulated more than 7,700 person-years of follow-up with RA.

RESULTS

Health Care Utilization

There were no systematic differences in health care utilization for RA between persons in the FFS and PGP sectors over the 11 years of the study. With respect to ambulatory care, both groups made about 90 visits to rheumatologists for RA during this time. Similarly, both groups made about 20 visits to all physicians other than rheumatologists for RA, or roughly 10 visits a year. The two groups did not differ in the distribution of visits to various medical specialties.

Of course, persons with RA have physician visits for reasons other than RA. When we evaluated the number of non-RA visits over the 11-year period among persons with RA in the FFS and PGP sectors, the difference almost reached the traditional criterion for statistical significance, with the former group reporting an additional 5 visits, for a total of 39. PGP physicians in our study attributed this finding to the fact that in most PGPs, rheumatologists provide primary care for rheumatoid arthritis patients during their visits for RA. In contrast, in the FFS sector, the physicians receive additional compensation when their patients have non-RA visits.

In RA treatment, the hospital accounts for the majority of all medical care costs. Persons with RA receiving care in the FFS and PGP settings did not differ in the number of RA-related hospital admissions over the 11 years of the study. They also did not differ significantly in the proportion with one or more hospitalizations; 55 percent among persons with RA in PGP settings and 54 percent among those in FFS.

On the hospital side of the cost ledger, total joint replacement is the single most expensive item. Persons with RA receiving care in the FFS and PGP sectors did not differ in the proportion receiving total joint replacement surgery, although there was a slight trend for the former group to have higher rates of joint replacement surgery. In contrast, there was a slight trend for those in the PGP sector to have higher rates for all kinds of surgeries. However, neither trend was sufficient to render invalid the overall conclusion that medical care utilization did not differ systematically in the two sectors.

In addition to evaluating the total number of ambulatory encounters, we analyzed differences in the content of these encounters in the two sectors of care. Persons with RA receiving care in PGPs were significantly more likely than those receiving care in FFS settings to receive an x-ray; those in FFS were significantly more likely to receive a complete physical exam. The two groups did not differ in the other eight characteristics of ambulatory encounters analyzed, including the proportion receiving gold injections, or urine and blood tests, the highest-cost items.

Health Outcomes

The RA panel study includes measures of symptomatology, including extent of pain, stiffness, and swelling; functional status; and global health status. In interpreting the outcomes for those receiving care in FFS and PGP settings, it is important to note that all analyses take into account differences in the baseline characteristics of the two groups, with the results reported presumably representing the long-term effects of the two systems of care.

With respect to symptomatology, the two groups did not differ significantly in the number of painful or swollen joints, the way in which they rated their overall pain, the duration of morning stiffness, and the proportion reporting improvement in the overall status of their RA. Persons with RA have traditionally rated functional capacity as the most important outcome of care. Of note, persons with RA receiving care in FFS and PGP settings also did not differ in the disease-specific functional status measure or the global measure of function. Finally, the two groups did not differ in the proportion reporting simultaneous improvement in all of the outcome measures, although there was a slight trend in the global measure of function favoring those in PGP settings.

Summary of FFS–PGP Comparisons

Thus, to summarize, the results for the comparison of FFS and PGP settings are broadly consistent with the MOS and other studies of discrete chronic conditions in finding no significant differences in ambulatory utilization, hospital admissions, and surgery, including joint replacement. There also were no clinically or statistically significant differences in outcome measures over 11 years of the study.

Comparisons of Care Provided by Rheumatologists and Nonrheumatologists

Over the course of the study, roughly 17 percent of the RA patients have migrated away from the practices of rheumatologists because they moved to a different area, experienced a change in health plan, were referred back to a primary care physician, or simply grew dissatisfied with the care they were receiving. As a result of these moves, we are able to evaluate differences in the amount and kind of content of care and outcomes for persons with rheumatologists and nonrheumatologists as the main physicians for the RA.

In contrast to the comparison between FFS and PGP, we could detect statistically significant differences in functional status, number of painful joints, rating of overall pain, proportion reporting improvement in overall RA status, and proportion experiencing simultaneous improvement in all measures. In each case, persons with RA in the care of rheumatologists fared better in the outcome measure than those in the care of nonrheumatologists. In addition, for outcome differences that did not meet the traditional criterion of statistical significance, the point estimate favored those in the care of rheumatologists.

When we evaluated the treatments used by rheumatologists and nonrheumatologists used in providing care for persons with RA, we found that the former were 50 percent more likely to use any form of disease-modifying agent as well as the current such agent of choice, methotrexate. In contrast, there was no difference in the proportion of persons with RA in the care of rheumatologists and nonrheumatologists who used nonsteroidal NSAIDS or the proportion receiving surgery in general and total joint replacement in particular.

Thus, to summarize results for the comparison of subspecialty versus generalist care, we found that persons with a rheumatologist as their main RA physician fared significantly better on several measures and that trends favored them on all other measures. We also found that these persons were more likely to receive a disease-modifying agent, especially methotrexate, the current therapy of choice for RA.

CONCLUSIONS

All of the large-scale studies of how persons with discrete chronic conditions fare in FFS and PGP settings fail to detect appreciable differences in outcome. The present study is no exception. However, we did find that persons with rheumatologists as their main RA physicians fared better on several measures of outcome. A contrast of the results for FFS versus PGP and subspecialist versus generalist suggests that the absence of a difference between FFS and PGP in this study may be due to the preponderance of rheumatologists in both settings. After all, we began the RA panel study with a random sample of rheumatologists. After rheumatologists have completed their fellowship training, they may be so highly socialized that the setting in which they practice does not affect the care they provide.

If so, the study of Feinglass and colleagues becomes especially germane to understanding the care of rheumatic diseases because they reported that newer forms of managed care, the ones with the greatest relative growth, are much less likely to use subspecialists.[83] In these plans the ratio of subspecialists to beneficiaries is much lower than in FFS or in the traditional PGP form of HMO such as Kaiser Permanente.

Finally, it is necessary to point out that few studies of the impact of these new and fast-growing forms of managed care exist. We experienced substantial difficulty when we approached several of these organizations to solicit their participation in our studies. First of all, they have not been around long enough to have sufficient numbers of persons with discrete chronic conditions for study and, just as importantly, because they are new, they have a rapid turnover in beneficiaries. Secondly, they do not have an infrastructure for supporting such studies. When we began our studies, we were able to solicit individual physicians because they were not part of larger plans. Now that most have contracts with plans, the individual physician has to receive the approval of the entire plan to participate in any studies. This suggests that if

---

[83]Feinglass J, J Schroeder, B Gifford, and L Manheim (1992). Gatekeepers and the medical specialist: The impact of managed care on rheumatologists. *Journal of the American Association of Preferred Provider Organizations, 2:* 13–36.

we are going to do a systematic evaluation of the newer forms of managed care, we may have to graft studies onto ongoing forms of quality assurance that either are mandated by the Health Care Finance Agency or are necessary if the health plan wants to market its services to large employers. The notion of grafting these kinds of studies onto quality assurance mechanisms makessense for another reason: the cost of replicating the current study comparing FFS and PGPs in multiple forms of managed care would be prohibitive, both because the individual plans may not have sufficient numbers of cases and because the plans change so quickly that it is difficult to follow persons with a discrete chronic condition and their physicians through time.

Invited Reaction

Elizabeth Badley

I was not really surprised that there were no differences in rheumatological care between the two payment systems. As a professional observer of rheumatological care, particularly in the United Kingdom and Canada, and in looking at the literature, I have observed that rheumatologists, on the whole, know how to do their job and do it well. The big difference when you go into clinics in different countries is consultation time. In Britain, it can be amazingly fast—a few minutes per patient. Consultation is more leisurely on this side of the Atlantic.

Dr. Yelin's study raises a question of other outcomes. Most of the outcome measures here and in other studies are much more measures of disease than of illness, if I can hark back to what Drs. Barondess and Holman said this morning. We must include the less tangible outcomes for patients namely, the ability to live a full daily life, to carry on working, to feel confident, and to have self-efficacy in the management of their diseases.

I think we have to take an integrated view, particularly when we are talking about changing the health care system. The patients Ed Yelin studied were very privileged, in that they were seen mainly by rheumatologists. It is interesting to note that there were, in fact, differences between those who were treated by rheumatologists and nonrheumatologists. The question that we have to ask is where the patients came from (i.e., what was the referral pathway).

We have talked a lot about gatekeepers, but we need to talk about appropriate referral. We have to realize that referral is not only governed by economic costs. There are a lot of reasons why a physician might refer a patient to a rheumatologist or decide not to refer. These might relate to continuity of care, a wish to do best by the patient, or a wish not to have to treat something as complicated as rheumatoid arthritis or lupus. In looking at the literature on primary care and our studies of primary care physicians in Canada, one of the big barriers to referral is lack of knowledge. Other than rheumatologists, doctors are not, in general, well trained in the examination of the musculoskeletal system or in the diagnosis and management of treatment of musculoskeletal diseases. Consider triage: if family doctors cannot even recognize lupus or rheumatoid disease when patients walk into their clinics, they are not going to refer—whatever the incentives or disincentives are. I think this points to the issue of continuing medical education for physicians, particularly those in a primary care situation.

Invited Reaction

Bradford H. Gray

The theme of a number of the papers and a lot of the commentary today has been that managed care has both promises and pitfalls. Dr. Yelin's data suggest that insofar as costs are driven by utilization, the cost savings of managed care—at least of the model that he was studying here, which was Kaiser—may be quite limited for rheumatoid arthritis. However, as he noted, the world has changed. All plans are now under cost containment pressures, and the differences across plans may occur in areas other than cost.

At least three other areas seem worthy of brief mention in considering the possible effects of different models of managed care. One is that managed care might provide a means for rapidly and effectively implementing state-of-the-art knowledge regarding diagnosis, treatment, and management as these things are reflected in professionally developed practice guidelines and standards. Another hypothesis is that managed care might improve the coordination of services. In fact, this is one of the hopes and ideals of the prepaid group practice model. Still another possibility is that managed care might steer patients to the proper sequence of high-quality providers. As we think about topics like this, it is clear that there may be important differences across managed care models.

The basic challenge that faces HMOs is that they must serve a population of enrollees for whom they are receiving capitated payments and must do so in a way that is satisfactory to purchasers. Let me comment briefly on both of these topics.

First, an elementary point is that the costs providing care to enrollees must be kept below the capitated payment rate. There are a lot of ways in which managed care organizations can pursue this. I will not go through them all, but let me just mention four or five. One is that they can remove the perverse incentives from fee-for-service practice and rely on medical professionalism. That, it seems to me, was the idea behind group and staff models, and it was enough to produce substantially lower utilization rates than traditional FFS medicine. It was not that many years ago that the lower costs of HMOs were described as something of a mystery, because the Kaisers and Group Health of Puget Sound didn't seem to have any formal mechanisms by which they achieved their cost savings. They just did.

This kind of a model may be ideal in many ways. It emphasizes professional processes of decision making. It allows for the use of practice guidelines. It has high potential for integration of services in ways that make sense and provide sound referral patterns. However, the problem is that these plans are losing market share, as we all have heard. Other models have been developed that are able to contain costs just as successfully. Large numbers of potential enrollees prefer the convenience and freedom of choice that are difficult to achieve in facility-based plans.

A second approach toward reducing costs is to employ various forms of utilization management. This doesn't require much in the way of collegial processes, but it does provide opportunities to move state-of-the-art knowledge into the forums in which it can be applied. However, insofar as utilization management is triggered by a particular high-cost event, it may not be particularly satisfactory as the solution to the problem of the patient with a chronic illness.

I will mention the third and fourth methods together: controlling costs by reducing the fees in FFS payments—that is a really popular one—and shifting risk downward. These are fairly easy for managed care organizations to do, but they have a number of negatives. They can create conflicts of interest, which have come up several times today. For purposes of this discussion, however, the important factor seems to be that by themselves, these methods do nothing to improve management of the care of the chronically ill, either by transmitting knowledge and practice guidelines, by improving the coordination or continuity of services, or by steering patients to high-quality providers. They may in fact excessively deter referrals to specialists for management or consultation.

The fifth method of controlling costs and trying to keep costs in line with premium is to control them through favorable enrollee selection. This has come up several times today, and Karen Davis will also discuss how the high costs are concentrated in a relatively small number of patients in any insured population. From the standpoint of care of the chronically ill, this is potentially the most dangerous cost containment option, because it implies that the organization will benefit from providing poor care to, and allocating resources away from, the chronically ill. I think this is a valid concern because plans may be able to exercise influence on services to the seriously ill through the strategies used in creating provider networks or through the structuring of incentives.

All in all, however, I think that it is not as easy to control costs by this method as one might assume. For one thing, chronic conditions are really pretty widespread in the population. I had a postdoctoral student analyze some data that had been collected from the Employee Health Value Survey, which was done a couple of years ago among employees of Xerox, GTE, and Digital. All of the people in the sample were active employees and were surveyed about their satisfaction with their health benefit programs.

A couple of questions asked about illness and disability: 80 percent of the people who were surveyed—all of whom were employed—reported that they had at least one chronic condition or illness, and 36 percent reported having at least three such conditions. Almost 50 percent of the employees reported moderate or severe problems with at least one activity of daily living, and 15 percent reported having problems with at least three activities. I would not contend that these are all disabled people who are having a hard time getting along in life. The point is simply that even a fully employed population is not just a bunch of healthy people. There are many people with serious ongoing illness in an employed population. A managed care organization that tries to follow a strategy of not providing service to people who get sick will soon acquire a pretty bad reputation. It is not as simple as it may seem to steer resources away from the people who need them in the hope that they will disenroll.

That brings us to the role of the purchaser. Purchasers do have a strong interest in seeing that they are getting what they pay for. They are paying a premium for services for their employees, and they expect the employees to be able to obtain the services paid for. Employers have led the demand for performance measurement and reporting by health plans. The initial versions of Health Plan Employer Data and Information Set (HEDIS) had only a few measures of performance relating to chronic illness, but there is no doubt that future versions of HEDIS will move in that direction. All the pressure is in that direction, and the purchasers are interested in doing so as well.

I will conclude with the observation that purchasers are the natural allies of providers who are committed to the development and provision of cost-effective services for people with chronic illness. They are a voice that belongs in discussions such as those being held today, and they are certainly a voice that belongs in discussions about the future of managed care and chronic illness.

Discussion

RONALD MACKENZIE: As an internist who practices at a rheumatic disease hospital, perhaps it did not disturb me as much as it did some of my colleagues to see this lack of differential between rheumatologists and internists in outcomes for people with rheumatoid arthritis. Still, it does run a little bit against what one would expect. Did you have any opportunity to look at subgroups of patients based on severity or complexity of disease?

A second question is whether we are to conclude from this that all one really has to do to negate the benefit of rheumatologists in the care of patients with rheumatoid arthritis is to increase the comfort level of the general internist in the use of methotrexate?

EDWARD YELIN: I will answer the second question first. We don't know the answer, but that is a testable hypothesis.

As to the first question, we did not have the statistical power to detect a small difference between rheumatologists and nonrheumatologists. We did find some differences that favored rheumatologists, and all the point estimates favored the them. My take on the data is a little different from what you were implying. It isn't much of a difference, but it is something. If you are a person with a chronic disease and you don't have much that you can control but could join a system with for example, a 10 percent increase in the proportion of people who say their RA has improved, or a 5 percent difference in function, or even a 2 percent difference in joint count—if that is something that you could control by the choice of a physician, it appears to me to be something you would do. Capturing that little difference may not be cost-effective from the perspective of plan administrators, but from the perspective of a person with the condition, it may be important to them.

BEVRA HAHN: I want to share another experience with the panel and get your reaction to it. At the University of California, Los Angeles (UCLA) multipurpose arthritis center we have started a different type of project, one in which we take a big population of people with rheumatoid arthritis and start defining them on the basis of whether or not they have seen a specialist, rather than starting with a specialist's identifying patients with rheumatoid arthritis.

Catherine McLean led this project, which has published data on RA cost in abstract form.[84] She looked at a large managed care organization database, where she found some 12,000 individuals coded in the International Classification of Diseases (ICD-9) as rheumatoid arthritis patients. Of that 12,000 people, more than 80 percent had never seen a rheumatologist. More than 50 percent were not receiving any antiinflammatory drug therapy (salicylates or NSAIDs) and were being managed with analgesics, usually narcotics. Only about 15 percent had ever received a disease-modifying antirheumatic drug during their care. So, if we take what rheumatologists think is a good approach to the care of an individual with rheumatoid arthritis, we would have to say that this large proportion of people was not receiving such care, which bring up some of the issues Dr. Badley raised in terms of education within our groups.

BRADFORD GRAY: There is an important point to be made about sample selection and research. The way in which a sample is selected does have consequences for the kinds of things you will find in the data. I am really sort of struck by those findings.

ELIZABETH BADLEY: The findings of our recent survey of family physicians in Ontario suggest that almost half would not refer an early rheumatoid arthritis patient to a rheumatologist in a situation where referral was indicated in the view of a current practice panel. Similarly, another study of Ontario family doctors with regard to referral for knee replacement surgery showed a reluctance to refer, often on grounds of old age or obesity, when such reluctance was not justified. This work was done as part of the Patient Outcome Research Team program, with parallel work in the United States.

We need to do more in medical schools to make sure that all who come through them are trained in the examination of the musculoskeletal system. Our study showed that family physicians have a similar level of confidence in examining the musculoskeletal system as they do for neurological exams. They are more confident with the cardiovascular system.

---

[84]MacLean et al., op. cit.

I think we have to start with our medical schools, trying to ensure that qualifying physicians have basic musculoskeletal examination skills. These probably do not have to be terribly sophisticated but should be sufficient to examine the major joints relatively comprehensively. We also have to give higher priority to continuing medical education in this area.

JEREMIAH BARONDESS: It is difficult for me to believe that this problem affects only rheumatic disorders. As a matter of fact, I think that education for clinical management of chronic disease is weak. It is not lacking. It is just lost in the enormous amount of biologically organized material that people are asked to absorb as the summum bonum of the educational process.

If you are able to understand the cardiac cycle, it seems to me that you ought to be able to figure out the nuances of clinical care and how to stay conversant with literature that will alert you to ways to alter a disease with some kind of reasonable intervention. So, I think the issues are broader, although you are right, of course, in suggesting that all new physicians should be able to examine joints.

BRADFORD GRAY: In theory, this is the sort of problem that should be easier to deal with in managed care. Presumably the McLean study that Bevra Hahn described used a managed care database. So, this gets back to the comments I made about certain forms of managed care not having the capability within them to do very much about this sort of problem at all, insofar as they rely on networks, discounts and so forth.

BEVRA HAHN: The study looks at a mix of all kinds of care structures and of people shuffling between one care structure and another. Only about 15 percent of the individuals were in fee for service. The others were all in some kind of managed care plan.

THEODORE FIELDS: Dr. Yelin, were there any practice guidelines at Kaiser at the time of the study? If not, will the newly published practice guidelines for rheumatoid arthritis be relevant to new studies, and how can they be incorporated looking at the kind of questions you examined?

EDWARD YELIN: I actually raised that issue with my colleagues in the Kaiser system. Rheumatologists there see so much RA, they say, that they would read the guidelines the day they came out and either find out that they were already pretty much adhering to them or shift their practices slightly to adhere to them.

It is more an issue for early RA in the system of care there. In the Kaiser system, RA patients get referred quite early because these people are not very appealing patients for the general internist, who doesn't see that much RA.

There, in that closed system, they have an opportunity to refer it, which is exactly the opposite of the incentive system in the fee for service, where they could get more money by taking care of these people.

This conference was organized around RA and SLE, but it would have been interesting to add osteoarthritis (OA) to the mix. OA, I think, is an example of where the promulgation of practice guidelines would have a far more profound impact in the Kaiser system, because it is a much more common disease and one that general internists, by and large, follow throughout care. I don't think rheumatologists see any but a handful of these cases and then mainly on a referral basis.

WILLIAM HAZZARD: There appears to me to be one sector of the health care industry that really understands the problem, and that is pharmaceutical companies. Rarely a day goes by that I don't have one of them offering to help me educate my residents on how to give sophisticated care for osteoarthritis, osteoporosis, dislipoproteinemia, and other sorts of problems that are underdiagnosed and undertreated until you get to a subspecialist.

LAURA ROBBINS: There are two studies, one done by the Arthritis Foundation in San Mateo and one done at Cornell, that have looked at patients' beliefs and attitudes in terms of the seriousness of arthritis and whether or not anything could be done about it. In summary, the findings were that it was seen as an old person's disease about which nothing could be done. One wonders if primary care physicians, based on their orientation and training and their own personal belief, do not see arthritis as something that is not a serious disease, and therefore referral patterns and treatments lag relative to diseases such as cancer.

EDWARD YELIN: Hal Holman and I were on the board at the San Mateo project. Indeed, a significant fraction of primary care physicians felt that osteoarthritis and most musculoskeletal conditions were not that difficult or important a problem, so they really didn't pay much attention to these diseases. A minority of physicians thought that these were important problems but weren't going to refer them because they were the bread and butter of their business.

ELIZABETH BADLEY: We have to go all the way to the general public with the message that there are different kinds of arthritis, some of them more serious than others, some requiring a specialist and some not. We need to tell them that there are things you can do for arthritis and that nobody should ever tell you to go home because nothing can be done. There are things we can do, even if only in self-management. I think if we had a more educated public, it would also act as pressure on doctors for referral and better services.

6

Measuring Medical Outcomes: Longitudinal Data on the Differential Impact of Health Care Systems on Chronic Disease

Introduction

Robert Newcomer

Empirical investigation of the health outcomes and quality of care in managed care systems for people with chronic health conditions has a short history. It traces back to the mid-1980s with the initiation of the Medical Outcomes Study (MOS) and various health maintenance organization (HMO) demonstration evaluations. These studies have generally been designed as comparisons between managed care patients and patients with similar conditions receiving care under fee-for-service reimbursement (FFS). The FFS system is used as the frame of reference to define appropriate access to tests and procedures, and patient outcomes such as functionality, readmission rates, and mortality levels. Issues such as these are given particular attention because of the patterns of lower service use—particularly hospitals, home health care, and specialist referrals—found among managed care members. A fundamental concern is whether reduced access to care (and the presumed lower expenditures) produces an adverse effect on health status or mortality.

The analysis comparing health outcomes between fee for service and managed care usually reports results for either nonelderly or only elderly patients. Although there are exceptions, the general pattern has been to find that managed care members are somewhat healthier at the time of enrollment in these plans than those remaining in fee for service and that health outcomes between these two groups are similar. Such findings have been reported for both elderly and nonelderly members. Many of these findings have come from the Medical Outcomes Study.

Alvin Tarlov presents new findings from the MOS, which compares physical health status change over four years. This measure is a composite index weighted by physical functioning, role performance, pain, general health perception, social functioning, change in health, sense of vitality, and mental health. Three sets of comparisons between managed care and FFS members are shown for the nonelderly, elderly, and poor versus nonpoor. The elderly, those in poverty, and those who were the most ill at the outset of the four-year period show less favorable change in status than comparable persons in fee for service. This finding is at variance with previous MOS and other analyses that have looked at more discrete outcomes. Nevertheless, it raises an important hypothesis about the relationship between health care expenditures (or utilization) and outcomes. Dr. Tarlov and his colleagues depict this relationship as an S-shaped curve, with expenditures or utilization on the horizontal axis and health gain on the vertical. They posit that many in the population (i.e., the nonelderly) are on the flat part of the S, meaning that expenditures and utilization can be reduced without adverse effects on health status. Other groups such as the elderly, as suggested by these findings, may be closer to the rising portions of the S—which makes them more vulnerable to reductions in expenditures or utilization.

One implication from these findings is that the formulas for reimbursing managed health care may have to be more sensitive to differences in historical patterns of utilization (and the marginal gains from this utilization) between the general population and those from more vulnerable segments of the population. This conclusion likely extends to a variety of chronic conditions such as rheumatoid arthritis and system lupus erythematosus. A second implication builds on recognition that the quality and the appropriateness of care are wholly determined by reimbursement. There remain the other concerns addresses by this conference: self-management, care coordination among physicians and ancillary providers, and ensuring access to prevention and rehabilitation. These objectives emerge as important priorities for medical education and health delivery refinement. Testing the efficacy of these refinements similarly emerges as the next stage in outcomes research.

Invited Address

Alvin R. Tarlov

This morning I am going to present data[85] from the Medical Outcomes Study. Begun in 1986, MOS is a longitudinal observational study of about 2,300 patients with chronic disease in three large metropolitan areas. The patients were selected from 28,000 doctor–patient interactions in those cities, based on having moderately severe or worse diseases in five different categories—hypertension, recovery from acute myocardial infarction, congestive heart failure, adult onset diabetes mellitus, and clinical depression. At entry into the study, patients were being cared for in either the fee-for-service system or some variation of the HMO system. The latter category was actually a combination of the different systems that John Eisenberg showed. The definition of HMO in the Medical Outcomes Study is a system in which patient care is prepaid and capitated, and in which there is some form of restraint on utilization. The MOS has already proven to be a valuable source of high-quality information.[86]

---

[85]A more complete report is now available in Ware JE, MS Bayliss, WH Rogers, M Kosinski, and AR Tarlov (1996). Differences in 4-year health outcomes for elderly and poor, chronically ill patients treated in HMO and fee-for-service systems. Results from the Medical Outcomes Study. *Journal of the American Medical Association, 276:* 1039–1047.

[86]Stewart, AL, JE Ware, Eds. (1992). *Measuring Functioning and Well-Being: The Medical Outcomes Study Approach.* Durham, NC: Duke University Press. Tarlov, AR, JE Ware, S Greenfield, EC Nelson, E Perrin, M Zubkoff (1989). The Medical Outcomes Study: An application of methods for monitoring the results of medical care. *Journal of the American Medical Association, 262:* 925–930. Wells, KB, RD Hays, MA Burnam, W Rogers, S Greenfield, JE Ware (1989). Detection of depressive disorder for patients receiving prepaid or fee-for-service care: Results from the Medical Outcomes Study. *Journal of the American Medical Association,*

In the MOS, functional health data were collected on the same patients in 1986, 1987, 1988, and 1990, and deaths up to 1994. The data presented today are four-year longitudinal data in patients with five chronic diseases aggregated. A focus is on baseline and four-year data (1986 and 1990).

The presentation concentrates on specific subgroups within the total patient population of 2,235. Patients are divided into those in HMO care and those in fee-for-service care; they are then subdivided further into elderly and nonelderly groups and into poverty and nonpoverty groups. Elderly is defined simply as 65 years old or greater. Poverty means income within 200 percent of the official federal poverty line.

As primary measures of physical and mental health, we used summary indices from the self-reported Short-Form Health Survey (SF-36).[87] The physical health score is a compilation of eight differentially weighted scales: physical functioning, role performance, physical pain, general health perception, social functioning, sense of vitality, role performance, emotional and mental health. For the physical health score, the scales are differentially

---

262: 3298–3302. Stewart, AL, S Greenfield, RD Hays, et al. (1989). Functional status and well-being of patients with chronic conditions: Results from the Medical Outcomes Study. *Journal of the American Medical Association, 262:* 907–913. Kravitz RL, S Greenfield, WH Rogers, WG Manning, Jr., M Zubkoff, EC Nelson, AR Tarlov, JE Ware, Jr. (1992). Differences in the mix of patients among medical specialties and systems of care: Results from the Medical Outcomes Study. *Journal of the American Medical Association, 267:* 1617–1623. Greenfield S, EC Nelson, M Zubkoff, WG Manning, W Rogers, RL Kravitz, A Keller, AR Tarlov, JE Ware, Jr. (1992). Variations in resource utilization among medical specialties and systems of care: Results from the Medical Outcomes Study. *Journal of the American Medical Association, 267:* 1624–1630. McHorney, CA, JE Ware, AE Raczek (1993). The MOS 36-Item Short-Form Health Survey (SF-36), II: Psychometric and clinical tests of validity in measuring physical and mental health constructs. *Medical Care, 31:* 247–263. Rubin, H, B Gandek, WH Rogers, M Kosinski, C McHorney, JE Ware (1993). Patient's ratings of outpatient visits in different practice settings: Results from the Medical Outcomes Study. *Journal of the American Medical Association, 207:* 836–840. Rogers, WH, KB Wells, LS Meredith, R Sturm, A Burnam (1993). Outcomes for adult outpatients with depression under prepaid or fee-for-service financing. *Archives of General Psychiatry, 50:* 517–525. Safran, D, AR Tarlov, WH Rogers (1994). Primary care performances in fee-for-service and prepaid health care systems: Results from the Medical Outcomes Study. *Journal of the American Medical Association, 271:* 1579–1586. Ware, JE, M Kosinski, SK Keller (1994). *SF-36 Physical and Mental Health Summary Scales: A User's Manual.* Boston: The Health Institute, New England Medical Center. Ware, JE, M Kosinski, MS Bayliss, CA McHorney, WH Rogers, A Raczek (1995). Comparison of methods for scoring and statistical analysis of SF-36 Health Profiles and Summary Measures: Summary of Results from the Medical Outcomes Study. *Medical Care, 33:4* AS264–AS279. Greenfield, S, WH Rogers, M Mangotich, MF Carney, AR Tarlov (1995). Outcomes of patients with hypertension and non-insulin-dependent diabetes mellitus treated by different systems and specialties: Results from the Medical Outcomes Study. *Journal of the American Medical Association, 274:* 1436–1474.

[87] Ware, JE, M Kosinski, SK Keller (1994). *SF-36 Physical and Mental Health Summary Scales: A User's Manual.* Boston: The Health Institute, New England Medical Center.

weighted to give greater importance to the physical health end of the scales and progressively less importance to the mental health end of the scales. Only the physical health data are given in this presentation. All data have been adjusted for sociodemographic factors, disease, and disease severity.

Baseline scores, change in scores in four years, and categorical change in four years are presented. Categorical change is the percentages of patients whose physical health scores worsened, stayed the same, and got better in four years. Worse physical health is defined as a decrease of at least 1 standard deviation in score at the end of four years. Better is defined as a gain of at least 1 standard deviation at the end of four years.

The U.S. population—a general, national probability sample—scores 50 on physical health because the instrument was calibrated that way, with a standard deviation of about 7. The MOS patient mean of 45 indicates that MOS patients are sicker than the general U.S. population, as expected from our selection of patients having chronic disease. In fact, a score of 45 in physical health places these patients in the 24th percentile of the U.S. population. Their mean score of 48.5 on mental health places these patients in the 35th percentile.

In tracking through the four years, the physical health score decreases by 3 points for the average MOS patient—a drop from the 24th to the 19th percentile. Mental health, on the other hand, increases—there is a rise in mental health with age with this instrument—from the 35th to the 38th percentile. The categorical change scores in physical health indicate that 15 percent of the total MOS population improved and 29 percent got worse.

The power of the Medical Outcomes Study is such that a change from 1 to 1.5 points, on either the physical or the mental health scale, is significant statistically and clinically. To put these scores in perspective, a patient whose SF-36 physical functioning score increases by 6.5 points, has had an improvement in function equivalent to a patient who received an aortic valve replacement to relieve congestive heart failure or a total hip arthroplasty. Patients who get worse on physical health are one-third more likely to lose their job in the next year because of health than patients whose scores are unchanged. MOS patients who declined on their physical health in four years—29 percent of them—are more likely to have experienced a new myocardial infarction, have a 50 percent chance of having had a weight loss sufficient to prompt a visit to a physician, and have a 60 percent chance of having experienced chest pain of sufficient severity to warrant hospitalization. The improvement in mental health scores by patients who improved is equivalent to a recovery from depression. The calibration is mentioned to indicate that the discerning power of becoming worse or getting better by using this methodology is powerful and meaningful and should be given appropriate attention, despite what appear to be small changes in the raw scores.

Turning to the main focus of the study, we found that HMO and fee-for-service patients on average were equivalent on physical health entry to the study, that their four-year change (decline of 3 points) is about equal, and that the categorical changes—worse, same, and better—were similar in the HMO and the FFS groups. This is essentially what Shelly Greenfield and colleagues reported in the *Journal of the American Medical Association* in 1995, with patients in HMO and FFS systems who have either hypertension or adult onset diabetes showing equivalent changes over time.[88]

The data from the 2,235 patients were separated into elderly and nonelderly groups (Table 6-1). As expected, at entry the elderly as a group score lower—a decrease of 5.8 points versus 1.9 for the nonelderly. The more rapid decline of the elderly in physical health is also reflected in categorical change scores, with fewer of the elderly getting better and more becoming worse over the four-year period.

TABLE 6-1 Physical Health Changes in MOS Patients over Four Years

Measure	Elderly (n = 822)	Nonelderly (n = 1,413)
Baseline SF-36 Scale	43.5	45.7
4-year change	–5.8	–1.9
Worse, same, better (%)	36, 53, 11	26, 58, 17

NOTE: All differences are statistically significant ($p < 0.001$).

The four-year transitions of elderly patients in HMOs showed a greater decline in physical functioning than those in the FFS system—a 7.0 point drop versus a 5.0-point drop for the fee-for-service group. That difference in the four-year change is statistically significant. For the nonelderly, we saw no such difference. The categorical change data (Table 6-2) are especially impressive. Physical health was more stable (the same percentage) by a factor of two in the fee-for-service system than in the prepaid system. Roughly twice as many HMO compared to FFS patients got worse in a four-year period, a statistically significant difference at the .01 level. We saw no such difference,

[88]Greenfield, S, WH Rogers, M Mangotich, MF Carney, AR Tarlov (1995). Outcomes of patients with hypertension and non-insulin-dependent diabetes mellitus treated by different systems and specialties: Results from the Medical Outcomes Study. *Journal of the American Medical Association, 274:* 1436–1474.

at least not a very impressive one with the sample size that we had, in the nonelderly in those two systems of care.

TABLE 6-2 Physical Changes in Elderly Patients over Four Years, by Type of Health Plan

Measure	HMO (n = 346)	FFS (n = 476)
Percent worse	54	28
Percent same	37	63
Percent better	9	9

NOTE: All differences are statistically significant ($p < 0.001$).

According to the physical health scores and categorical changes of poor patients, 18 percent of patients in the FFS system improved over the four-year period, whereas only 9 percent improved in the HMO system (Table 6-3). This was significant at the .05 level. The nonpoverty groups in HMO and in FFS didn't show that difference.

Poor patients who were most sick at the onset of the study in 1986 (bottom third on physical health score) were analyzed separately. At baseline, the physical functioning of the sickest was about 10 points lower than the average poor patient.

TABLE 6-3 Physical Changes in MOS Patients over Four Years, by Income Level and Type of Health Plan

	Poor Patients		Nonpoor Patients	
Measure	HMO (n = 295)	FFS (n = 194)	HMO (n = 879)	FFS (n = 867)
SF-36 change	–4.0	–3.3	–2.2	–3.4
Percent worse	32	36	24	30
Percent same	58	46	62	57
Percent better	9	18	13	12

NOTE: All differences are statistically significant ($p < 0.05$).

Of more interest to the committee's deliberations, HMO patients got worse (−2.0), whereas the FFS patients improved (+5.4 points), significant at a probability level of < 0.001 (Table 6-4). A similar pattern is seen in the categorical change data: in the FFS system, roughly two-and-a-half times as many patients improved in the HMO system, 33 percent of patients in HMOs got worse, and 5 percent of those in fee for service system, a differential of six- or sevenfold (Table 6-4).

TABLE 6-4 Physical Changes in the Sickest Third of Poor Patients over Four Years, by Type of Health Plan

Measure	HMO (n = 90)	FFS (n = 126)
SF-36 change	–2.0	5.4
Percent worse	33	5
Percent same	45	38
Percent better	22	57

All differences are statistically significant ($p < 0.05$).

I'd like to close by summarizing my subjective sense of the state of health care in a hypothetical curve (Figure 6-1) describing the relationship between health utilization or expenditures on the horizontal axis and health gain on the vertical axis. This relation, I think, is expressed in an S-shaped curve with a long flat plateau at the top. The average U.S. population is on the flat of the curve, I speculate, perhaps $100 billion dollars or more from the point of inflection. If the total U.S. health care expenditure was reduced 10 percent, there would be no change in the *average* health gain or *average* health of the entire population. However, that subset of the U.S. population with chronic disease is likely to be at the point of inflection of this curve (C), so reduction in utilization of its medical services is likely to result in a decline in health. The elderly with chronic disease (E) and the poor with chronic disease (P) may be further to the left, on the downslope of the curve, perhaps needing more services than they are presently receiving and perhaps more vulnerable to decrements in health services. I think that the MOS data are telling us that although for the average American, decreases in health care services will not be detrimental to health, elderly and poor people with chronic disease should be monitored separately to ensure that their health is not being jeopardized by cost-restraining mechanisms.

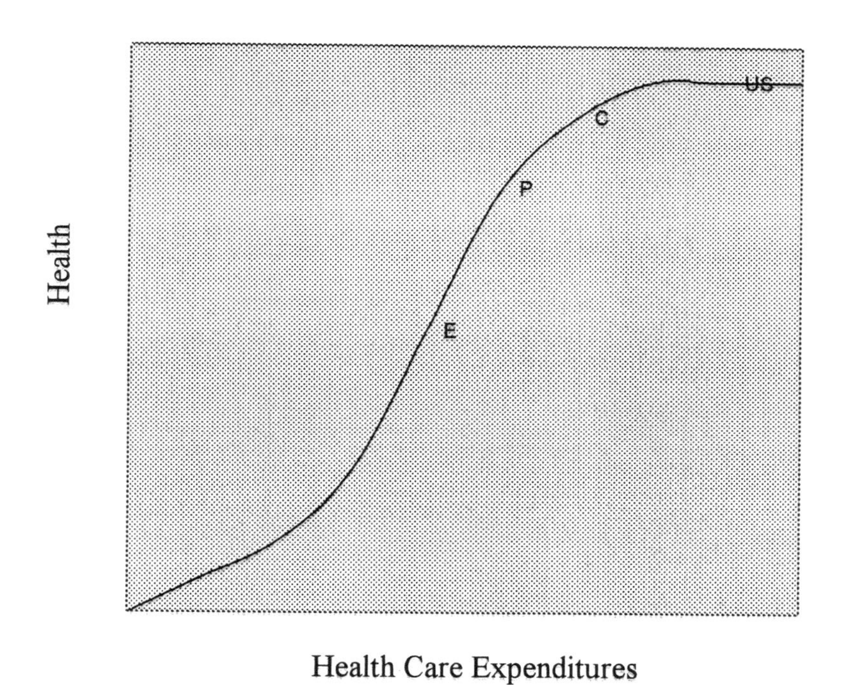

FIGURE 6-1 Hypothesized relationship between health care expenditures and health in the United States (see text for explanation of E, P, C, and US).

Invited Reaction

Carolyn Clancy

I want to share some good news and some bad news about where we stand right now in terms of tools available to assess performance and quality in organized systems of care. The good news is that, along with a growing public concern that what some people call the epidemic of managed care may get us to an end point where less is not more but simply less, has come an intense interest in actually developing and using tools to assess quality. This really is good news. The bad news is that it is a lot harder to do than we thought. I would challenge any of you to try to come up with some tools that are easily used but would reflect the quality of care given a population of patients with any condition in rheumatology.

I know Matt Liang is working on some tools for the Foundation for Accountability, but the number of tools that are ready to use right now is actually quite limited. For the past couple of years, an effort that grew out of health care reform to actually have a list of conditions and performance measures has grown into a database that we will make publicly available soon. Clinicians, health care organizations, and others can use this database to identify tools and even create their own measures for assessing quality. This is also good news.

Again, the bad news is actually making this happen in the real world. Some of the problems that arise are fairly obvious: How do you identify the right eligible patient population? You have to use diagnostic coding data for the most part, which are quite flawed in many systems of care. The diagnostic codes were not created to identify clinical conditions, they were meant to simplify billing.

Frankly, the list of conditions for which there is a very clear link between the process of care and the outcomes of that care is very short. I think this is an important challenge for all of you, as we start to think about the impact of changing health care organizations on rheumatologic diseases.

Many of you are familiar with the report cards that exist now. I heard these recently described as being something like the Wright brothers airplane: simultaneously an astonishing achievement, but astonishingly primitive as well. We are working very hard with National Committee for Quality Assurance (NCQA) and other groups to try to push the science in this field, but it will remain a challenge, I think, for the foreseeable future.

What is the fuel, if you will, for these performance measures? That, I think, very much comes out of our outcomes research program. As many of you are probably aware, the Agency for Health Care Policy and Research (AHCPR) has had sort of a politically disastrous year this past year, but we are still here. That is the good news. The not-so-good news, of course, is that we are functioning on a much lower budget and trying to prioritize as carefully as possible. After six years, a fairly substantial investment in outcomes research, I think the good news is that we have built a tremendous capacity to perform this kind of research and have tried to establish a growing interest in it. The Institute of Medicine now tells us that there is actually a shortage of outcomes researchers, which I think is all very, very good news. I certainly hope that resources will be forthcoming to keep the researchers busy and productive.

The bad news is that we find ourselves in a situation with which, I think, the field of rheumatology has been familiar for a long time. That is to say, although our knowledge has expanded, we find ourselves in a situation with more questions than answers.

One of the questions that challenges us as we try to assess quality of care for rheumatology and other fields is, What are the best kinds of measures? Are they disease-specific or general measures? I am sure that Dr. Tarlov has a very clear opinion about that, but there are many people doing research in this area who believe that clinicians are much more persuaded by disease-specific measures.

Another big issue relates to the timing of assessments. How often do you use the instruments you have? I often run into people at meetings who say, "We think the SF-36 is the greatest thing we have ever found, but we actually don't know how often to give it out and whom we should ask to take it."

Invited Reaction

Matthew H. Liang

Dr. Tarlov's data are very important. In fact, they probably underestimate the true magnitude of the problem. I say this because generic health status measures were used, and disease-specific measures would be even more sensitive to change for groups of patients and would show greater differences. After 20 years of work, partly funded by the National Institutes of Health (NIH) and the Arthritis Foundation, we have a collection of fine, disease–specific instruments that are valid in measuring what they purport to measure, are reproducible, and are sensitive in clinical trials of medications, surgery, or rehabilitation.[89] Disease-specific measures for lupus, for example, would include the following:

1. Activity-related:
    - SLE—Disease Activity Index
    - SLE—Activity Measure
    - British Isles Lupus Assessment Group
    - European Consensus Lupus Activity Measure
    - Lupus Activity Index

---

[89]Karlson, EW, JN Katz and MH Liang (1996). Chronic rheumatic disease. In: Spiler, B (ed), *Quality of Life and Pharmacoeconomics in Clinical Trials* (2nd Edition), 1029-1037. Philadelphia: Lippencott-Raven. Gladman, DD, E Ginzler, CH Goldsmith, et al (1996). The development and initial validation of the SLICC/ACR damage index for SLE. *Arthritis and Rheumatism, 39:* 363-369. Gladman, DD, CH Goldsmith, MB Urowitz, et al. (1994). Sensitivity to change of 3 systemic lupus erythmatosus disease activity indices: international validation. *Journal of Rheumatology, 21:* 1468-1471.

2. Organ damage related:
   Systemic Lupus International Collaborative Clinics

A list of disease-specific measures that have been developed for rheumatoid arthritis would include the following:

- Arthritis Impact Measurement Scales (AIMS)
- Health Assessment Questionnaire (HAQ)
- Functional Status Index (FSI)
- MACTAR Questionnaire
- Lee Functional Status Instrument
- Toronto Functional Capacity Questionnaire
- Convery Polyarticular Disability Index
- Modified Health Assessment Questionnaire
- Shortened Arthritis Impact Measurement Scale

The best measures we have, however, are frequently insensitive at the patient level. One example involves grip strength. When one compares pounds of pressure generated in a grip strength test to a response to a question about how difficult it is to do a power grip, a significant number of people who by objective physical measurement are unable to do a power grip say they have no problems.

Another example is a 70-year-old gentleman seen on house call for arthritis. His apartment was completely denuded except for a cockpit of items around the sofa where he sat. Many years before my visit his wife had died. Shortly thereafter he was admitted to a hospital with a urinary tract infection, came home in a weakened condition, and stumbled as he went into the apartment. He was convinced that something bad had happened and basically lived on his couch for 17 years, developing severe flexion contractures of the hip and knee. Nevertheless, on a reliable, valid measure of function he reported no functional problems. New measures work in groups but are insensitive at the individual level because of the multiple determinants of self-expressed dysfunction or disability.

Tarlov's data are extremely important and probably underestimate the extent of the problem for those with chronic rheumatic diseases—particularly at the individual level. For individuals at risk, we are trying to get scientific answers to what I think are basically political and business questions. We have the tools, although we can not really capture the true impact on individuals, but we don't have the time to study the situation in a changing environment.

Discussion

MARK ROBBINS: One of the challenges to outcome studies is that health care delivery systems and the incentives that work at the system or provider level are changing so rapidly that by the time we actually get a measure and follow diseases long enough to be able to make some conclusions, the incentives have already changed. Hence, some of the studies that have been done with staff and group model HMOs may not be relevant now.

The second issue is that we have no idea how patients select health plans and what kind of report cards they are going to need. This is even more problematic for outcomes measures. What kind of outcomes measures will make a difference to patients in the way they select things?

CAROLYN CLANCY: I have noticed that when a study reports news that sounds very good to the industry the study is praised, whatever analysis is being presented. When the news is not so good or might be interpreted in a different light somebody says, "What do you want, this was in the late 1980s?" as if the study were conducted 100 years ago.

AHCPR actually has a fairly large investment in trying to understand how consumers make choices about health care plans, which I agree is an enormously difficult problem. Right now in some markets the big problem is that even if you had perfect measures and tools, with the turnover in plans it is very difficult to actually assess care for the very small population that stays in one place long enough to be measured twice.

ROBERT EPSTEIN: Given the plethora of both generic and disease-specific measures that have been published in this field—at least nine different generic measures have been used—what are your feelings about people coming to some consensus for folks like me who are administering benefits to millions of individuals and would like to use the same methodology and the same instruments?

A second question is somewhat related to Jack Rowe's comment about patient report cards. What evidence is there to suggest that within-person variability is so large that collecting information on individuals and tracking them over time isn't as good as group-level information?

MATTHEW LIANG: I don't think we should spend much time on this question of which is the preferred measure. Any one of these measures is fine. I think the question is more important than the measure.

ROBERT EPSTEIN: What about the variability issue within person versus within group? This is a big problem, and I wonder if people feel comfortable with reporting individual scores back to patients?

CAROLYN CLANCY: I think that is an open question, and it is very unclear what the right level of accountability is. Right now there is a lot of interest in tracking accountability at the plan level. However, if a plan gets a score that is the equivalent of a B-minus and wants to fix that score, the question is where the problem is. A lot of our measures and current methods aren't very good at helping plans determine figure that. We assume they will figure it out internally, but exactly how you would look at the level of the provider or another level, is, I think, a big challenge.

In terms of consensus, I do think that this is the value of the report card movement. It will create some consensus. I think the greater challenge is the actual state of data systems. For most of the measures that exist in rheumatology now, you would have a very hard time going to most health care systems and actually being able to get the data that you need.

MATTHEW LIANG: Could I just add one comment about the Health Plan Employer Data and Information Set (HEDIS), which is the industry standard? If you look at it, it is very frightening for people who are interested in rheumatic and musculoskeletal disease. The measures are mostly process oriented, and there is not one single item that reflects how people on a population level might be doing in terms of getting care for arthritis and musculoskeletal disease. I think that really must be corrected given the morbidity of the population.

ROBERT NEWCOMER: Dr. Tarlov, your S-shaped curve is a very appealing concept to me. My question is whether you have any optimism about risk-adjusted reimbursement as a way to solve what may be the cost and access to care issue indicated by your data?

ALVIN TARLOV: I think that when the nation established the managed care system it was to solve a problem, runaway costs. Managed care has done that. Now I think managed care has become the normative system, we are stuck with it, and it is going to take a couple of decades to work out the problems with it and to arrive at a health services state in which we are confident that we are working for quality and improved health outcomes.

Will risk-adjusted reimbursement do that? I don't think so. I think that the methodology does exist right now to risk-adjust, but it is complex and subject to perversion. From a practical point of view I don't think that this is a worthwhile approach to improving the nation's health. I do think that outcomes-driven systems with proper incentives to achieve good results are desirable.

7

Changing Health Care Systems and Access to Care for the Chronically Ill

Introduction

Naomi Rothfield

Karen Davis and Cathy Schoen focus on the potential of managed care to provide better care for patients with chronic diseases and on potential for leaving these patients with less or no care. The risks that come with managed care are described; that is, the financial risk that plans attracting the chronically ill will do poorly compared to plans attracting healthy patients; the risk of having physicians unable to act in the best interests of their patients; the risk of patients being denied entry into a plan or dropped; and the risk of limits on referrals or appropirateness of care.

The potential for systemic lupus erythematosus (SLE) or rheumatoid arthritis (RA) patients to have better care could come from having a physician who manages all of the care of that patient. However, currently, the rheumatologist is the primary care giver for most patients with SLE and, as such, coordinates all of the care by all care givers. For patients with rheumatoid arthritis, the rheumatologist may or may not be the primary care giver.

The potential risk for both SLE and RA patients is great. These patients are high users of care and may be terminated from plans or denied access to them. Many of these patients have been denied health insurance, and this has been going on for years. For-profit and nonprofit plans do not want to attract patients such as SLE or RA patients who are chronically ill and will cost the plan money. The plans would much rather attract "healthy" patients so that they can make a profit or at least not have a loss. Thus, having skilled practitioners for the care of SLE or RA patients is not a priority of managed care plans because they might attract patients.

It is widely believed (judging by the *New York Times* and other newspaper reports and TV programs) that physicians in some plans are not allowed to act as the patient's advocate and may not be allowed to tell the patient about all therapeutic or diagnostic possibilities.

At present, we are seeing a definite limit on referrals in some managed care plans. Although we do not have adequate data, it is the perception of most physicians and of most patients that physicians having the most experience with a specific disease provide the best care, which leads to the best outcome for the patient.

Research on outcomes of comparable SLE and RA patients treated by rheumatologists and by internists or family physicians is needed to document the above perceptions.

Invited Address

Karen Davis and Cathy Schoen

Today's evolving U.S. health care system poses new risks and uncertainties for access to quality care, particularly for those suffering from chronic disease. Although an era of managed care and more integrated systems in theory offers much promise for those with long-term or complex illness, the chronically ill are likely to face new barriers to access to appropriate care, given current market dynamics and insurance trends. The risks are especially high for the 40 million people without insurance coverage and the 29 million with inadequate or unstable coverage.[90]

This workshop offers a timely opportunity to discuss access barriers intrinsic to current market dynamics and changing systems as well as ongoing and new challenges to serving vulnerable populations well. This goal of this paper is to stimulate discussion about the likelihood of new barriers to care and policy implications. Throughout, the focus is on those populations with chronic illness that we know are likely to be at high risk: the frail elderly, low-income people, minority Americans, and women. To frame the discussion, the paper is organized into four sections:

1. A discussion of characteristics of the chronically ill and new access barriers in an era of competing, capitated, managed care health "systems;"
2. An analysis of current coverage and insurance trends that are likely to undermine access and continuity of care, particularly with increased enrollment of the insured in managed care organizations,

---

[90]Short, PF, and J Banthin (1995). New estimates of the underinsured younger than 65 years. *Journal of the American Medical Association, 274:* 1302–1306.

3. A review of populations likely to be at particular risk, and
4. An outline of policy implications and possible strategies to address emerging concerns.

The paper's central argument is that policy changes are needed to match or anticipate the changing times. Whether or not the nation's changing health care system will evolve to improve health and quality of life for those with chronic illness, particularly the vulnerable populations, is likely to depend critically on policy responses. The paper's concluding remarks suggest directions for change that would hold new organizations accountable, reward efforts to improve health and quality of life, and improve insurance coverage and stability.

THE CHRONICALLY ILL: PROMISES AND RISKS IN AN ERA OF MANAGED CARE AND COMPETITIVE MARKETS

Chronic Illness

Chronic illness poses particular challenges for medical and health care systems. As noted in a recent paper by Stan Jones, chronically ill patients typically require specialized as well as primary care with a varied team of providers, and needs persist and fluctuate over time.[91] Care and treatment of chronic illness tend to focus on preventing or slowing the progression of illness rather than curing disease and require that patients work in partnership with physicians in following often complex care regimes.

For sicker patients, coordination and continuity of care are particularly important factors in access to quality care. To serve and care for patients with chronic illness, medical and health systems need the time to care, the flexibility to combine multiple medical and support services (varying by patient), and the ability to coordinate care, often across multiple sites or types of medical or health services.

For care systems to work well, patients and their families must have the ability to get to and pay for services, and delivery systems must be concerned with maintaining or improving the quality of life and functioning, not just treating disease. Measures of quality care or standards of appropriate care often require subtle distinctions, varying with the particular patient's condition and aimed at avoiding acute care episodes or deterioration in health status, as well as improving health or functioning.

---

[91]Jones, SB (1996). *Why Not the Best for the Chronically Ill?* Research Agenda Brief, George Washington University Health Insurance Reform Project. Washington, DC: George Washington University.

Risk and Current Managed Care Market Dynamics

Given the ongoing and at times extensive use of health care services by the chronically ill, the minority of those in any population group with chronic illness accounts for a substantial share of total health care expenses for the group. As a result, the distribution of health care expenses is highly skewed. For children, for example, recent estimates indicate that the 70 percent of children who are relatively healthy account for only 10 percent of total expenses, whereas the 20 percent of children with minor chronic problems and the 10 percent with serious illness or severe chronic disease account for 90 percent of expenses.[92] As a result, children with chronic illness are two to five times more expensive than "average."

Costs are similarly and dramatically skewed at the other end of the age spectrum (See Figure 7-1).

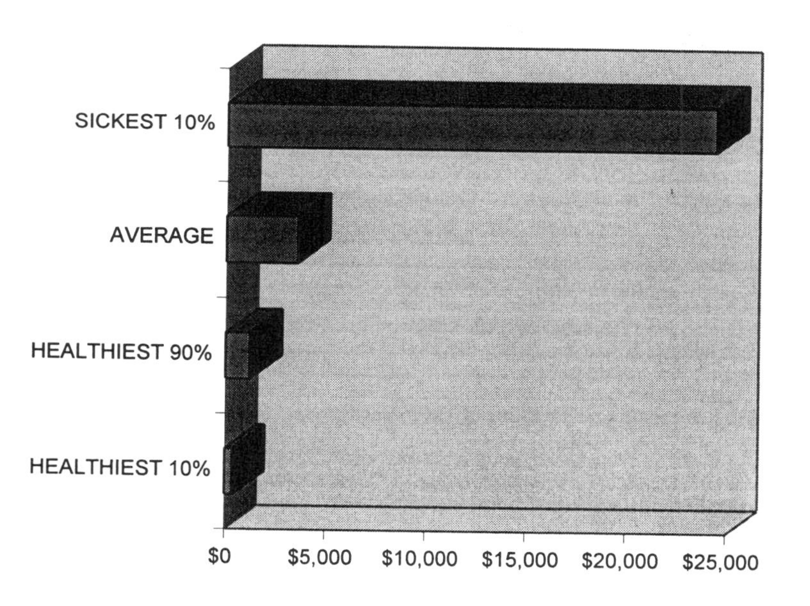

FIGURE 7-1 Average per capita costs for subgroups of Medicare beneficiaries, 1993 (authors' calculations are based on *Health Care Financing Review, Statistical Supplement, 1995*).

---

[92]Neff, JM, and G Anderson (1995). Protecting children with chronic illness in a competitive market. *Journal of the American Medical Association, 274:* 1866–1869.

The sickest 5 percent of Medicare beneficiaries account for half of total spending, while the healthiest 90 percent account for only 30 percent of total spending. Average costs for the sickest 5 percent came to more than $24,000 per person in 1994, compared to $3,561 per person for all Medicare beneficiaries.[93] Unlike costs for more episodic illness or accidents, higher costs for care for the chronically ill persist over time, with fluctuations depending on severity.

Managed care and integrated delivery systems should, in theory, offer much promise for the chronically ill. Such plans can move the burden of coordinating care from the patient to case managers and, with capitated payments, allow physicians and case managers to operate under more flexible budgets to arrange and pay for services as needed, without regard to narrowly defined covered benefits or providers. More highly integrated plans also offer the potential of shared medical records and close coordination of care by teams. By taking on the responsibility of providing care over time, managed care organizations should have a significant incentive to invest in improvements in cost-effective care centered on patient concerns and circumstances. In theory, markets could be structured to encourage plans to compete with one another on their reputations for quality as well as costs and to give plans strong incentives to invest in improving care while lowering costs. The emphasis would be on effective care and system improvements.

In practice, current market dynamics are more likely to reward those plans that succeed in avoiding risk and penalize those that gain a reputation for outstanding care for the seriously or chronically ill. With most public and private purchasers paying plans on the basis of average costs, with only minor adjustment for risk (usually age, sex, and disability status), managed care plans have an incentive to attract those at the low end of the expense distribution and, at best, keep quiet about aspects of care systems that in practice, might attract a disproportionate share of the chronically ill.

In today's markets, we are probably just at the beginning of seeing the impact of intense competition among capitated plans. In most markets across the country, the industry is still relatively new and has enjoyed the favorable risk advantage of relatively new market entrants. The existence of fee-for-service (FFS) plans (whether Medicaid, Medicare, or an employer's residual indemnity plan) as the preferred choice for those with a long-standing provider relationship or in the midst of ongoing care has skewed risk in favor of newer plans and moderated competitive pressures and incentives to adopt more aggressive measures to avoid risk. Studies repeatedly find that when more limited managed care network plans are offered side by side with an FFS option, fee for service, with its broad community coverage, tends to absorb a

---

[93] Health Care Financing Administration (1996). *Medicare: A Profile*. Baltimore.

disproportionate share of higher-cost, older populations with more chronic, severe conditions.[94]

Plans to date have also typically sought to offer as broad a network as possible in order to increase market share. Trend data within the health maintenance organization (HMO) field, for example, show almost all the growth has come in broader-based association models. Similarly, among the employed population, the jump from 54 percent enrolled in managed care in 1993 to 70 percent in 1995 has come almost entirely from the growth in preferred provider organization (PPO) enrollment and plans offering point-of-service (POS) options.[95]

As market penetration deepens in the coming years and a greater proportion of the seriously and chronically are enrolled in managed care plans, competition among managed care organizations is likely to intensify, with individual plans less able to gain advantage through discount arrangements alone.' Network composition and control and the health status of plan members will more directly influence each plan's comparative advantages.

It is at this point in market competition that intensified competition among capitated plans threatens to erect new barriers to care. The list of opportunities to market or "de-market" based on expected risk is long and ranges from more subtle to more aggressive.[96] Moreover, rather than encouraging investment care advances for the sickest patients, competitive forces may deter investment in managing care well in order to avoid a reputation for being the best for the sickest. Unless purchasers structure payments to adjust for higher expected costs based on health status, plans that seek to compete on the high end of quality and to promote reputations for caring for the chronically ill are likely to be at a competitive disadvantage

Reports from recent efforts of a California purchasing alliance to adjust for risk indicate that a disproportionate share of patients with chronic illness can result in significant pricing disadvantage, outweighing the potential gain from managing care more effectively. The plan with the highest concentration of those with chronic disease or serious illness required a 20 percent adjustment in its premium based on the underlying health status of its membership.[97]

---

[94]For examples from the Federal Employees Heath Benefits Plan and state employee plan experiences, see Schoen, C, and L Zacharias (1994). Federal and state public employees health benefits programs. In E Ginzberg, Ed., *Critical Issues in U.S. Health Reform.* Boulder, CO: Westview Press.

[95]Statistics are for firms with 200 or more workers. KPMG Peat Marwick (1996). *Health Benefits in 1995: Executive Summary.* Newark, NJ.

[96]Jones, ibid.

[97]Shewry, S, S Hunt, J Ramey, J Bertko (1996). Risk adjustment: The missing piece of market competition. *Health Affairs, 15:* 171–181.

Capitation: Moving to the Provider Level?

Capitation and competition for patients put in motion a dramatically different set of incentives than fee for service, particularly if risks are shifted downward to physicians or physician groups. Under fee for service, physician income depends on attracting patients in need of care. Generally, the sicker the patient and more intense the care needs, the higher is the physician or physician group income. Capitation at the physician group or individual level reverses this equation. The more care required by patients covered by capitated rates, the more physicians are at risk if they see a sicker mix of patients than their colleagues. The broader the scope of services covered by capitated rates, the greater is the potential for conflict of interest between the health and welfare of the patient and that of the physician.

We have little historical experience with which to judge the future. Today, capitation as a method of paying physicians remains a growing but small share of the managed care market. Group or staff HMOs traditionally have paid physicians salaries, with possible end-of-the-year adjustments depending on overall plan performance. Global budgets and salary payments are essentially neutral regarding delivery of care to individual patients since the physician neither gains nor loses income in deciding what services are necessary. Group or staff model HMOs historically have relied on organizational culture and supply controls to stay within capitated plan payments at the plan level.

As recently as 1994, a Physicians Payment Review Commission (PPRC) survey of plans found that Independent Provider Associations (IPAs) and network HMOs continue to pay specialists on a discounted fee-for-service or fee schedule (often a modification of Medicare's resource-based relative value scale (RBRVS), with capitation spreading mainly for primary care physicians for primary care services. Capitation for primary care services alone, however, leaves in place primary care and specialist incentives to "do more." FFS payment without risk sharing remains the norm for PPOs. Although managed care plans typically require varying mixes of withholds or bonuses to give physicians financial incentives to stay within budget targets, to date, payment incentives at the provider level in IPA or network model HMOs and PPOs continue to reward physicians who see sicker and more complex patients.[98]

The next few years will offer an opportunity to monitor what happens as plans seek to move risk downward in more mature, managed care markets. Capitation at the physician level, unless adjusted for risk, will give physicians as well as plans incentives to avoid the chronically ill—a major shift in current

---

[98]Gold, M, R Hurley, T Lake et al. (1995). *Arrangements Between Managed Care Plans and Physicians: Results from a 1994 Study of Managed Care Plans.* Washington, DC: Mathematica Policy Research Inc.

care paradigms.

Our ability to monitor quality of care is especially weak as incentives shift from doing more to doing less. Protocols for caring for those with long term or even life-threatening disease are highly dependent on knowing the individual patient's condition and relate to functional status as well as medical condition. A recent study comparing outcomes for frail elderly patients in need of home health care, for example, found that overly restrictive managed care practices reduced care for the chronically ill elderly in need of such care and, as a result, led to poorer outcomes. To detect differences and to control for case mix, however, the study required access to medical records and details of the patients' functional status (ability to feed, dress, etc.) over time to contrast outcomes of those enrolled in managed care with those of more traditional Medicare enrollees.[99]

Access barriers arising from risk selection are intrinsic to competitive, capitated markets. The challenge we face today is how to encourage and support managed care plans that earn a reputation for providing access and quality care to their enrollees. Even if such plans can demonstrate that they provide lower-cost, higher-quality care for sicker patients, their total plan costs are likely to be higher than average. Without methods and standards to hold plans accountable for access and incentives to enroll and care for the chronically ill, we are likely to see new sets of access concerns in the future.

STANDARDS OF COMPARISON

In the past, managed care plans could be compared to the dominant fee-for-service, indemnity sector as a check point for access and care. Studies finding that managed care enrollees lower ratings for access and for various dimensions of quality of care have helped keep the pressure on plans to improve their performance.

As the FFS sector dwindles and indemnity plan benefit coverage worsens (higher deductibles and copayments), traditional plans will become less useful as a standard of comparison. The task today is to develop standards and measures capable of comparing and differentiating managed care plans and sensitive to the minority of enrollees with chronic and serious illness. Patient reports on care from those with chronic illness in different managed care plans, as well as comparisons with broad-access FFS coverage are needed to evaluate variations.

A recent Commonwealth Fund study of experiences in three cities, for

---

[99]Shaughnessy, PW, RE Schlenker, DF Hittle (1994). Home health care outcomes under capitated and fee-for-service payments. *Health Care Financing Review, 16:* 187–222.

example, found significantly different ratings by families with chronic or serious illness when comparing ratings by type of HMO (group or staff, IPA or network, or mixed model) or PPO (Figure 7-2). Better tracking of markets at the community level will be essential to hold plans to high standards rather than let ratings shift downward.

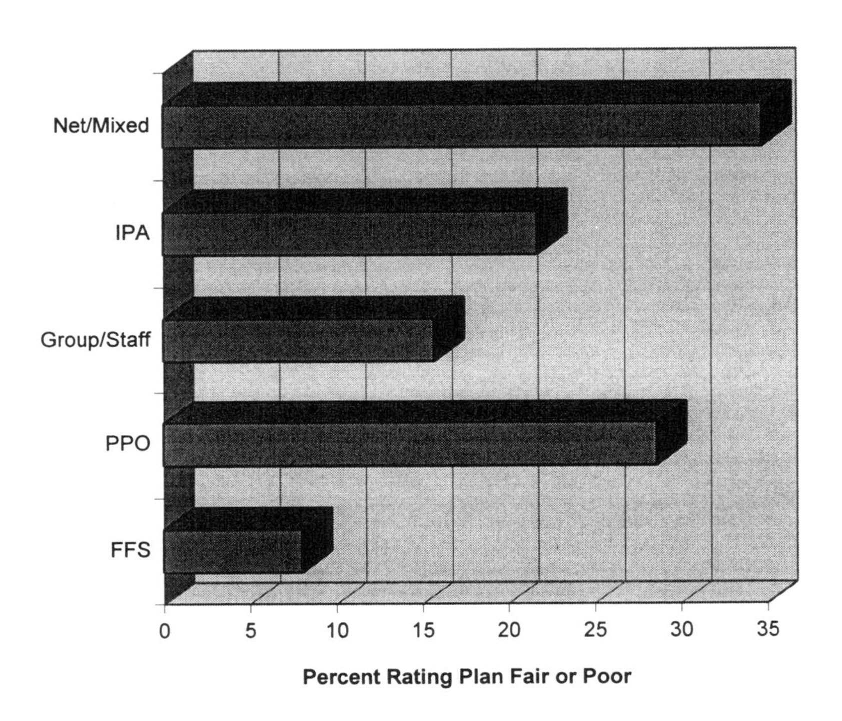

FIGURE 7-2 Percentage of families in poor health rating access to specialists in their health plan as fair or poor, by type of health plan. SOURCE: Commonwealth Fund Managed Care Survey, 1994.

The National Committee on Quality Assurance (NCQA) is the major organization setting standards for managed care plans. It accredits HMOs and promulgates managed care plan quality indicators known as HEDIS (Health Plan Employer Data and Information Set). Additional development of HEDIS indicators for patients with chronic conditions is an important step.

INADEQUATELY INSURED CHRONICALLY ILL: A HARSHER FUTURE

Broad coverage trends threaten severe access barriers, even if we could solve the problem of risk incentives and accountability standards tomorrow. Efforts by managed care networks and public programs to reduce fees paid for insured patients, combined with the slow but steady increase in the number of uninsured and underinsured, are undermining the capacity of community health systems to provide care for those unable to pay. The inadequately insured face an increasingly bleak and harsh future given current market trends.

Measured over a two-year period, 64 million people were uninsured for at least one month during 1991–1993. More than two-thirds of those with a gap in coverage were uninsured for at least eight months. As of 1994, 40 million people were uninsured during the year, and another 29 million were inadequately protected against costs of a long-term or serious illness.[100] In combination, this amounts to one-third of the under-65 population without adequate insurance.

Most of the uninsured lack insurance because they can not afford premium costs and because, if they are employed, their employer does not offer a plan or does not pay for coverage. Incomes are generally low: three in five of the uninsured have incomes below 200 percent of poverty.[101] Not surprisingly, given low income and no insurance, studies repeatedly find reports of significant access barriers to care for the uninsured and for those in and out of insurance coverage.

Mounting pressures on safety net health providers—public hospitals, community health centers, and physicians dedicated to providing at least some free care—are rapidly eroding the capacity of communities to subsidize care for the growing ranks of those without adequate insurance. In communities with a high penetration of managed care plans, market forces are cutting deeply into resources for uncompensated care. As these pressures drain resources and the ability to cross-subsidize with revenues from insured patients, we are likely to see significantly greater access barriers, with traditional entry points to free care closing their doors.

For the chronically ill, spells without insurance as well as being uninsured raise access barriers and undermine care. Those with gaps in health insurance are less likely to have a regular source of care and more likely to use multiple,

---

[100]Short and Banthin, op. cit.

[101]Davis, K, and C Schoen (1996). Uninsured in America: Causes, consequences, and coverage options. Paper presented at conference on *The Future U.S. Health Care System: Who Will Finance and Deliver Care for the Poor and Uninsured?*, sponsored by the Council on the Economic Impact of Health System Change, Princeton, NJ, May 10–11.

fragmented sources.[102] In an era of managed care, changing jobs or changing plans, moving from Medicaid coverage to private insurance, and spells without insurance increase the likelihood that care and relationships will be disrupted. In contrast to indemnity coverage or traditional Medicaid, changing insurance coverage is no longer merely a matter of changing claims processors and reimbursement rates. Now a change in plans is likely to require a change in physician and a change in referral networks as well.

Several trends in combination are increasing the likelihood that a change in family circumstances or employment will trigger a change in physicians and care systems. Insurance for the working population is still based largely at the employer level, and employers are moving to decrease rather than expand choice of plans. RAND surveys in 1993 found that nearly half of private sector insured employees had only one plan offered by their employer, and only 18 percent had a choice of three or more plans.[103] A Commonwealth Fund study found that nearly one-third of those enrolled in managed care plans in three cities did not have a choice of an alternative plan.[104] Today even larger employers are seeking to narrow the range of choices in order to minimize administrative complexity, avoid adverse risk issues, and improve control. Employers have not yet moved into larger purchaser alliances capable of offering a broader range of plans meeting group standards. Thus, employer-based coverage typically offers at best a few of the managed care networks operating in each market.

As of 1995, one-third (11.6 million) of Medicaid beneficiaries were enrolled in managed care plans, nearly triple the number enrolled in 1993.[105] Beneficiaries move on and off the program frequently due to changing employment (loss or gain of a job, increase or decrease in hours and wages) or family circumstances (poor health, pregnancy, age).[106] See Figure 7-3 and Figure 7-4.

---

[102]Kogan, MD, GR Alexander, MA Teitelbaum, BW Jack, M Kotelchuck, G Pappas (1995). The effect of gaps in health insurance on continuity of a regular source of care among preschool-aged children in the United States. *Journal of the American Medical Association, 274:* 1429–1435.

[103]Cited by L Etheredge at the Institute of Medicine workshop on Medicare and Managed Care, December 1995, from preliminary tabulations by S Long of the 1993 Robert Wood Johnson Foundation Employer Health Insurance Survey.

[104]Davis, K, KS Collins, C Schoen, C Morris (1995). Choice matters: Enrollees' views of their health plans. *Health Affairs, 14:* 99–112.

[105]Health Care Financing Administration, Office of Managed Care, June 30, 1995.

[106]Short, PF (1996). *Medicaid's Role in Insuring Low Income Women,* prepared under a grant from the Commonwealth Fund, April 23.

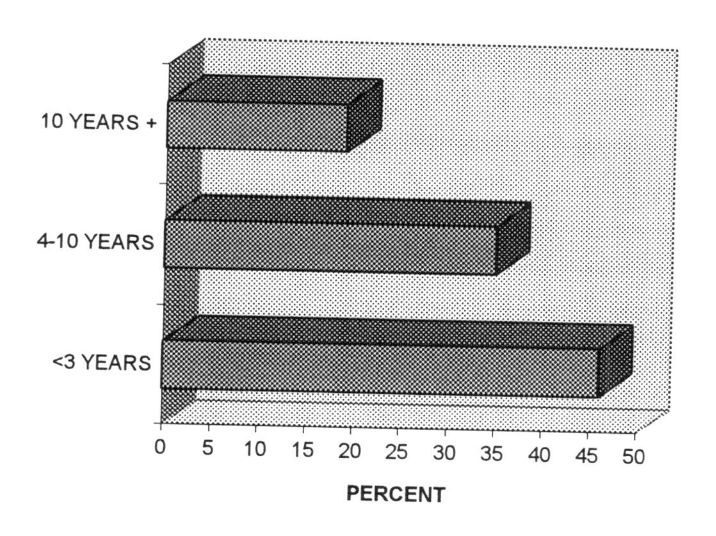

FIGURE 7-3 Length of time in employee health insurance plans. Data from the Commonwealth Fund Managed Care Survey, 1994.

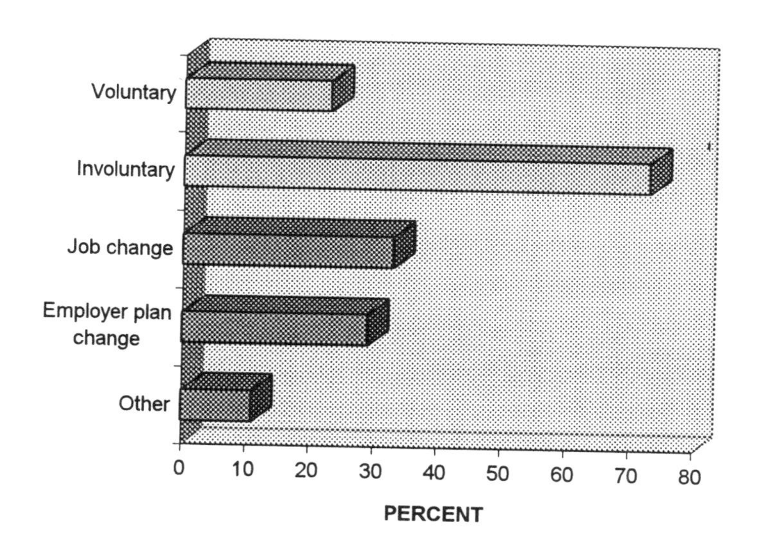

FIGURE 7-4 Reasons for change of health plans reported by employees changing plans within the previous three years. Data from the Commonwealth Fund Managed Care Survey, 1994.

Still, many Medicaid managed care plans are not offered on the commercial market, and Medicaid does not contract with all commercial plans. As a result, moving on and off Medicaid, even into a private job with insurance, is likely to mean a change in care networks. More typically, moving off Medicaid means becoming uninsured: nearly two-thirds of low income women leaving Medicaid over a two-year period lost their insurance.[107]

Recent Commonwealth Fund surveys indicate that frequent, usually involuntary changes in plans today are the norm rather than the exception. In a survey of employed, insured adults in three cities, nearly half of those surveyed had been in their current plan less than three years.[108] Three out of four who had changed plans reported that their recent change had been involuntary, due to their employer changing plans, a change in jobs, or a change in family status. Preliminary data from a survey of low-income adults indicate even more frequent plan changes: 57 percent have been in their current plans three years or less.[109] Rates of change are similarly high among low-income families whose members have chronic health conditions.

Basing eligibility for health insurance on individual employers, income, and family status has always meant frequent switching of plans and coverage. In an era of managed care and more restricted care networks, frequent change now may regularly disrupt and shift patterns of care systems and, in the process, raise new barriers to continuous care.

At the same time, managed care plans' networks are also in a state of flux. Care systems are being "dis-organized" and recreated, often with fairly high turnover in participating physicians. In newer managed care organizations, financial contracts rather than the patient's past history or immediate concerns tend to set the parameters of referrals. Physicians are now referring patients to specialists on plan lists rather than to past teams used by the physician and her or his patient in the past.

VULNERABLE POPULATIONS

The time, resources, and care required by patients with chronic illness vary with social, cultural, and economic factors as well as with age and severity of disease. Repeated studies over the past decade have shown that even with

---

[107]Short, PF (1996). *Medicaid's Role in Insuring Low Income Women,* prepared for the Commonwealth Fund, March 17. Based on analysis of the 1990 cohort of the Survey of Income and Program Participation.

[108]Davis, Collins, et al., op. cit.

[109]Louis Harris and Associates, Inc (1996). *Preliminary Tabulations of the Kaiser/ Commonwealth Five State Low-Income Surveys*. Washington, D.C.

insurance, poor, near-poor, and minority populations tend to lack other resources necessary to access health care. Unless health care systems build in outreach, education, and support services, low-income families may be unable to "comply" with health plan rules and medical care instructions, however willing.

Managed care's emphasis on planning ahead to make appointments, calling before using services, and moving care out of hospitals into ambulatory care centers and the home by design poses barriers for low-income families or chronically ill patients (including the frail elderly) living alone. Families without telephones, transportation, other family members with time and training to care, or the ability to take time off from work during the day to get to medical care for themselves or family members are less likely to be able to navigate through to needed care. Inconvenient location of a plan's network providers (including distance to public transportation) or its hours of operation may exacerbate organizational barriers and result either in patients' continuing to rely on the nearest emergency room for episodic care or in missed appointments and delayed or postponed care.

Copayments for services in managed care plans, which seem relatively modest to middle-income families, may erect financial barriers to care for families living on already stretched or poverty budgets. Preliminary results of a Commonwealth Fund survey of families with young children find that low-income families are having trouble paying for the basic needs of their infants (formula, diapers, and clothes), much less medical care.[110] Poverty leaves little room for paying even nominal fees, such as copayments for drugs or follow-up visits.

Studies also indicate that low-income and minority populations may be less prepared to negotiate the bureaucracy of managed care. Following referral rules and guidelines for making appointments and getting care may at times require considerable patient or family initiative. An early RAND study and, more recently, the Commonwealth Fund three-city survey found evidence that low-income enrollees fared less well than others enrolled in similar managed care organizations.[111]

The transition to managed care is likely to require time, education, and outreach efforts to ensure that new enrollees understand plan guidelines and link up with new care systems. Case studies of managed care plans with a long history of caring for lower-income and minority Medicaid populations have found that the adjustment process is a two-way street—managed care

---

[110] Commonwealth Fund (1996). *Survey of Parents with Young Children*. New York.

[111] Ware, J, WH Rogers, AR Davies, GA Goldberg, RH Brook, et al. (1986). Comparison of health outcome in health maintenance organizations with those for fee for service care, *Lancet, 1(8488):* 1017–1022.

plans discover over time that providing support services is essential to providing medical care.[112] The characteristics of frail elderly, low-income, and minority populations that have historically undermined access under more traditional fee-for-service insurance are likely to continue to challenge evolving care systems. Commonwealth Fund and other studies of low-income populations find that low-income and minority populations are accustomed to episodic and fragmented care: they are more likely to cite the emergency room, hospital outpatient department, or urgent care clinics as their regular source of care; less likely to report regular use of preventive care services; and more likely to postpone getting needed care even when insured.[113] Commercial plans originally developed to serve a relatively healthy, working population are finding that they need to develop services and skills to serve populations living on low incomes, facing debilitating disease, or facing hurdles due to cultural or ethnic concerns.

In most states, the transition to managed care for Medicaid beneficiaries has been so rapid that neither state agencies, plans, nor beneficiaries have had time to prepare and adjust. The rapid pace of change itself has introduced short-term access concerns that may or may not ease over time.

Minorities are also more likely to report discrimination or feeling "unwelcome" by virtue of race or ethnicity. In a recent Commonwealth Fund survey of minority health, 15 percent of minority adults believed they would have received better care if they were of a different race or ethnic group.[114] Only two-thirds of minority adults felt "very" welcome at their doctors' offices. To the extent that community providers have succeeded in building more welcoming systems of care, rupturing relationships will decrease access. On the other hand, if enrollment in new networks removes past stigmas of inferior or second-class care, access may improve.

---

[112]Gold M, M Sparer, and K Chu (1996). Medicaid managed care: Lessons from five states. *Health Affairs, 15:* 153–166. The following 5 reports were all published jointly by the Henry J. Kaiser Family Foundation (Washington, DC) and Commonwealth Fund (New York): Sparer, M, M Gold and L Simon (1996). *Managed Care and Low-Income Populations: A Case Study of Managed Care in California.* Sparer, M and K Chu (1996). *Managed Care and Low-Income Populations: A Case Study of Managed Care in New York.* Sparer, M, M Ellwood, and C Schoen (1995). *Managed Care and Low-Income Populations: A Case Study of Managed Care in Minnesota.* Gold, M, K Chu, and B Lyons (1995). *Managed Care and Low-Income Populations: A Case Study of Managed Care in Oregon.* Gold, M, H Frazer, and C Schoen (1995). *Managed Care and Low-Income Populations: A Case Study of Managed Care in Tennessee.*

[113]Lillie-Blanton, M, and A Alfaro-Correa (1995). *In The Nation's Interest: Equity in Access to Health Care.* Washington, DC: Joint Center for Political and Economic Studies.

[114]Commonwealth Fund (1995). *National Comparative Survey of Minority Health Care.* New York.

For those with chronic disease, the challenge of matching care systems for vulnerable populations is doubly complex. With care requiring a varied team of providers, referral and team arrangements—not just the site of the primary care physician—are important to building an ongoing relationship of trust and partnership with primary care providers. Patients are no longer choosing just a personal physician but an entire system of care. Similar challenges exist for serving the frail elderly and homebound.

POLICY IMPLICATIONS

The above review of trends in coverage and managed care market dynamics implies that, absent new policies to match the changing times, access barriers are likely to grow worse for the chronically ill, particularly for the poor and those without adequate insurance. In the past, we have relied on a complex system of hidden subsidies to sustain a health care system that was for the most part accessible, at least in an emergency. As public and private purchasers reduce payments for the insured and encourage enrollment in managed care plans, resources to sustain care for those without insurance are at risk. For the insured, the dynamic of competing, capitated plans plus disruptions in coverage could move us rapidly from an era of excessive care to underservice, with plans particularly reluctant to take on care of the chronically ill. Populations that have historically been at risk for barriers to care are likely to be particularly at risk.

Three types of policy initiatives appear necessary to counteract the trend toward increased access barriers:

1. incremental expansions of coverage to the uninsured most at risk;
2. new methods of paying for care in managed care plans that give plans an incentive or at least neutralize disincentives to provide access and care for the chronically ill; and
3. Standards, data reporting, and monitoring to hold plans accountable for quality care for sicker, more vulnerable populations.

Invited Reaction

Leigh F. Callahan

A number of today's speakers present different perspectives, depending on where they are sitting in the medical care community. Fogelman and Eisenberg focused primarily on the role of the physician and the system in this changing health care arena. Brady, Allaire, and Holman certainly highlighted the role of the patient, and Davis has highlighted both groups in looking at the problem of barriers and access to health care for the chronically ill. She noted in her paper the central argument that policy changes are needed to match or anticipate the changing times. Together with Holman's point that the health care system is attempting to deal with a set of problems it was not originally created to deal with, these are two important points to look at when we examine the barriers to health care.

Most of the speakers have focused on chronic illness and the difference between chronic and acute illness. Davis nicely summarized some of the thoughts by pointing out that the care and treatment of chronic illness tend to focus on preventing or slowing the progression of illness, rather than curing disease. The care and treatment of chronic illness require that patients work in partnership with physicians in following often complex care regimens.

That is the area I want to focus on—the complexity of this system and how it affects this issue of care versus cure, the patient's role, and the nature of the services that the patient is being asked to handle. There has been considerable discussion regarding the role of the patient as the director of medical care and the role of the patient in self-management. As Bevra Hahn pointed out, we may be a bit narrow in our thinking about the patient's role, particularly if we focus primarily on Caucasian populations.

There are a number of potential barriers facing vulnerable populations in the changing health care system. This has been an area of considerable interest to me in rheumatoid arthritis and systemic lupus erythematosus.[115] Numerous studies have demonstrated that individuals with lower socioeconomic status have increased prevalence of, and increased morbidity and mortality in, rheumatic disease and most chronic diseases. These associations of lower socioeconomic status and poor health status outcomes have been noted in many different countries with varying health care systems. Individuals with lower socioeconomic status are those individuals who are vulnerable and at risk. They are going to need the most help in dealing with the complexities of the services and the changes. In studies that have looked at potential mediators of the association between socioeconomic status and health status outcomes, measures of psychological status account for a portion of the association. This will influence the capability of the patient as the case manager.

Davis's data, not all of which appear in this volume, show that people who are at risk, who are in the poverty group or lower level, when they are in managed care settings, reported that they were not receiving care (17 percent compared to 11 percent in the FFS sector). Forty-two percent reported that they put off getting needed care. Also, a much smaller percentage of people who were in the poor, more vulnerable populations reported that they had received fair or poor service in fee for service, and the figure was close to 30 percent for some of the managed care models. Tarlov also pointed out that the nonpoor group had better outcomes in prepaid systems, whereas the poverty group had better outcomes in the fee-for-service system.

We are seeing differences in outcomes according to the type of population. We have to look at the differences in these vulnerable populations and evaluate what needs to be addressed as we change the health care system. Clearly, a lot of the issues that were brought out in terms of the role of the patient are very important. However, when we have a varied population of patients—not simply the white, upper middle class model that has been looked at so frequently in the self- management role—we are going to have to look at what the role of the system is going to be and what policy initiatives are necessary to target those at-risk and vulnerable groups.

---

[115]Pincus, T, LF Callahan (1995). What explains the association between socioeconomic status and health: Primarily access to medical care or mind-body variables? *Advances: The Journal of Mind-Body Health, 11:* 4–36.

Invited Reaction

Norman G. Levinsky

I would like to combine my two interests (a very amateur ethicist but a professional nephrologist) and say a word about some of the ethical issues I perceive in managed care, and then share with you certain analogies that I think are not too far-fetched between another chronic illness—namely, end stage renal disease—and some of the issues you were discussing with regard to rheumatic diseases.

First of all, it seems to me that managed care really is management of physicians. This isn't usually the way it is described, but the key to managed care is to manage physician behavior, physician time, and all other aspects of what physicians do as professionals. This inserts into the traditional dyad between physician and patient, where the physician's ethics determine the most appropriate care, a third party—one that has a different set of motivations.

The for-profit organization has obvious responsibilities to stockholders, but even a not-for-profit organization has responsibilities to manage costs within a set premium. A marketplace morality can be exerted in important ways by limiting what physicians can do, for example, through threats such as disenrollment, through limitation of access to a plan's patients, and through bribes (i.e., large payments for limiting care). Thus, there is an opportunity for a third party to insert a nonprofessional morality into the interchange between a physician and a patient.

What I think is especially relevant to the management of patients with chronic illnesses is the management of physician time. In most plans, physicians work on a relatively tight schedule—certainly in staff model HMOs—and managers tell them how much time they can spend with patients. As a quick anecdote, I would point out that my wife, who is a mental health professional, receives a significant minority of her patients from one of the largest managed care programs in Massachusetts. That program allows three 20-minute visits for patients with anxiety. Fortunately for both my wife and the patient, these patients are willing and able to pay for additional counseling from her.

There are also market forces, of course, even in the fee-for-service environment. For example, we all are aware of some of the ethical tensions in recommending hip prosthesis for patients who choose hip replacements. There are prostheses varying from a few hundred dollars to several thousand dollars in cost. Because the diagnosis related group (DRG) payment for hospitals is fixed, hospital administrators have leaned on orthopedic surgeons to select prostheses without informing the patient about which prosthesis they will use or the criteria for the choice.

As I mentioned, we have had an experiment in managed care in end stage renal disease for the last 23 years. In 1973, the federal government undertook to care for virtually all Americans with end stage renal disease. There are a couple of points about patients on chronic dialysis that are perhaps worth comparison with rheumatic diseases. In effect, the cost of dialysis has been capitated for the past 23 years, although other aspects of the care of these patients is on a fee-for-service basis. The facilities that perform dialysis and the physicians who supervise it are paid a set sum for each of the three weekly dialysis episodes. This is really an annual managed care fee. The fee has never been adjusted upward for inflation. In fact, it has been adjusted downward in absolute dollars twice in the last 23 years. So, if one looks at it in inflation-corrected dollars, the fees now paid are 30 percent of those that were paid in 1973. What has been the response of the medical care system in caring for patients with chronic disease?

First, and most importantly in terms of patient outcome perhaps, there has been a gradual reduction in the amount of time for each episode of dialysis. This, of course, permits a given group of nurses to dialyze more patients, because each patient is dialyzed for a shorter period of time. Secondly, many units moved from having nurses deliver dialysis to having technicians deliver dialysis. Technicians are quite competent to perform the mechanics of dialysis, but they aren't clinicians and they can't handle some of the clinical issues. Third, social work support and nutritional support, which are very important for these patients, have been minimized to the point where there is really a slapdash, minimalist type of access for patients in these very important areas. There is some, although controversial, evidence that all of these changes have resulted in increases in mortality and increases in hospitalization.

In all of this 23-year period with a single payer and with access to information about all patients, there has been no real measurement of quality in the program until very recently. We know from cost reports that dialysis facilities are required to file that mortality varies from 30 percent less than the mean to 30 percent more than the mean among different units—a 60 percent swing in mortality from the best to the worst. Similarly, the cost of a single dialysis treatment varies from $35 less than the federal payment to $35 more than the federal payment among different units. No one has tried to link these two pieces of information and see whether those facilities that cost more provide better service or simply skim off money and make a profit. 70 percent of the units doing dialysis are for-profit units).

Discussion

JOHN ROWE: Karen, you showed data that indicated that a small proportion of beneficiaries is responsible for a very large proportion of health care utilization. In the case you mentioned, 10 percent of the Medicare population used 70 percent of the dollars. This can lead to the assumption that because these are the sickest patients, they must have chronic disease. I wonder if a lot of those patients are not acutely ill—whether a lot of that utilization is not by chronically ill elderly people but by people who were previously well and had a heart attack or emergency major surgery or something similar.

KAREN DAVIS: The studies are underway, but I don't really have any answers for you. Gerard Anderson at Johns Hopkins is looking at the Medicare database and trying to sort out the health conditions of those who are in the costliest 10 percent. We have also sponsored some work by Alan Barker at the National Bureau of Economic Research on the persistence of large outlays over time. They are finding that the patients that have big expenses this year are those who will have big expenses next year. However, there is some regression to the mean, meaning that some of the people who are high health care users today are low tomorrow, and some of those who are low health care users today are high tomorrow. Therefore, if you look at three-year expenses, you don't get quite the same 10 percent of patients accounting for 70 percent of expenses, but there is still a fair amount of persistence of this high-cost-today, high-cost-tomorrow kind of patient.

NORMAN LEVINSKY: It happens that we are studying a related issue, the high-cost elderly, using the 1992 Medicare database. I can answer part of what you asked based on unpublished data: 50 percent of the cost incurred by the most costly patients—the 5 percent who account for 50 percent of the total cost of the Medicare system—is for hospital care. About 70 percent of that 50 percent appears to be related to general medical diseases. Only 30 percent is for episodes involving a procedure, for example, a myocardial infarct followed by angioplasty or something like that.

LEIGH CALLAHAN: When you look at a specific rheumatic condition, a small percentage of the individuals account for a large percentage of the cost, even when you are just looking within the chronic disease.

DEBORAH FREUND: We heard the anecdote from someone about how specialists under carve-outs don't want to refer patients back to primary care physicians. Karen Davis told us about the barriers to access that face the elderly and the poor. Now we have heard about endstage renal disease, which in its own way and time involved a carve-out plan.

My question for Karen, and whoever else may want to answer, is the following: Is there any evidence in the Medicaid data that when you carve some subset of patients out of managed care, especially at-risk populations with chronic diseases, they do any better than if they were not carved out? Is there any relation to whether the carve-out is prepaid in and of itself?

KAREN DAVIS: I don't believe that there is a lot of literature on that yet. I think of this as merely a financial arrangement—just a different way in which the state Medicaid program would pay a health plan for care of patients with a particular disease. It would not necessarily mean that these patients would shift their sources of care.

However, in following the *New York Times* coverage of this issue, certainly you get a sense that many HIV patients are not faring very well in managed care plans because they can't get to their infectious disease specialists or their physicians haven't had enough experience with HIV patients and aren't up on the latest techniques.

WILLIAM HAZZARD: The exponential rise in cost per capita in the sickest resembles the exponential rise in cost per capita in the final illness. To what extent do the Medicare concentrations of cost represent terminal illness, and does that apply to rheumatological disease?

KAREN DAVIS: About 6 percent of Medicare beneficiaries die in a given year and account for 24 percent of Medicare outlays, so they don't explain the entire phenomenon of high-cost patients. Obviously part of those terminally ill do fall within the high-cost patient populations, but approximately 20 percent of those who die have not been hospitalized in the last year. So, it is not the case that everyone who dies does so in a very expensive way.

RONALD MACKENZIE: This question is perhaps best directed at Dr. Davis. It concerns the problem of accountability. Managed care companies seem to be in the process of enhancing the vulnerability of our already vulnerable patients with rheumatic diseases. Do you think that as managed care participates more in Medicare and Medicaid, which are institutions that may be a little more sensitive to the political process, we will see some redressing or influence on the broader base of managed care and the way patients are being insured?

KAREN DAVIS: I am optimistic that Medicare and also Medicaid, at least in some states, will provide a leadership role in setting regulations or rules of the game that govern managed care practice. I think that should be required for accreditation of HMOs participating in Medicare and Medicaid by an organization such as the National Committee on Quality Accreditation (NCQA). The Health Care Financing Administration (HCFA) ought to require that plans submit the HEDIS indicators. They are not currently required to submit such data. HCFA should also require the data be audited and that the results of the audit be publicly available.

HCFA has in fact worked with NCQA to develop Medicaid-specific HEDIS indicators. For example, there is a glycosylated hemoglobin test for diabetics, so they are starting to develop some specific indicators for specific conditions. I haven't seen anything yet on Medicare HEDIS, but I know that it is under development. I think it is beginning to move us in the right direction. Basically we need accreditation, quality measures, reporting of those quality measures, right of patients to appeal, a grievance process, some right to care in an emergency situation without waiting to have it approved by a plan, right of physicians to act in their patients' best interests, and appropriate payment methods for managed care plans—methods that eliminate financial disincentives or penalties for caring for the chronically ill. This is basically my list of the rules that are needed. I think that Medicare and Medicaid may well help us to move that agenda along.

BEVRA HAHN: Given that it is cheapest for people to die quickly, what would the members of the panel see as optimal measures of value?

NORMAN LEVINSKY: It seems to me that value must ultimately lie in the patients' perceptions that they are receiving something that contributes to their quality of life and ability to function. In the renal disease literature there is a well-known study that contrasts patients' perception of their functional status and quality of life with the judgment of outside observers using well-known psychometric and other tests. The two perceptions are totally disparate. The objective analysis indicates that dialysis patients are closer to dead than to normal, whereas the patients rate themselves on a par with the average person in the United States. That is why I would focus on the patient's perception.

THEODORE FIELDS: Dr. Davis, you mentioned that it is probably not in the interests of managed care companies to advertise that they have services for the chronically ill, particularly if an expensive service is involved. How would we go about making sure that patients in managed care, particularly the chronically ill, get the information about which companies are connected with which services? Someone else previously mentioned the importance of having centers of specialized service. This may be a way in which such patients are kept away from those services, because they are not advertised.

KAREN DAVIS: In a broad way, again, in marketing for Medicare and Medicaid, I think the enrollment process should be managed by the Medicare and Medicaid programs. They are the ones that should be providing equal information on all of the plans and their capacity, quality, specialists available, credentials, and so forth, rather than door-to-door marketing or a lot of these decisions being swayed by advertising. We are a long way away from being there.

JEREMIAH BARONDESS: As clinical decisions get modified by nonphysicians and, for that matter, by nonclinicians and by computer programs, is there any information about the inclusion of managed care entities in the tort system with regard to malpractice or liability issues? If a system says that you can't have a magnetic resonance image (MRI) for a suspected acoustic neuroma, only have a computed tomography (CT) scan, and it misses the tumor, who is legally responsible?

NORMAN LEVINSKY: Actually, some very striking legal judgments have already indicated that not only HMOs but physicians are liable for their actions, even when the plan prevents them from taking the action they think is in the patient's best interests. I don't know how far that will spread or whether it will become a mechanism for improving the clinical process in some of these plans.

JOHN ROWE: There is another answer emerging as well. In the State of Maine, if you come to the emergency room as a patient with a head injury and the physician follows the approved Maine practice guideline in deciding whether you get a CT scan, the physician cannot be sued, regardless of the outcome. That experiment has been going on now for a couple of years, and the State of Florida is beginning to consider it. This approach uses practice guidelines to immunize clinicians against inevitable, but unpredictable, adverse effects and their legal consequence.

KAREN DAVIS: Let me add one thing to that last point. In fee for service, when something is denied under Medicare the physician is often the patient's best advocate, explaining why it is really needed. In managed care the physician no longer advocates on behalf of the patient, and the patient must try to go through a grievance procedure without such help.

8

Training and Utilization of Generalists and Subspecialists at the University of California, Los Angeles

Introduction

William R. Hazzard

The environment that dictates reappraisal of the management of rheumatic disease is changing rapidly and is the principal force behind the present study. Nowhere are these forces of change felt more acutely than in the academic health center wherein advances in the diagnosis and treatment of rheumatic disorders have been concentrated in recent decades of major biomedical research. In no rheumatic disorders more than rheumatoid arthritis and systemic lupus erythematosus have the coincidence of biomedical research and highly focused, subspecialized diagnosis been more concentrated than in these academic health centers. Thus, it is important to examine the approach of one major academic health center to the reorientation and reorganization necessary to survive the whirlwind changes in health care delivery and financing so as to permit its continued focus on excellence in fulfilling its historical tripartite mission of research, teaching, and clinical care.

A particularly instructive and reassuring example is the leadership of the University of California, Los Angeles (UCLA) Medical Center in reorganizing to address the forces of managed care market domination in a manner so as to preserve its commitment to academic excellence. Thus, the report by Alan Fogelman, chairman of the Department of Medicine at UCLA, presents an approach that appears promising, logical, well designed, and rational. It is also useful to examine this approach in the context of a previously articulated plan to reorganize the department in a manner that preserves its historical excellence in biomedical research and the training of both future physician scientists and an even greater number of primary care internists at the medical student and resident levels. Thus, UCLA Internal Medicine under Alan Fogelman appears likely to survive—indeed flourish—through a rational, enlightened process of planning and commitment to change (with considerable shared sacrifice), allowing transition to a model of prosperity in the most demanding environment of competitive managed care. Biomedical scientists, academic physicians, administrators, and planners at the local and national level have much to learn from Dr. Fogelman's thoughtful, scholarly, and clearly articulated approach to the challenge faced by all academic health centers.

Invited Address

Alan M. Fogelman

A central theme of our system at UCLA is that it is based on the education of physicians, of patients, and of the staff that participate. With this in mind, I am going to tell you how the Department of Medicine component of our UCLA health system is approaching some of the problems you are grappling with today.

In response to economic pressures, as we have all heard, health care delivery has shifted significantly toward primary care. By July 1992, when I became department chair, our department had only four full-time practicing primary care physicians. These full-time physicians spent fewer than 20 hours a week on direct patient contact. As the future importance of primary care became evident, we developed a strategy to create a positive environment for primary care, and to recruit a sufficient number of primary care physicians on the Westwood campus to care for the number of lives necessary to compete for contracts and preserve both our teaching mission and our subspecialty practices. This strategy is described in detail in an article published in the *Annals of Internal Medicine*,[116] and I will not repeat the details here.

Our initial goals have largely been met. We successfully persuaded the university to eliminate the requirement for regional and national recognition as prerequisites for advancement and promotion of these clinician educators. They are now judged on their achievements and creative contributions to local education and patient care. We have established productivity standards that are similar to those of a staff model HMO. That is, the clinician educators that

---

[116] Fogelman, AM (1994). Strategies for training generalists and subspecialists. *Annals of Internal Medicine, 120:* 579–583.

are primary care doctors, as well as our subspecialist clinician educators, are scheduled to spend 32 hours each week in direct outpatient contact when not assigned to an inpatient service.

One result has been a dramatic increase in patient visits to our primary care clinician educators since initiation of the program. As a result of this tremendous increase in primary care, our subspecialty practice has also grown, although at a slower rate, 10 percent per year. This modest growth in subspecialty practice needs to be taken in the context of the West Los Angeles market, where subspecialty activity and incomes have declined on the order of 25–50 percent in the past two years. In contrast, our net cash continues to grow and our faculty has received, on average, a 5 percent increase in salary this year.

A major principle of primary care is that it is provided in the neighborhoods where people live. Having largely met our goals for primary care on the Westwood campus, we have begun to establish neighborhood facilities. We have opened three community sites already: in Marina Del Rey, in Culver City, and at our Eichenbohm site in the Fairfax district, which is a geriatrics facility. We have negotiated leases on three additional sites, one of which, in Manhattan Beach, is almost ready to open. We are renovating or negotiating for facilities in four other sites, including two in Beverly Hills and one in the Valley in Sherman Oaks. The area west of UCLA in Santa Monica is being developed with the Huntington Provider Group and the Santa Monica independent practice associations (IPAs), an affiliation established by UCLA. We anticipate having five neighborhood satellites open before the end of this academic year and 10 open by July 1, 1997. The goal of the department is to open 20 neighborhood satellites. All of the offices are in small buildings. This is not UCLA Medical Center. These are simply offices.

To accomplish our goals we have established the following principles and infrastructure; they are the backbone of a primary care strategy for transitioning to all-payer capitation. Our mission statement is to develop a high-quality patient-focused system for providing primary care in geographic proximity to the neighborhoods where people live, but with the capability of providing state-of-the-art, world-class knowledge and technology for those individuals with conditions warranting such resources, that is, the infrastructure and support systems to provide care in the most appropriate and cost-effective setting in an all-payer capitated system.

As I have indicated, our outpatient sites are stand-alone buildings with easy parking. We find that former bank buildings are particularly good, and there are a lot of those in southern California; we are making them small, dedicated medical buildings. Our sites are of sufficient size to accommodate two to five physicians, one to two medical residents, and one to two visiting subspecialists accompanied by a trainee.

Inpatient treatment for patients outside the catchment area of UCLA

Medical Center is done at local hospitals for low-acuity conditions, unless the patient requests otherwise. Patients are admitted to UCLA for higher-acuity conditions or are transferred to UCLA Medical Center if appropriate facilities do not exist at the local hospital.

PRIMARY CARE PHYSICIANS

Primary care physicians are general internists or subspecialists with heavy general internal medicine practices—that is, greater than 50 percent. All internist physicians are full-time faculty in the Department of Medicine in the clinical compensated series, and they are expected to spend a minimum of 32 hours each week in direct patient contact. Physicians recruited with existent practices are paired with recent graduates who have been trained in general internal medicine in a managed care environment.

An inpatient team of general internists has been created, which is responsible for caring for hospitalized patients at local hospitals. The community subspecialists and specialists on staff at these hospitals are utilized. Our team of internists is also responsible for arranging for transfer of patients to UCLA Medical Center when this is appropriate.

SUBSPECIALTY AND SPECIALTY CONSULTATION

The subspecialty divisions provide regular consultative services on-site in neighborhood facilities one-half day per week for the more common disorders requiring consultation. This has allowed the establishment of relationships with primary care physicians so that urgent consultation can be provided in Westwood on nonscheduled days. Communication systems have been established so that the primary care physicians can request a consultation by E-mail or pager from a consultant who has been designated as being on call. E-mail is, in many ways, preferable to the phone, because you don't have to make the connection at the same time.

Consultants outside the Department of Medicine are chosen in consultation with the medical group. Often, immediate consultations are not required for patient treatment, but an extended E-mail dialogue will result. We are encouraging this system, even though capitation is only about 8 percent of our business. We are trying to prepare for the future. Even though we are not reimbursed, we are encouraging our faculty to communicate and to seek consultation in easy ways that present no barriers, without regard to compensation. A visit may be scheduled for the regular day on which the consultant visits the neighborhood facility. However, if the consultant or the primary care physician feels that urgent consultation is required, this is arranged, together with transportation to bring the patient to Westwood for the consultation.

To facilitate these matters and to keep the system focused on the patient, the Department of Medicine has hired personnel who are responsible for seeing that the physicians have communicated—and that is the key word—prior to the patient's visit. They see to it that appointments have been made, that transportation has been arranged, that the patient has been contacted prior to the visit, that the patient is greeted on arrival at UCLA and transported back after the visit, that the consultant communicates with the primary care physician after the consult, and that the patient is also contacted by phone after the visit to be sure that all went well and that the patient understands what has been recommended and what the next steps in treatment will be. It is expensive to have these patient facilitators, but it has made all the difference in the world in terms of both the perceived and what we think is the real quality of care that is provided.

These personnel also work with the inpatient team to facilitate notification of the team and arrange admission to the local hospital, track patients in local hospitals, and participate in discharge planning and organizing return visits to the primary care physician and subsequent consultation with UCLA subspecialists and specialists.

A system is being devised to increase the efficiency of ambulatory care and to track electronically the medical problems of all patients in the system. It will include allergy and drug information referrals and key process variables that will allow a continuous quality assessment and improvement process. This is being undertaken as a joint venture among our department, our medical group, and our medical center.

TRANSPORTATION SYSTEMS

An important component of our system, transportation, has been developed as a joint venture with UCLA Medical Group and Medical Center and includes the transport of patients for routine, subacute, and emergent care from neighborhood facilities or local hospitals to UCLA Medical Center. We find that senior patients like to be able to drive to the neighborhood office, get out, go in and talk to the staff, and have a van pick them up there to take them up to UCLA. They are greeted by one of our greeters, walked to their consultation, and walked back to the van. They come back to the office, walk in and talk to the staff, and perhaps see the doctor briefly. We have found that this has made an enormous difference in the ability of patients to participate in a system as complex as ours.

EDUCATION SYSTEMS

Subspecialty divisions have been charged with developing programs for educating patients and primary care physicians in new developments related to practice in their particular subspecialty areas. These education modules are being developed in conjunction with the Division of General Internal Medicine and focus on improved outcomes from processes that can be delivered at the primary care provider or patient level.

A new position, director of communications, has been posted for the Department of Medicine. We are interviewing right now. Among the duties of this individual will be responsibility for developing patient education materials, which we think are critical to enable us to provide high quality care.

GRADUATE MEDICAL EDUCATION

General internal medicine residents rotate to neighborhood facilities as part of their ambulatory medicine experience and ultimately have continuity of care clinics at a neighborhood facility. A new track for training general internists in critical care is being incorporated into the inpatient team.

INTEGRATING SUBSPECIALTY MEDICINE INTO GENERAL INTERNAL MEDICINE

The challenge to fee-for-service medicine has been to prevent overutilization. The challenge to capitation is not to provide incentives for underutilization. A health system such as ours, based on primary care, must learn how to include subspecialty and specialty care in an appropriate balance.

Starting with the curriculum issue of how best to teach general internal medicine, the department has embarked on an expanded role as the integrator of subspecialty science and practice. Our department has created a series of small working groups composed of general internists and representatives from each of the subspecialty divisions charged with designing the subspecialty content of the general internal medicine curriculum. These working groups include both clinician educators and health services researchers. In addition to designing the curriculum, they will also be charged with designing and implementing clinical guidelines, deciding on medications for our formulary, determining measures of quality indicators and outcomes, and designing patient education modules. Thus, the department has assumed the task of integrating the talents of the faculty in general internal medicine and in medical subspecialties to create a new paradigm for a primary care based health system for adults.

CONTINUING MEDICAL EDUCATION

Building on our approach to the residency curriculum, we have committed to a new program in continuing medical education. We have asked Dr. Roy Young to develop a new system of continuing medical education for our clinician educators. To this end, we are establishing an educational center where Roy, who is a general internist, will bring our clinician educators for seminars in continuing medical education on a variety of topics related to practice.

For example, Roy may decide to present a diabetes module. A group of our primary care clinician educators, perhaps from one of our neighborhood offices or from one of the Westwood firms (we use a firm system) will be invited to provide a list of their diabetic patients. Prior to the seminar, Roy's staff will collect the hemoglobin A_{1C} levels on these patients. At the seminar, Roy will review the treatment approach utilizing a diabetes specialist and will outline appropriate follow-up reading materials. Subsequently, this group's hemoglobin A_{1C} levels will be sampled again, and when the group reconvenes, the data will be reviewed as a positive reinforcement to better practice. Our goal is to develop a system in which we practice what we preach and teach. To accomplish this, we feel we must incorporate continuing medical education into the work week, realizing that a primary care practice cannot fit into a 40-hour work week.

In preparation for this workshop, I met with members of our primary care group and with David Klashman, a rheumatologist clinician educator who works in Bevra Hahn's Division of Rheumatology. I asked them to tell me how they would approach the two diseases that you are considering. For early rheumatoid arthritis (RA), the consensus was that a patient with symptoms compatible with early mild RA without erosions would likely be started on nonsteroidal antiinflammatory drugs (NSAIDs) by our general internist. If the symptoms disappeared completely within two to eight weeks and the RA factor was negative, a referral to a rheumatologist was unlikely. If the symptoms did not resolve or if the serology was positive, a referral would likely result. Parenthetically, our general internists are comfortable aspirating knees, and some will aspirate an ankle, but none will aspirate a shoulder or wrist. Our general internists are comfortable injecting bursa in some joints, but not others.

What about advanced RA? If a patient has advanced RA upon presentation to one of our internists, is on a disease modifier other than an NSAID, or has marked deformities, a referral is likely to be made to a rheumatologist. If a patient has nonactive RA and is not on chloroquine, methotrexate or gold, and there is no question of the need for surgery, a rheumatologist is not likely to be consulted. When consultation is made, the follow-up is decided by discussions between the general internist and the consulting rheumatologist. Rheumatologists often act as the principal care givers for patients with active RA when the patient is on methotrexate or gold. The key principle, however, is co-management. What appears to have changed in the past few years is that subspecialist-to-subspecialist referrals have been replaced by a co-management approach between the principal subspecialist and the general internist.

What about sytemic lupus erythematosus (SLE)? The diagnosis of SLE or suspected SLE is usually carried out by a general internist who orders the appropriate serologies. If the diagnosis is entertained seriously, a rheumatology consultation is usually obtained. Definite SLE is almost always referred to a rheumatologist before treatment is started. The treatment of active SLE is almost always managed by a rheumatologist in our practice. If the disease progresses to renal failure, the nephrologist usually becomes the principal caregiver. If the disease burns out without the need for dialysis, care is returned to the general internist.

From my discussions with our generalists and rheumatologic consultants, I believe that a system that fosters regular communication between the general internist and the subspecialist is more important than trying to establish who is a primary care giver and who is a principal care giver.

Invited Reaction

Jerome H. Grossman

I have just come from a meeting of the executive committee of the National Alliance of Business, and I am struck by the fact that Dr. Fogelman's presentation could have been a description of the new paradigm for running any industry: team-based and quality-based—in a constantly changing environment.

I would like to make three points. First, I will go back to what Al Tarlov was commenting about. That is, although we have captured, I believe, the issue of cost, we have not matched it at all with what in other market environments is called the quality or value trade-off. He mentioned that this was beginning but was only very modestly process related.

Al Tarlov also made the comment that he worries a little bit about how managed care will work out. I guess the second point I would make is that, although we have been talking about full capitation risk and co-management and no specific limit on visits to specialists, those are, I think, critical, really forward-thinking views about co-management. However, let me tell you, I have now looked at four companies in California that are subspecialty and specialty carve-outs. The specialists don't want to leave the work to primary care. They don't want primary care people making decisions about when they get used and who gets to keep the benefit of not using them. As a result, they are now arguing for a carve-out capitation, saying they are better at diagnosing and better at treating. So, we are not done with this issue yet.

My final comment relates to the fact that we have been talking about economics, about medical science and technical medicine, and about medical care giving. What is missing so far, but very relevant to today's discussion, is some recognition of the importance of relationships: medical caring is often dependent on a quality relationship between two individuals. It is not at all clear that this must involve one sort of physician or another, but knowing a patient as a human being is a critical part of success in managing these chronic relapsing diseases. A successful medical outcome is quite often a function of the quality of that relationship.

What we are discovering in an Institute of Medicine (IOM) committee that I chair, which is looking at managed care of mental illness and substance abuse, and I am sure it is true here as well, is that the social infrastructure that supports a patient with a chronic, declining, or relapsing disease is critical to that person and his or her family's ability to cope with those diseases. Thus, when we think about capitation, we need to be thinking not only about the medical and the caring part of it, but about the wrap-around social infrastructure that is so important.

Invited Reaction

William Arnold

I have several remarks, the first of which is a follow-up on Jerry Grossman's point about the societal infrastructure. I work in, and am on the board of directors, of an integrated delivery system (Advocate Health Care System) that is faith based. We are a product of the Evangelical Lutheran Church and the United Church of Christ. In the true tradition of faith beliefs, we believe that faith-based care has a place and adds value, particularly to the care of patients with chronic illness, because we go into the community where these patients live. One of the things we are currently about is trying to quantify that value, which is, as you can imagine, a daunting task.

The second area I would like to cover is a lesson I learned 25 years ago in my first days as a consulting rheumatologist in the hospital where I now practice. I learned it from an experienced consultant who taught me as a medical student when he was a resident. He said, "Billy, if you want to be a successful consultant, remember the three A's. You must be **available**, you must be **able,** and most important, you must be **affable**. You must be able to talk to your doctors and your patients; you have got to be there for them; and you have got to be able."

I have remembered that, but I would submit to you that, after this morning, particularly after Alan's talk, it should be the six A's. The new six A's of being a rheumatologist and a consultant in this era of managed care could guide us as we seek to optimize the care of the patient with rheumatic disease in an integrated delivery system by optimizing at least one member of the caregiver team, the rheumatologist.

The first of the new A's—**adaptability**—is a prime requirement in this era of rapid change. Rheumatologists must be willing to change continuously during their careers to better serve the needs of their patients with arthritis.

Whether these changes involve going directly to the offices of internists to provide services, as in Dr. Fogelman's construct, or being able to function as a consulting specialist, a principal care physician, or a combination of the above, rheumatologists must adapt to the changing environment. In fact, I would have said that rheumatologists should check all four options on Dr. Eisenberg's choices, even the one that includes driving a taxi, particularly if the taxi is bringing a patient with arthritis to a needed service! In addition, our curriculum and fellowship training programs must produce rheumatologists who are adaptable and comfortable with the experience of lifelong learning. In my own situation, long after my rheumatology fellowship experience I acquired the skills to provide diagnostic and therapeutic arthroscopic services for patients with arthritis. I'm pleased to say that I've also had an opportunity to train rheumatologists who are now providing similar services at several centers. Both Drs. Hahn and Rothfield now have rheumatologists on their faculties who provide diagnostic and therapeutic arthroscopy services. Other examples of the continued learning and incorporation into practice that are necessary include the management of patients with rehabilitation needs and the diagnosis and management of osteoporosis.

Even the most adaptable rheumatologist, however, will not be allowed to care for patients unless she or he is "aligned." The second A—**alignment**—refers to both financial and clinical alignment. Financial alignment is most simply understood as becoming a member of as many provider panels as possible for insurance and managed care products. Since this often involves considerable administrative burden, many rheumatologists find it easier to simply become aligned with a group, either a rheumatology practice group or a multispecialty group. In this setting, the administrative aspects of alignment generally are handled by the management of the group or organization. Clinical alignment comes through participating in devising and implementing clinical care pathways for patients with arthritis. Together with internists and other allied health professionals, rheumatologists need to understand and help direct the overall care of the patient with rheumatic disease in a setting where the paradigm is value added, not quantity equals quality.

The third A—**accountability**—makes explicit what all rheumatologists have done implicitly for years (i.e., accept responsibility for the care of patients with arthritis). Its explicit nature means that we must be accountable in a quantitative fashion for outcomes, both financial and clinical. Financial outcomes, of course, include cost of care and must fit within reasonable parameters. Clinical outcomes are easy to talk about and difficult to determine or measure. Nonetheless, our patients, insurers, employers, and the government are demanding that we provide explicit outcome measures to illustrate the quality of our care, and we must do this. If rheumatologists do achieve better outcomes than generalists, we must document this, not merely claim it.

Finally, I don't know if women physicians make a difference, but I do know that in the care of my patients with rheumatic diseases, the characteristics that are most notably associated with being female definitely make a difference. Males can have these characteristics too, but the so-called female characteristics that, in my opinion, predict success in the management of chronic disease include the ability to share one's feelings in an open manner, often with multiple people. I continue to be impressed with the fact that I can sit in a room and talk with a good male friend for an hour, and we will share less about what is really important about our families than our wives will do in five minutes. The female side of us is also used to working in groups, has high levels of compassion, and—I think very importantly in chronic illness—uses a very spiritual approach.

Discussion

RICHARD FINKBINER: The Health Plan Employer Data and Information Set (HEDIS) has been mentioned a couple of times, and I wanted to make a comment. HEDIS is not a static process. It is ongoing, and we staff at the National Committee for Quality Assurance are very sympathetic to the perception that process measures dominated earlier versions. I am now project director for a Robert Wood Johnson chronic disease initiative to develop quality indicators. This is an enormously complicated area. You have different model types within managed care trying to achieve uniformity there. You have the issue of the ebb and flow of chronic disease, as has been mentioned. For rheumatic disease, I am aware of nothing that has come forward from the call for measures for the next versions of HEDIS. However, those of us working with HEDIS are very interested in processes and dialogues like these.

BEVRA HAHN: I want to ask Dr. Grossman two questions. The more important one is what you think that salarying physicians would give them incentives to communicate. How likely do you think it is that physicians would be salaried under some of these coming health programs? Second, what is the content of your software in terms of how you are going to evaluate quality?

JEROME GROSSMAN: In answer to your question about salaried positions, let me just give you the latest example. In Boston last week, Harvard Pilgrim Health Plan announced that its health centers with salaried positions would be spun off into group practices. Kaiser in California, the largest salaried practice, is having a very complicated, difficult time making the transition to being adaptable. Frankly, I don't think salary is the issue. The issue is whether you want to be at risk, be fully capitated, or be a carve out. We will be testing a thousand different strategies, because we don't know what the answer is yet. They will keep evolving, but I do not think that straight salary is going to turn out to be the dominant model.

To answer your question about quality measures, I am very much interested in making patient-based assessments, which Al Tarlov alluded to—quality of functioning and satisfaction, as well as the technical, disease-specific measures of well-being. I have a strong belief that such assessments can make a large contribution to the quality of the relationship between caretaker and patient, if those measures are included in the day-to-day care of patients.

THEODORE FIELDS: I have a question related to the co-management of patients with rheumatic disease. Where does patient preference fit into that? Two speakers with rheumatoid arthritis described very different feelings about how often they wanted to see their rheumatologist. Where does the factor of patient preference fit? I see it as a factor in different patient payment systems.

ALAN FOGELMAN: For us patient preference is always an important component. It really becomes known when the patient communicates either to the primary care physician or to the consultant. If the consultant and the primary care doctor are talking to each other, this is one of the things they will discuss, and it has worked out. We don't have complete control over this, because of the multiplicity of plans that we must work with. In some plans we don't have absolute control over access to some of the diagnostic modalities without preapproved authorization. However, in terms of flow between the doctors, at least for us, that is pretty easy.

THEODORE FIELDS: You wonder if some of the incentives that may be set up over time may influence the ability to carry out the patient's preference.

ALAN FOGELMAN: We are trying to find the right incentives. For our primary care doctors, incentives are going to include three components: availability, productivity, and patient satisfaction. We just hired somebody for our small group—actually, more than one person—whose full-time job is to sample patient satisfaction. We are trying to develop a component of salary for our primary care doctors that is incentive based. I happen to agree with Dr. Grossman that incentives have to be there. The key is to find the right incentives.

CAROLYN CLANCY: I wanted to reinforce a point that Dr. Grossman made about who is in charge, whether it is the specialist or the primary care physician. I think an open question now for many kinds of chronic disease is the extent to which the carve-outs we have seen for mental health will be extended to other conditions as well. On the one hand, you can make a very appealing case for doing so. After all, if you have a constellation of services organized tightly for patients with rheumatic disease, who would not like that? What is there not to like? On the other hand, there are patients who, of course, don't have just one condition. I think the other benchmark is how well services are coordinated, because the more doctors a patient sees, the more opportunities there are for error.

WILLIAM HAZZARD: First of all, you said that these activities cannot fit into a 40-hour week. How long is the week for a full time equivalent in your model? A second question stems from what must be a continuing need for capital to develop your system. Where is that capital coming from?

ALAN FOGELMAN: The answer to the first question is that it is probably on the order of 50 to 55 hours a week. The incentive is the educational component of practicing with us and the requirement for doing creative work. We find that helps to make that long work week as enjoyable as it can be. In terms of capital, we decided as a faculty—a collection of people committed to scholarship, research, and education—that we would take a portion of our income, a significant portion, and reinvest it in developing this primary care system. We are putting about $3 million a year of faculty money into this system right now. The vast majority comes from the fact that we are still largely in a fee-for-service market, and that, instead of the subspecialists taking the money home, we are reinvesting it in the system.

9

How Easily Do Health Care Systems Adopt New Knowledge, and What Are the Likely Future Developments?

Introduction

Michael R. McGarvey

Larry Manheim was invited to address the question, How easily do health care systems adopt new knowledge? His charge was further broadened to address the questions What are the likely future developments in the care of rheumatoid arthritis and lupus, and in managed care? Manheim's remarks and those of the invited reactors (Mark Robbins and Michael McGarvey) are formulated against the overall theme of the conference: What overall impact on the care of patients with chronic diseases are the dramatic alterations occurring in the health care system, particularly the rapid growth of managed care likely to have?

Like other speakers, Manheim reflects on the positive and negative incentives inherent in the basic modes of physician or provider reimbursement, fee for service, and capitation. His own review of the literature suggests that actual outcomes for patients with chronic diseases in fee-for-service (FFS) and managed care systems yielded little difference, with the possible exception of slightly decreased patient satisfaction in managed care associated with access to services. Offsetting this is the potential opportunity within the managed care setting for the more organized and creative use of nonphysician providers to assist in continuity of care for patients with chronic illness. However, the current rapid consolidation among managed care organizations and the propensity of premium payors to shop for the plan with the lowest price work against continuity of doctor–patient relationships and of services for patients. Future developments in the care of patients with lupus and rheumatoid arthritis were, from a scientific and technology point of view, predicted to be incremental.

Invited reactor Mark Robbins emphasizes the impact of the rapid evolution of managed care, including consolidation in the industry. Michael McGarvey points out that the organized nature of managed care provides at least a theoretical opportunity for a more orderly approach to technology assessment and adoption than currently exists in the FFS system. Both Robbins and McGarvey point out that managed care can neither substitute for nor adequately address health care issues that are essentially social in nature, including coverage of the uninsured.

Invited Address

Larry M. Manheim

How easily do health care systems adopt new knowledge? There are a number of issues here, but I will try to keep the focus on how financial incentives are likely to impact adoption of new organizational knowledge by managed care organizations. I also will review the characteristics of evolving "model systems" that appear to provide good, integrated services at reasonable cost to frail elderly patients in managed care. I would suggest that these might serve as a model for rheumatologist service delivery.

Although discussions of managed care are often phrased in terms of comparisons of capitated (HMOs) versus other service models, this can blur the critical questions of who the decision-makers are and what their incentives, constraints, training, and interests are in learning about, and adopting, new knowledge.

I am an economist, not a physician, so I will not talk much about questions of training and the nature of medical knowledge in rheumatology. I cannot really speculate on the specifics of likely biomedical advances in treatment, except to say that breakthroughs are likely to be on the margin rather than in the form of cures. Treatment of rheumatoid arthritis and lupus usually involves multiple drugs. Changing medical technology often affects physician decisions with respect to whether one or multiple drugs are administered in situations in which one drug works better than another in limiting progression of disease, minimizing symptoms, or minimizing toxicity. Choice among which of these qualities of a drug to stress will often change depending on the ebb and flow of the disease. For rheumatoid arthritis, and even more for lupus, providers worry about systemic effects, monitoring organ system involvement, and changing the treatment as required.

As with other chronic diseases, physicians often work to achieve marginal improvements. At least for the foreseeable future, medical improvements are likely to increase the need to manage the patient over time. Therefore, the more important questions in terms of organizations adopting new knowledge, are those concerning changes an organization can adopt to manage chronic diseases more efficiently. In this regard, the knowledge base is growing as "model systems" are identified and studied.

Before looking at the characteristics of some model systems that I believe hold promise for the management of chronic diseases such as rheumatoid arthritis and lupus, we need to ask whether the decision-makers will be interested in this new knowledge? Who are the decision-makers? At a minimum, they are the patient, the physician or other care provider, and the organization responsible for managing the patient.

The patient will often be dissatisfied with treatment, simply because of the nature of these chronic diseases. Patients may go through a number of drugs, have physical therapy at different times, and go through some pain management. Some of these will work now, but not later. Some may not work now, or at least may not relieve symptoms to the satisfaction of the patient, leading to the question of trying an array of alternative treatments. Patient participation in these decisions may depend on socioeconomic or educational status, and patients (rightly or wrongly) may think they know more about their needs than their primary care physician and want to be managed by a physician who specializes in the patient's particular disease, which can cause tension if the primary care physician acts as gatekeeper.

The physician is another decisionmaker. In fact, multiple physicians and allied health professionals are often involved, given the systemic nature of these diseases. What is the optimal relationship among the rheumatologist, other specialists and allied health professionals, and the primary care physician? To a large extent this is determined by the structure, incentives, and hiring practices of the managed care organization.

The financial value of the patient to the HMO depends on the expected financial remuneration from treating that patient, compared with the expected costs of treatment. The HMO will also worry about the financial risks of certain types of patients turning out to be very high-cost patients. Many have pointed out that chronically ill individuals are not people that HMOs will necessarily want to attract, at least if they are not paid a capitation rate that is viewed as reflective of the cost of that type of patient.

A lupus patient, for example, might apply for disability benefits under Social Security Disability Insurance (SSDI). Patients receiving coverage under SSDI, and therefore eligible for Medicare capitation rates based on the average cost of a disabled person in that county, may have a capitation rate far higher than a similar individual who does not receive SSDI eligibility—and physicians say eligibility determination can be quite arbitrary for a disease such as lupus. In the first case the patient may be viewed by the HMO as a financially profitable patient, on average, while at a lower capitation rate the patient may be viewed as a financial liability.

There is also the incentive question: who bears the cost of bad patient outcomes? Clearly, the HMO bears these costs to the extent that it is responsible for medical costs or has its reputation tarnished among people it wants to attract as members. In many cases the managed care organization may not bear the cost of bad outcomes from care (e.g., needed domiciliary long-term care costs if access to joint replacement is limited). For lupus patients, renal failure is a major complication that may occur because of poor chronic care management. However, transplantation and renal dialysis are covered under separate Medicare programs so that the cost of providing less-than-optimal care, which results in renal failure, may not be borne by the patient's care plan. Thus, the incentives to provide good care are reduced. There are numerous cases in which such fragmentation distorts incentives when an HMO has a chronic care patient at risk for long-term care services.

More generally, Medicare patients are not locked into their current plan, and even in private plans, employees are generally allowed to change plans annually. Given the high disenrollment rates for Medicare and Medicaid managed care patients, good, comprehensive medical care that prevents expensive utilization in the long term is not likely to be viewed as of much financial value to the HMO unless it generally enhances the HMO's reputation. Indeed, by making it difficult for costly, chronic care patients to access certain types of services, the HMO may be able to increase disenrollment and decrease future enrollment of these less profitable patients. Of course, this strategy is only financially successful if healthier patients do not also leave the HMO.

With reference to training, I would stress the need for physicians to understand that the appropriate use of allied health personnel is likely to be a valued attribute of managed care subspecialists. Providing the care that practitioners in a chronic care field feel is first rate, either under the current system or under managed care, will have to involve, I think, less costly providers. Regardless of provider, appropriate use of social supports is very important both in physician training and in setting incentives for the system. Finally, because the nature of new knowledge in rheumatoid arthritis and lupus is often equivocal and requires complex long-term management (e.g., use of multiple drugs with toxic effects that must be monitored), an ongoing provider-patient relationship that enhances patient monitoring will continue to be essential to good chronic care management.

To help manage disease, patients need access to someone who they believe specializes in their disease, but it may be too expensive if that is always a rheumatologist. A useful approach is to use the rheumatologist as an ongoing consultant and part of a multidisciplinary team that includes less expensive allied health professionals who become the primary contact for individuals with rheumatoid arthritis and lupus. This model for managing chronic care fits with a number of examples of best-practice models for providing care to the chronically disabled and frail elderly. We heard about the system at the University of California, Los Angeles, which is one example. Other models that seem to work in managed care systems involve gerontologists. In each case, subspecialists act as consultants to primary care physicians and as head of a team that will take over management when long-term care services are required. Physician assistants and allied health professionals working in the team are assigned to given patients and have the most direct contact with them.

The key to such an approach is the notion of a team of health professionals, which includes someone knowledgeable in the disease (and directly responsible to the subspecialist) that a patient can readily access. A case manager might then be viewed by the patient as a facilitator rather than a gatekeeper. There also would be someone on the team through whom social and educational programs could be coordinated. The patient then accesses this system when he or she becomes problematic in terms of independent living.

The same approach would seem to be possible in the management of rheumatologic chronic diseases. This may provide a system with good access to care and with costs that are reasonable relative to what the managed care organization sees as the program's value added. However, there is always likely to be tension between the notion that value is added by these additional services and the realization that both the value added and the funds available may be modest.

Like everyone, I have been focusing on traditional managed care systems. Systemic lupus erythematosus (SLE) disproportionately affects African American women—nine out of ten cases of SLE are women, and the incidence of SLE is between two and five times greater for African American women than for white women. A lot of these women seek care in public institutions or in private institutions covered under Medicaid. Given low payments and declining budgets, more attention needs to be given to the management of chronic disease in the public sector. The shift to Medicaid case management might seem to offer hope for more comprehensive care for Medicaid eligibles, but this might prove illusory if Medicaid payments are insufficient to support true case management. Thus, it is important to continue research to monitor access to medical care received by chronic care patients under Medicaid or with no insurance coverage.

Invited Reaction

Mark L. Robbins

I would like to react to Dr. Manheim's presentation by providing an overview of the forces that are shaping the health care industry, the incentives that are influencing decisions at the patient and provider levels, and the changing nature of these incentives. I think that only by understanding these forces and their dynamics can we acquire insight into the critical issue of whether competition in health care will take place on the basis of innovations designed to enhance quality, thereby encouraging the adoption of new knowledge and improved chronic disease management, or based on potentially less desirable factors. Many of the comments that follow are based on my work on a study funded by the Robert Wood Johnson Foundation that is looking at private sector health care reform in four different U.S. markets.

Economic recession, health care inflation, and an increasing uninsured population stimulated national health care reform efforts, which drove early changes in the market but ultimately did not proceed. The failure of federal health care reform left the purchasers of health care—large employers such as state governments and corporations—to fend for themselves in containing health care costs. Managed care and managed competition in a variety of forms appeared to be the best systematic approach by which these purchasers of health care could contain costs without introducing substantial cuts in health benefits.

However, managed competition evolved primarily for large employers and state governments. As a result, some of our discussions and concerns today about where the unemployed, unregistered, or uninsured go for continuing health care. Employers generally wanted to maximize their purchasing power, avoid internal risk shifting, and provide wide geographic access for their employees. This drove managed care organizations to develop larger and larger provider networks. The accelerated and sometimes frenetic cascade of mergers and acquisitions among health plans and hospitals has led to new and sometimes dysfunctional delivery systems and has raised the critical issue of what the essential components of a truly integrated delivery system are. It has also raised the questions of what is the most effective model or mixture of models (independent practice association(IPA), preferred provider organization (PPO), staff or group health maintenance organization) to deliver integrated care.

This is particularly important for the continuing care of chronic disease patients. In some health markets, such as Minneapolis, the level of consolidation was so complete that the end result was an anticompetitive oligopoly of only three major remaining health delivery systems. The Minnesota business coalition is taking active steps to reverse this trend by shifting the focus of decision making, quality measurement and improvement, and incentives away from oversized health plans back to the clinic and provider levels. In response to this challenge, insurers and health plans are reassessing the value and services they add to the process of health care delivery. A significant part of their future contribution will be in the areas of technology assessment and innovation, development of clinical guidelines, and refinement of health information systems, because of their significant technical expertise and financial reserves.

Large purchasers of health care and their employees also influenced the market by demanding the widest possible choice of providers. This contributed significantly to the dwindling enrollments of closed panel staff and group model managed care organizations and to the emergence of point-of-service (POS) options and rapidly expanding IPA networks.

Overlapping IPAs, in which one provider may be listed with an infinite number of insurers, potentially represent a significant force against competition based on quality and innovation. First, quality indicators measured at the health plan level lose their significance and blunt the power of consumer choice based on quality reporting. If a difference between health plans did arise on a particular quality indicator that essentially derives from the same providers in the same offices with the same systems and support, it becomes a challenge to explain the measurement difference. Second, there is little incentive for these overlapping IPA health plans to introduce innovations. Innovations introduced by the health plan, which previously might have been associated with an exclusive provider network and provided brand identity, now diffuse rapidly through the overlapping provider network. For example, if an insurer develops a new clinical guideline or pathway, offers a new service, or develops a new chronic disease management technique that the provider finds of value, these innovations are likely to be adopted for patients in the providers' practices who are covered by other insurers or health plans.

In some markets such as California, the dominance of nonexclusive overlapping provider networks has led to extreme price sensitivity. There is evidence that people in these markets will switch health plans to save as little as four dollars a month on their premium payments because, despite the health plan change, they can still maintain their providers. One can certainly argue that the growth of overlapping IPAs is an effective way to force health plans to compete on price. Cost containment is something we have been talking about quite negatively today—the shift from inpatient to outpatient treatment; primary care gatekeepers limiting specialty access; the heavily discounted fee-for-service policies that were initially tried to control costs; and capitation, which followed and is gradually marching from west to east.

In summary, I want again to emphasize that managed competition was not intended for and is not likely to address many key public policy and public health issues. It does not deal adequately with the public health system, social safety net issues, teaching and research, and the uninsured. It does not systematically address issues of technology assessment and innovation, and it does not provide an ethical framework for managing care while containing costs. For quality and innovation in chronic disease management to take place, a number of important developments are necessary. Purchasers of health care will have to recognize that payment for health services must include risk adjustment. Current payment systems create economic disincentives for health plans or provider networks to develop centers of excellence for the management of rheumatologic or other chronic diseases. Quality measurement related to chronic disease management will have to be improved and its focal point shifted from health plan to exclusive multispecialty provider groups. Capitation or risk payment for providers and health plans will have to be based on better chronic disease management rather than on measures of decreased utilization and costs.

Invited Reaction

Michael R. McGarvey

I speak as an individual with responsibility, among other things, for one of the most rapidly growing HMOs in the State of New Jersey (Blue Cross and Blue Shield of New Jersey). We currently have about 500,000 people covered either in our HMO or in our point-of-service product. You won't be surprised to hear that this is our most rapidly growing line of business.

To get to the question that was just posed, whether purchasers are going to be buying largely on the basis of quality or of price, I am afraid that at the moment the answer tends to be price. A few very sophisticated, large organizations have worked a bit to see if they can't identify one organization from another on the basis of quality. However, for the most part, we are certainly finding in our marketplace that individuals and organizations, large and small, are buying on price, not on quality, even to the extent that we can manifest some degree of quality and are trying all the time to do a better job at that.

I think Larry Manheim asked a very important question concerning the basic modes of adopting new technology in different managed care systems. That is, who is the decision maker? I think the fact of the matter is that in standard, traditional fee-for-service medicine, the decision maker has essentially always been the individual practicing physician. I think that depending on his or her reading habits and conscientiousness about continuing education, the individual physician has been in a good position to make a decision on whether to adopt the latest treatment modalities. Such decisions could involve whether or not, in the case of rheumatoid arthritis, to move to a fairly early trial of methotrexate, given current knowledge that its toxicity is much less than we originally feared; or whether antibiotics should be used for the treatment of peptic ulcer rather than continuing to dole out Maalox in copious quantities.

In the managed care system, however, the decision maker, more often than not, is the medical director of the managed care organization. More often than not, a real part of his or her responsibility is trying to keep up with literature, trying to tap into technology assessment capabilities, and trying to bring that information into the organization. Again, more often than not, this individual is guided in decisionmaking by a series of physician panels that represent enrolled physicians—subspecialty groups, specialty groups, and primary care physicians of various types, usually collected in a variety of advisory panels.

Thus, new technology can be addressed, assessed, adopted or rejected in a reasonably organized manner, and transmitted and communicated in a reasonably organized manner. Then, based on how the organization does or does not monitor the performance of its physicians, their adoption and application of new technology can be assessed.

On balance then, I would say, just as Karen Davis outlined a number of theoretical pros and cons of managed care, that one of the pros is that in a managed care environment there is, in fact, a structured approach to technology assessment, adoption of new technology, and investing in new technology for actual application by practicing physicians helping to shape that system.

One of the myths I would like to address here is that managed care organizations behave without any clinical input. Certainly I think some have and do; those tend to be the plans that have bitten the dust. The ones that are surviving and thriving tend to have a fairly well structured approach for developing physician input into the decision making and policies adopted.

A very interesting new development is the concept of disease management, fundamentally the identification of patients who have a specific disease and the treatment of these patients according to guidelines and protocols that, again, have been adopted by the clinical decision-making capability of the managed care organization. Many organizations are now describing themselves as disease managers. Right from the beginning, my own belief has been that, frankly, the only organizational structure in which disease management made very much sense at all was, in fact, managed care, and the better managed care organizations have, in fact, been doing their own brand of disease management for quite some time.

Another major development—several speakers have made reference to it—is specialty capitation. Our own organization is, in fact, moving in that direction. Last year we did a statewide capitated network for radiology. This year we are looking to do very much the same kind of thing in cardiology, gastrointestinal services, and allergy. We may even address orthopedics. I am very sorry to say that rheumatology has not been on our screen, simply because it has not been one of those areas that has involved many of our patients or costs us large amounts.

My final point is that I was really struck by the as yet unpublished data reported today by Karen Davis and Al Tarlov, highlighting the potential vulnerability in a managed care structure of populations in this country that have always been vulnerable—the old, the sick, and the poor.

I think it is important to remember that the prepaid group practices that were the progenitors of our managed care entities today developed essentially to take care of working populations—younger people who were involved in a job and needed health care, and whose organizations paid for it. It is very much in the tradition of American insurance that it has been employment based. To the extent that these organizations are now being drawn, in a variety of ways, into the care of vulnerable populations—the Medicaid population and the aged population—I think this is still unfamiliar ground and a learning experience for them. The kind of data that we are beginning to educe are extremely important if thereis to be an adaptive mechanism by which these organizations can address such issues in either a private sector or a public sector regulatory environment.

Discussion

ROBERT NEWCOMER: In terms of innovations, we have not talked about community care systems and social services more generally. They typically are not funded under health insurance or Medicare but sometimes are funded under Medicaid or other kinds of state-controlled services. Particularly since we are talking about vulnerable populations, do you see any incentives or disincentives, or any problems with that community care safety net and the integration of health plans into it, utilizing its resources or augmenting them for their own benefit?

LARRY MANHEIM: To the extent that community care will save money on some cost that these plans would otherwise bear, capitated care systems might put money there. I think it would be limited, though, because the disenrollment rate can be so high. Most of the things you are talking about, such as long-term care, are not included in current coverage. Although we might place that requirement on the system, for the funder it is really a question of breaking even.

MICHAEL MCGARVEY: From a philosophical point of view, I find utilization of community care very attractive, but it is not the sort of thing that many of the people who pay our premiums are asking for.

MARK ROBBINS: The Harvard Community Health Plan has always dedicated a percentage of its premium to research and public health efforts. As a result, violence education, violence prevention, and other kinds of community efforts are taking place within the HMO. However, this percentage of premiums is under constant attack from within the plan. As the market becomes more and more competitive in terms of price, it is becoming more difficult to defend this practice to employers and others, but so far it has been protected.

WILLIAM HAZZARD: It was reassuring to hear that physicians are becoming more and more involved in direction of some HMOs' policies and guidelines. What about rheumatic disease, in which we hear that patients are so critical? To what extent are patient—consumers being involved in the design of these programs?

MICHAEL MCGARVEY: We do have a panel of enrolled patients who we consult on a regular basis, although I am not aware that we have as yet had anybody with a rheumatic problem.

JEREMIAH BARONDESS: How do they relate to the putative topic of this section of the program: which system adapts more effectively and more efficiently to new information, new knowledge, and new techniques?

MICHAEL MCGARVEY: That is a good question, but I am not sure there is much in the way of a structured method for involving patients in the non-managed system. They can certainly get to their individual physicians and should do so on a regular basis.

JEREMIAH BARONDESS: Should we be pushing for patient engagement in selection or prioritization or adoption of new techniques? Does anybody have a view on that?

LARRY MANHEIM: The only problem is that if you consider the average plan member, who is healthy, it is not clear that such a person would want to pay higher premiums to improve the system. I think it would be good to involve chronic disease patients, but you must have a payment system that supports that kind of interaction.

NORMAN LEVINSKY: With regard to the issue of the disadvantaged, I would mention that there is an experiment going on, largely funded by Medicare, dealing with the frail elderly. It goes by the acronym PACE, Program for the All-Inclusive Care of the Elderly. One of the programs is related to Boston University, to one of its neighborhood health centers. This program involves socially responsible and very motivated physicians, along with a team of professionals and nonprofessional community workers. Together they provide all-inclusive care to the frail elderly. In terms of the cost potential for standard HMOs and managed care to provide that level of service and dedication, I wonder whether one could expect comparable outcomes. There is a price, however, and the price is not in dollars, which is approximately the same as the standard Medicare costs. The price is very tight control of the patient's access to the health care system. Patients must use a limited group of practitioners and a limited group of hospitals; basically are putting their care totally in the hands of these—we hope—well-motivated and ethical physicians and associates.

LARRY MANHEIM: I would just note that under PACE, providers are often paid as if the patients were in a nursing home, because they qualify. So, the capitation rate is quite high.

LEIGH CALLAHAN: Alan Fogelman noted several things that I think are very important to vulnerable populations: patient facilitators, transportation, and education about their disease and its management. When someone asked him how he does this, the answer was capital, but a unique form of capital, in that the physicians are foregoing a percentage of their income to fund this comprehensive system. Do you think managed care organizations would put a portion of their income into government systems to enhance the care for the vulnerable populations?

MICHAEL MCGARVEY: Although our HMO is technically a for-profit subsidiary, any sensible financial analyst looking at our medical loss ratio would question whether this is an accurate characterization. I think that changes are likely to come as managed care organizations acquire more and more experience with fragile populations. We have now been in Medicaid managed care activity for about two years. In fact, the leadership of that particular subsidiary of ours is now beginning to recognize that we need to have some people on staff who provide the type of facilitating role that Alan Fogelman described, and we are prepared to do it.

We are even newer in the Medicare business, although we have used our traditional Medigap population as the target population for marketing. We are finding that our enrollees are considerably older than the group we had originally expected to enroll. We feel that we will probably have to make some of these investments ourselves. I think this kind of investment—this kind of programmatic development—sort of follows from what one perceives as the needs and requirements of covered populations.

SUSANA SERRATE-SZTEIN: We heard today that there are no cures for either lupus or rheumatoid arthritis. I would like to get your opinions on the impact of the changing health care system on the availability of patients for clinical studies, especially large, multicenter clinical trials.

MICHAEL MCGARVEY: It certainly has occurred to me that managed care organizations would be the ideal places to tap in order to identify patients for enrollment in such controlled studies. I did some work last year reviewing operations at the National Institutes of Health Clinical Center. One of the recommendations, in fact, was that the clinical center be a little more aggressive about contacting managed care organizations for case finding. If things were structured properly and if people understood the ground rules, this it would be a very fertile area for patient identification.

10

Issues and Insights Regarding Research, Education, and Training

Introduction

Deborah A. Freund

Medical schools and the hospitals in which predoctoral and postdoctoral physicians train are important institutions today, and they will continue to be in the future. However the financial support that they have to train physicians and to undertake research, both basic and clinical, will continue to erode. Traditional sources of support for internally funded training and research include the teaching pass-through of diagnosis-related group (DRGs) and Medicaid payments, fellowship and research grants from the public and private sectors, and reimbursements from private insurers that are higher than marginal costs. Together, these streams of funding have allowed training programs to offer treatments that "do not pay for themselves" to all in need. Such monies historically have provided plentiful opportunities for physicians at various stages to observe the most cutting-edge therapies, do research on them, or refine them. Meenan discusses how the new managed care environment may affect the training of physicians, opportunities for research, and the potential impact of these effects on outcomes. He contends that when all of these sources are cut, it is questionable if the number of physicians who can train and the opportunities to practice with expensive therapies can be maintained at current levels. It also is unlikely that managed care and integrated care entities, whether they eventually affiliate with teaching hospitals or not, will continue to provide the revenue now given in other forms to make cross-subsidies for care provision and research possible. Meenan contends that dollars made available by managed care are likely to come with the contingency that the focus be on cost-efficient practices rather than those simply improve or refine current techniques but do not improve patient outcomes.

Meenan foresees a world in which medical education and the research performed along with it occur in very different configurations than they do today. He contends that it is unclear whether our teaching hospitals as configured today can respond quickly enough to supply managed care entities with the appropriate mix of physicians (e.g., more generalists and fewer specialists) having the necessary clinical competencies in cost-effective medical practices. If not, managed care organizations may start their own training programs alone or in concert with affiliated hospitals. For example, Kaiser has had its own residencies for a long time. Teaching hospitals that are unable to respond may shrink in size or close. Medical schools may decide to affiliate with managed care to form vertically integrated health systems and use managed care practices as training sites for students and residents, or as pointed out by Meenan, they may elect to be free-standing educational enterprises without their complicated missions of today.

In his mind the ultimate questions then boil down to the following: (1) What is the evidence that the questions tackled by researchers and the medicine practiced in the future under managed care will actually result in less favorable outcomes for the population? Why should we presume that the current fee-for-service system really is better than or preferable to the alternative?, (2) How will medical schools and other training institutions actually be configured to do research and take care of patients when the "dust settles"?

Invited Address

Robert F. Meenan

Uwe Reinhardt has pointed out that what is generally referred to as "managed care" actually consists of three relatively distinct elements of health care system change. The first, managed care, involves the oversight and proctoring of medical decisions. Such oversight is not new: it has been prevalent for decades in the form of utilization review and related approaches. Practice guidelines and practice profiles are simply new approaches to the management of care. Reinhardt's second element of health care system change is financing, which increasingly emphasizes capitation and risk bearing. These approaches essentially reverse the financial incentives in health care from over utilization to underutilization. The third element of health care system change is market competition based on price and coverage. This competition is increasingly characterized by classic market behaviors. It is not in any real sense "managed competition" because the competition is not seriously constrained by government regulation.

Most of the impacts of health care system change on medical care process and outcome for people with chronic rheumatic diseases will result from two of Reinhardt's factors: management of care and risk-based financing. The major impacts of change on medical research, education, and training, however, will derive primarily from market competition and its direct and indirect effects on academic medical organizations. Three key factors will be especially critical in determining the future status of medical research, education, and training: (1) the new form of the academic medical organization; (2) the underlying philosophy driving government policies; and (3) the market power of managed care organizations. Competition in health care will play the primary role in shaping each of these factors.

The prevailing form of today's academic medical organization is the academic medical center, essentially a medical school linked to a teaching hospital. This form will undoubtedly change in the face of the dual pressures of declining clinical incomes and stagnant research funding. In the future, some medical schools will break their close links with clinical service organizations and will come to look more like business schools and law schools. Other will become components of large, integrated health care delivery systems. Although the second model is appealing to many in academic medicine, it is not clear that such an organization can be successful in the increasingly competitive environment of health care. It is also unclear to what extent such an entity would actually pursue a classical academic mission of research, education and teaching. On the other hand, if the "medical school as medical school" model becomes the prevailing form of academic medical organization, it is not clear how medical research, education, and training will be supported.

Government policies of various types have played a major role in the growth of medical education, research, and training over the past five decades. These policies include Hill–Burton funds for postwar hospital construction in the 1950s, Medicare support for graduate medical education beginning in the 1960s, capitation support for increased medical school class sizes in the 1970s, and consistent support for medical research funded by the National Institutes of Health (NIH) over four decades. In the 1990s and beyond, government policy will continue to play a critical role in determining the nature and magnitude of the impacts of health care system change on medical education, research, and training. If the traditional view of these activities as public goods prevails, government policies may substantially blunt the impact of health system change. If the newer view prevails—that these activities, particularly education and training, should and can be determined by the market—then government policies (or the lack of them) may exacerbate the detrimental effects of health system change.

Finally, medical research, education, and training will be affected in major ways by the growing market power of managed care organizations in an increasingly competitive health care system. As these entities become major customers for academic medical organizations and as they become progressively larger corporations with growing influence on a range of public and private policies, they will increasingly define their own agendas for research, education, and training. As these large corporations utilize capital markets to finance their growth, they will have little or no interest in subsidizing the traditional activities of academic medical organizations, because they will derive no clear stockholder benefit from doing so.

RESEARCH

Different types of medical research will be affected differently by health system change, but there is no reason to believe that research into rheumatic diseases will be affected differently from medical research in general. Basic biomedical research in rheumatology and in all areas of medicine will shrink. Medical schools currently underwrite basic research with cross-subsidies from clinical income. As the clinical incomes of academic medical organizations continue to decrease, this cross-subsidization will be markedly attenuated, if not eliminated. Stagnating federal support for basic research, decreases in grant overheads to academic organizations, and limits on the percentage of a faculty member's salary that can be charged to research grants will all reinforce the shrinking of biomedical research.

There is little likelihood that managed care organizations will fund basic research because it produces no short- or intermediate-term payoffs for them. Although a convincing argument can be made that basic biomedical research is a public good, it is unlikely that government support for such research can be substantially expanded in the face of increasing pressures to cut government spending. Academic medical organizations will increasingly turn to private industry, particularly the pharmaceutical and biotechnology industries, as sources of support for biomedical research. Such support will focus more on applied than on basic research, and it will increasingly raise issues about the appropriate boundaries and relationships between academic and business organizations. Regardless of the new models that might develop, it seems inevitable that total support for basic biomedical research will decline and the number of faculty involved in this activity will decrease. This will necessarily delay the discovery of markedly better treatments for rheumatoid arthritis and systemic lupus erythematosus, but it is impossible to predict if this postponement will be a particularly lengthy one.

The effects of health system change on clinical research are difficult to predict. On the negative side, there are a number of reasons why support for clinical research is apt to decrease in an increasingly competitive health care system. Clinical incomes that previously supported such research will continue to fall, and this will be accelerated by the ongoing shift of public health care plans (Medicare and Medicaid) to a managed care approach. The pressures to maintain clinical incomes will also decrease the amount of time that clinical investigators can devote to research and to the training of future clinical investigators. On the positive side, managed care organizations have the potential to be excellent sites for clinical research because of their large size and their increasingly sophisticated data systems. Certain forms of clinical research may also produce short-term benefits for managed care organizations in terms of better patient care.

Academic medical organizations will also turn to business corporations for the support of clinical research. The obvious targets for such efforts will be drug and device manufacturers. Once again, these companies will emphasize very applied, product-oriented clinical research. To the extent that they do support clinical research, they will do so only in academic organizations that possess certain key attributes. These will include large patient populations that support both the conduct of clinical research and the eventual marketing of approved products; efficient research processes that facilitate the rapid approval and conduct of clinical research; and sophisticated data systems that identify potential subjects and permit the efficient collection of high-quality data. Since academic medical organizations possess these attributes in varying degrees, it is likely that clinical research will grow substantially in some academic medical organizations while declining dramatically in others.

Support for health care research may actually increase under managed care. Managed care organizations have fairly direct incentives to carry out health care research that examines the cost and effectiveness of alternative approaches to medical care. Furthermore, managed care organizations can increase their competitiveness by supporting research into cost-effectiveness, clinical pathways, outcomes measurement, and other aspects of health care. The results of such studies may well provide proprietary advantages to the sponsoring company. Unfortunately, this point has been used as a primary argument for decreasing government support for health care research through agencies such as the Agency for Health Care Policy and Research (AHCPR).

In fact, the health care research needs of managed care organizations are so substantial that alternative arrangements are developing to support such studies. These include major in-house units in larger managed care organizations and numerous private sector companies that are building their health care research capacities. Both of these developments represent direct competition with academic medical organizations in the search for health care research dollars. Once again, patient populations, efficient research operations and information technology capacity will determine which academic medical organizations are able to compete for health care research dollars.

EDUCATION

Medical education, as distinct from medical training, refers to the preparation of medical students that culminates in the awarding of an M.D. degree. Medical school education is generally a four-year program, with the first two years focused on classroom-based, didactic education and the second two years emphasizing clinic-based practical training. This general approach to medical education dates from the Flexner report, issued early in this century, which transformed medical education from an apprenticeship model to an academic model. Since the 1960s, the didactic components of medical education have increasingly been taught by basic science faculty, while the clinical elements have increasingly been taught by specialist physicians in hospital-based settings.

Health system change has profound implications for medical education. Once again, the most immediate and obvious impact of such change will be a progressive, competition-driven decrease in clinical income to medical schools and their clinical faculties. A combination of competition from nonacademic medical care providers and decreases in reimbursement levels from payers will cost academic medical organizations billions of dollars per year in clinical income. These losses will soon produce substantial decreases in the number of clinical faculty as well as reductions in the time that remaining faculty can devote to the teaching of medical students. There is no reason to expect that either managed care organizations or government will take steps to mitigate these financial strains on medical education. In fact, the basic premise in government policy toward medicine and other professions is that the choice to pursue professional education should be made by each individual based on classic market considerations of cost and eventual income.

Government, accrediting bodies, and managed care organizations all have an interest in the content of medical education. Each is interested in making medical education more relevant to the practice of medicine in the evolving health care system, making the content of medical education more relevant to the evolving demographic and disease burdens of society, making medical education more oriented toward preventive care, and making medical education more balanced in its attentions to population health and individual patient health. Changes in these directions would all represent positive steps for medical education in general and for rheumatology education in particular. In fact, it is arguably more important to change the content of medical education than it is to change the number of medical students. However, it remains to be seen whether medical schools can respond effectively to the pressures of the new medical care market by making medical education more outpatient oriented, more chronic disease oriented, more cost control oriented, and more prevention oriented.

TRAINING

Training refers to the post graduate education of physicians. In the current system, the vast majority of medical school graduates pursue clinical training for three or more years in order to become medical specialists or subspecialists. In rheumatology, the training program is five years long, requiring three years of training in internal medicine followed by two years of training in rheumatology. For most trainees, the two years of rheumatology training are a combination of clinical and research experiences. The modest salaries of rheumatology trainees have traditionally been supported by a mix of training grants, research grants, and clinical income.

Health system change has already had substantial impact on rheumatology training. Once again, the impact has been driven primarily by financial factors. The clinical incomes of rheumatology divisions have decreased in line with the overall decrease in academic clinical incomes. Tighter research budgets do not allow for support of trainees. Funds for training grants have been cut. Medical care competition also has decreased the incomes of practicing rheumatologists, which in turn has decreased the economic returns to rheumatology training. As a result, the number of applicants for rheumatology training has dropped steadily and markedly over the past decade.

This decrease in the number of rheumatology trainees will not necessarily have adverse effects on the health care outcomes of people with rheumatic diseases. Managed care organizations increasingly strive to have specialists serve only as specialists. In this model, rheumatologists are utilized primarily for the care of complex rheumatic disorders such as rheumatoid arthritis and systemic lupus erythematosus. Substantially fewer rheumatologists are needed in this model than in the old fee-for-service model. Thus, a reduction in the number of rheumatology trainees and practitioners need not produce access or outcome problems for the most pertinent patients.

Like medical education, the content of medical training should change to reflect the changing needs of the competitive health care system. Rheumatology training should increasingly emphasize clinical skills and the care of complex rheumatic disorders. Given the realities of a competitive health care system, the number of training slots should be decreased to alleviate an impending oversupply of rheumatologists. It remains to be seen, however, whether rheumatology training programs will have the foresight and the will to make such changes.

Managed care organizations have an interest in well-trained physicians. To the extent that academic medical organizations do not change their approaches to training, it is possible that managed care organizations will set up their own training programs, particularly for generalist physicians. It is unlikely, however, that managed care organizations will ever directly support rheumatology training. Rheumatologists will continue to be trained in the academic medical organization of the future, but the organization and the content of training will both be substantially different.

CONCLUSION

The changes occurring in the health care system are profound, and they will be permanent. Health care competition represents a new era in American medicine, not just a minor adjustment in the old system. As the new, competition-driven system takes form, approaches to research, education, and training will arise that are most appropriate for the new system. The question is not how current approaches to research, education, and training can be supported under the new system. They cannot and should not be. The onus is on the old system to change and adapt, not on the new system to preserve.

Invited Reaction

Robert Mechanic

We all agree that markets are changing. The question many are focusing on is whether academic medical centers will prosper or even survive in this new environment and, if so, what that means for research and education. I will give you a few numbers with which to gauge the magnitude of what is going on right now and help separate some of the rhetoric from the current reality. Then I will talk a bit about how managed care plans and academic medical centers might come together in productive ways.

Federal grants for research have been growing at about 9 percent a year over the past decade. The NIH received an increase of about 6 percent for FY 1996. Although the rate of growth in federal grants may slow down, clinical cross-subsidy of research is the funding source that is most threatened by the changing market environment. If you look at medical schools, about half the funding today is clinical revenue.

Government policy is important, perhaps more important than what is going on in the private market. Here are some of the things that we need to think about. First is the rate of growth in federal research funding. Second is consideration of an all-payer indirect medical education (IME) and direct medical education (DME) funding pool for teaching hospitals. Even though you hear less about this concept in Washington, many states, driven by either their medical centers, their universities, or their state legislators, are looking into dedicated medical education funding pools, although to my knowledge no legislation has actually been passed.

Medicare payment is still very important. For the 225 major teaching hospitals, about one-third of their DRG payment is based on indirect medical education and disproportionate share hospital (DSH) payments. In the most recent year for which data are available, 1993, major teaching hospitals did well under Medicare, with an average margin of 11.7 percent compared with the average for all hospitals of 0.3 percent. The congressional budget resolution that was passed but vetoed early in 1996 proposed a 35 percent cut in IME and DSH payments. A cut of that size would have reduced Medicare payments to major teaching hospitals by about $1.3 billion and would have lowered the average Medicare margin from 11.7 percent to less than 2 percent.

In terms of market impacts, two things are happening. Over the last 10 years, there has been a reduction in inpatient utilization of about 30 percent. A number of scholars, including The Lewin Group, have done projections for the year 2000, and the number that seems to fall out—a midrange estimate—is a further decline in inpatient utilization of about 35 percent. That could have a profound impact on academic health centers (AHCs).

The Association of American Medical Colleges (AAMC) shows AHC total margins in the 4 percent range for 1991. This is higher than the historical average, so it is difficult to say that AHCs are in dire financial straits right now. On the other hand, I think there will be a great deal of variation in AHC financial status on a market-by-market basis, and I agree with Meenan's suggestion that it will be the "marketers" that do well in this new market. Being a "seller" will be a losing proposition.

Now I want to very quickly talk about a relevant study we just completed. We did seven site visits to assess the question of how managed care is affecting clinical research. Two hypotheses were investigated. One was that managed care plans are denying more research-related care. The second was that market change is affecting the overall ability of institutions to attract patients and fund research.

We found, in general, that managed care was not denying more research-related care than fee-for-service systems, but there was a lot of pressure due to aggressive price negotiations in competetive markets. Many plans also try to direct people into low-cost provider networks. These general financial pressures affect the level of support available for faculty.

What managed care plans want is efficient, patient-friendly care; a work force that can practice in a managed care setting; and research results that help them produce better outcomes at lower cost for their enrollee populations. If academic health centers are going to stay in the forefront of research as power shifts to managed care organizations, they will have to devote greater attention to those goals.

Discussion

WILLIAM HAZZARD: What about international medical graduates and how they perhaps confound or complicate the issue of a rational plan for graduate medical education?

ROBERT MEENAN: They do complicate things. This is one of those balloon-like problems where you press on one end to reduce it and it simply pops out someplace else. International medical graduates not only raise issues about rational planning for graduate medical education, but also raise central questions about the purpose of medical schools in the evolving health care system.

If you utilize the market model for the evolving health care system, you might ask who the customers of medical schools are. One of the products they produce is medical students. What attributes should those medical students have? Obviously, it depends on the customer. If the customer is a hospital-oriented residency training program, medical schools should produce students with certain skills. If the customer is a managed care organization, the content of medical school education ought to be different. If graduates actually went from medical schools to their ultimate places of employment, the content of medical school education probably would be very different.

Jerry Barondess has talked about the difficulty of teaching clinical skills when students are overwhelmed with the mass of biomedical knowledge they are being fed. I think everyone recognizes that there must be changes in terms of where medical students are taught, who teaches them, and what they are taught. We currently have a specialist-driven clinical education system and a basic scientist-driven first two years. Neither one is an appropriate way to teach medical students what they need to know to be effective care providers in the evolving health care system. Rheumatology training is not unique in its dependence on less-than-appropriate teachers, settings, and content.

One issue that must be addressed in any restructuring of medical education and training is the consistent instillation of a mind-set that physicians should maximize total benefit without regard for marginal benefit and the cost of the next increment of benefit. A key point I make when I talk to medical students about clinical decisionmaking is that one can look at medical practice as a giant two-by-two table, in which "positive/positive" and "negative/negative" are the preferred boxes to be in. When it comes to choosing between the other two boxes, however, every medical student and trainee is taught to avoid the "disease present/no action" box, which represents an error of omission. Students and trainees are taught that it is alright to do many, many tests in which nothing is found, but it is a terrible thing to miss a diagnosis when every possible test was not done.

Teaching students and trainees that it is acceptable to look at the issue of marginal benefits and the cost of marginal benefits is relevant because, as health care continues to evolve, we are likely to lose some ground in terms of the intensity of evaluation and therapy we can provide in our medical care system. We will undoubtedly move back on Dr. Tarlov's S-shaped curve. It drives most physicians insane to contemplate that: to think that they might be giving up some benefit at the margin by not using every test or therapy. As we train physicians for the future, we must make them understand and become more comfortable with the issues of marginal benefit and marginal cost. This will help them function in an environment in which we may not be able to give a hip replacement to that next person in line or train that next rheumatology specialist.

MATTHEW LIANG: Let me introduce the notion of a type III error, an extension of types I and II, which involves giving the right answer to the wrong question. As one who has tried to do economic analyses of health practices, I realize that assigning a dollar value sometimes is a excuse for not assigning a moral value, which is much more difficult to do and may be more contentious. I also realize that in many cases we are trying to sweep out the sea in attempting to resist change, but some of the changes that we are trying to resist concern things of real value, public health concerns. How do we introduce these issues into the public debate and decision making, when the entire debate is centered around dollars and assignment of dollars?

ROBERT MEENAN: I think we must accept that this is really a paradigm shift that will be fundamental and long-lasting. We must recognize that the dynamics and values of the market will determine much of what happens in health care, so we should try to focus public policy on aspects of health care that we know will not be handled well in a system dominated by market characteristics. The market has some positive aspects, including driving excess costs and capacity out of the system and forcing us to ask relevant questions about costs and benefits. The challenge will be to build on some of the positive aspects of a market-oriented system—to craft a synthesis between the thesis of traditional care and the antithesis of managed care.

If we as clinicians had a drug that we thought had modest positive effects but also had substantial toxicity, would we simply throw it out? Of course we wouldn't. In rheumatology, we faced this issue with the early evidence about methotrexate for rheumatoid arthritis. We handled it the way we handle many new drugs for rheumatic diseases, where treatment options are limited and not very effective. We studied it, tried various dosing regimens, and eventually developed a major new treatment for rheumatoid arthritis. We should do the same thing with managed care: look at it as a treatment for the ills of our health care system that is effective but has toxicity. We need to study it, refine it, and use it to build an effective new approach to a complex problem.

Let us never forget that the good old days were not all that good. The approaches that prevailed have led us to the point at which we are paying 14 percent of our gross national product for health care. As economists point out, it is not so much that we are paying 14 percent, but that we are not getting acceptable value for those dollars. If one looks at the results of managed care, it is very clear that there is substantial excess capacity in the clinical care system. If we translate this insight into research, education, and training, we can easily conclude that the good old days have led to excess capacity in those systems as well. The problem is to decide on a new balance point between quantity and quality in our medical education and research systems.

One of the key insights in adapting to a market-oriented system is recognizing that we must stop being believers in medical care or sellers of medical care and that we must become marketers of medical care. The believer is one who feels that the work that he or she does should be funded because it is valuable. It is work with intrinsic value (in some sense, God's work) that should be supported. Many, if not most, medical researchers are believers. A seller is someone who decides what people ought to buy. Usually what people ought to by is what the seller is willing to offer, and the whole idea of selling is to convince people that they want what you make. Most professionals and organizations in health care have been sellers. They decide what tests and treatments the customer should buy, and they determine the time, place, and price at which these services are available. The health care marketer, on the other hand, asks what people out there are looking for. The health care marketer asks what service, approach, or product can I produce that will have enough value for the market to buy it? One positive result of the evolving health care system would be to produce more marketing and less selling and believing.

I also want to point out that public policy is likely to be far more important in the areas of research, education, and training than it has been or will be in the clinical delivery area. We need to help policy makers recognize those aspects of research, education, and training that will not survive well in a market-oriented system. They are the aspects that have elements of a public good, like a national park, in which group benefits outweigh the benefits to any individual. Public policy must be developed to support these aspects.

JEREMIAH BARONDESS: Let me take a minute to tell you an illuminating story about paradigm shift. When I was a "puppy" in medicine, the state-of-the-art treatment for acute myocardial infarction was strict bed rest. People were fed. They were not even permitted to turn over in bed by themselves; two people came and turned them. They lay in bed until their sedimentation rate was normal, this being the index that the inflammatory process had subsided. The treatment took six weeks on average. I can't tell you with what awe we approached those extraordinarily fragile people. They were literally not allowed to cut their own meat.

When the insurers said they would no longer pay for care of that duration, the system responded, and hospital stays for acute myocardial infarctions were cut in half fairly rapidly. Like Kuhn said, progress is not made in a logical, sequential order in which each step is based on the revelations of the prior step. It comes in jumps, and sometimes we jump for surprising reasons.

BEVRA HAHN: Do you think we should be teaching two separate groups in medical school: one group for efficient outpatient care in a managed care setting and the other for intensive inpatient care, so that the physician groups are different, as they are in Britain?

ROBERT MEENNAN: I don't know, Bevra. That is one step further than I would be prepared to go at this point. I think there are some basic steps that we need to take before we consider a two-track system. If we look at the current system with its basic science-driven first two years and its clinical specialist-controlled second two years, there are many aspects of it that we could change in terms of content, teachers, and learning sites. Such changes would go a long way toward producing medical school graduates who are prepared more appropriately for work in the new health care system. I would be concerned that the approach you suggest would spark debate and resistance that would actually make it more difficult to implement these other, more general changes in medical education.

JEREMIAH BARONDESS: I would add one codicil to that, in relation to medical education and especially residency training. I think that complex challenges in differential diagnosis and triage arise with every complaint presented by patients. We should be very careful, as we train the next generations of generalists, to be sure of two things. The first is that they should be trained rigorously for the complicated real-world challenges presented by ambulatory patients. The second is that generalists should expect of themselves a capacity to handle clinical problems of more than minimal levels of complexity. Whether we can effectively train people to do this by concentrating heavily on ambulatory care training environments is a serious question. Implicit in the idea of training people oriented around lesser clinical challenges, if you will, is the pressure to continue to train large numbers of subspecialists to whom generalists can refer people with more complex disorders. The cost implications of excessive numbers of subspecialists have been commented on very widely. The impact on the quality of care—especially that deriving from fragmentation and the resulting lack of coherence—has not achieved as high a profile.

11

Commentary on the Day's Papers

John W. Rowe

I have 10 things to say, and I am going to take only one minute for each, which means that my entire presentation will be substantially shorter than some of the three minute presentations of today's reactors.

First, I would agree with that contention of Bob Meenan and others that managed care is not inherently evil, and that, despite the moral hazard associated with the incentive for underuse, it has several attractive design features with respect to patients with chronic diseases such as rheumatoid arthritis or lupus. These include a tendency to decrease the perils of overuse or even misuse of services and the promose of continuity of care. I think of patients with rheumatoid arthritis seeing a different fellow in the clinic of an academic medical center every 6 months for the last 40 years. I am sure that is not the best possible arrangement. Vertical integration of care and more reliance on non-physician resources might be valuable. An increased focus on prevention and rehabilitation will certainly be valuable.

Secondly, we have heard that managed care is changing. As data are presented by individuals who have done very nice studies in this field, they are quick to tell us that their data are 6 months old and therefore may not be relevant to the current situation. We have also heard that many of the managed care entities are increasingly seeing that they need to add some support services and other services specifically for certain chronic disease populations. So, in addition to not being inherently evil, managed care is rapidly changing.

Third, health care, overall, appears to be just as good under managed care as it is when unmanaged. We can cut the pie some way to demonstrate that it is not as good as the old way of delivering care, but overall it seems to be pretty good. There are special populations that don't do nearly as well—the elderly and the poor in particular. However, both the Medical Outcomes Study and Ed Yelin's study, as well as Hal Holman's very nice studies on utilization and cost for osteoarthritis all show that overall, outcomes are pretty good in prepaid group/staff HMO settings.

However, these special populations—my fourth point—are very, very important. There seem to be two different parts to this and I think both are worth emphasizing. We heard from Karen Davis and again from Mick McGarvey that these populations have access problems, first in getting into and staying in any system, and then, after they are in, they have access problems related to the process of obtaining care within the system. I think those are two different things. Getting in and staying in the health care system is difficult for some individuals, but equally important is getting access to care if, for example, you don't have a telephone or transportation, a network of friends with these things, and so forth.

My fifth point is that, as Brad Gray, Karen Davis, and others pointed out, managed care entities are very variable. They are variable with respect to their content, their organization, their incentives, their training, and their results. I think that we should not even talk about managed care entities in general. Those of us in geriatric medicine like to say that the elderly aren't all the same, and that if you have seen one old person, you have seen one old person. We might want to think about managed care programs and entities in that same way, and try not to paint with such a broad brush. I suspect that new models will evolve as well.

It seemed to me that some of the data that were presented, and many of the concepts dicsussed, coalesced around four structural issues, my items six through nine, that are relevant to chronic disease and managed care.

The first of these, from what I heard, was practice guidelines. It seems to me that it is important for us to understand that there are at least three different kinds of practice guidelines. There are behavioral practice guidelines, which really were not mentioned but are really important in chronic disease. These are guidelines like "You should exercise," and getting you to understand that you should exercise. Then there are medical practice guidelines: "This is *how* you should exercise." The third type of practice guidelines are psychosocial, helping people deal with adaptation to chronic illness. These are very specific, and very different, and nowhere more important than in chronic disease.

The second structural aspect of managed care I heard about today that is important to chronic disease has to do with information systems. I think these are very important. That should be the front page, because one of the real advantages of managed care is the ability to follow patients. Providers can track medication use, for example, to see if their patients are using narcotics for pain. That should be routine in a good managed care entity with a good information system. It is a huge advantage to see how often patients are calling in, to see how often they are coming in, to be able to develop those report cards, to feed back the information, and to establish some quality assurance programs. An information system is a very important part of what needs to be done.

The third structural element is sustained patient education and support, and I heard two parts to this in different fragments of the discussion. The first part was how important that education is for vulnerable populations. The second is based on some specific data from the ver impressive study of Hal Holman and Kate Lorig on the self-management program for arthritis. This program decreases pain, decreases depression, decreases use of health care resources, and improves function. Such a program is a very important part of sustained management of all arthritis patients. It is probably not provided by many managed care entities, but it really should be.

The last structural element is practice redesign, teamwork, changing the way we practice. I loved the example that we heard earlier from the John Wasson study at the White River Junction VA, in which he increased the quality and decreased the cost simply by calling the patients on the phone. What a novel idea.

Let me leave you with a recommendation as my final point, number ten. Because it is always good to have something specific to recommend at the end of an day at the Institute of Medicine (IOM), I pondered as I sat there at the edge of my seat all day about what I could say that would be a specific recommendation. How could we do something specific, use our muscle, use our leverage?

An idea finally emerged, and I tried it on Karen Davis before she left. She didn't laugh, so I will try it on you. Karen's third recommendation was to try to establish standards for monitoring HMOs and what they do. We talked about the National Committee for Quality Assurance (NCQA) and the Health Plan Employer Data and Information Set (HEDIS) and how we need better, disease specific measures. It seems to me that there is a better, quicker, market driven opportunity that the IOM might push. The American Association of Retired Persons (AARP) decided two weeks ago that they were going to sell the AARP seal of approval to HMOs. HMOs will be very anxious to get that approval, and they will be willing to pay dearly for it. We should get AARP our view of programs to guarantee access, measure quality, keep track of patients with chronic disease, improve rheumatologists, and so forth. We should get those views written into the requirements that AARP sends out to these HMOs in their requests, demands, or specifications. These HMOs will have to say, this is what we are going to do for patients with RA or SLE in order to get the AARP seal of approval.

We can use the market and use our leverage at no cost, take the results of this day and this committee's work and get it incorporated into a program which might possibly influence a huge number of people. There are more members of AARP than there are citizens of Canada. That is my last point and my only recommendation.

12

Conclusions and Recommendations

The charge to this committee, and the basis for the workshop reported in the previous sections, entails the following questions:

1. Does the model of managed care or integrated delivery system (e.g., fully capitated managed care, gatekeeper-only model of managed care, discounted fee for service) influence (a) the types of interventions provided to patients with chronic conditions such as rheumatoid arthritis (RA) and systemic lupus erythematosus (SLE), and (b) the clinical and health status outcomes of those interventions?
2. If so, are these effects quantitatively and clinically significant, compared to the effects that other variables (such as income, education, or ethnicity) have on patient outcomes?
3. If the mode of health care delivery system appears to be related to patient care and outcomes, can specific organizational, financial, or other variables be identified to account for the relationships?
4. If not, what research agenda should be pursued to provide critical information about the relationship between types of health care systems and the processes and outcomes of care delivered to populations with serious chronic conditions?

As noted in the introduction to this report, the published evidence for differences in treatment received or outcomes achieved by RA and SLE patients in various health care delivery systems is practically nonexistent. The committee was unable to locate any such studies involving SLE. The most extensive comparison of delivery models and RA is that of Yelin and his colleagues, which he summarized for the committee at the workshop. They were unable to demonstrate significant differences between RA patients treated in fee-for-service (FFS) relationships and those treated in prepaid group practice health maintenance organizations (HMOs). All patients received some care from a specialist (rheumatologist). This finding is consistent with a larger body of data from studies of chronic diseases other than RA and SLE, although the data presented by Tarlov suggest that this may not hold true for certain vulnerable subsets of the chronically ill. The committee notes that lack of evidence for an effect does not constitute evidence for the absence of an effect, but the essentially negative answer to the first of the four questions in the charge would seem to rule out meaningful responses to questions 2 and 3, since they presuppose a positive answer to question 1. The rest of this chapter is therefore organized as a series of conclusions that the committee feels are justified by the current state of knowledge, and as recommendations for research that flow from these conclusions. The reader is referred to relevant portions of the workshop proceedings as appropriate. However, the committee was selected to bring a wide spectrum of experience and knowledge to bear on the task of answering these questions, and its conclusions and recommendations reflect the committee's own expertise as well as the data and opinions provided to it by the workshop's invited speakers and other participants. The committee alone bears full responsibility for the conclusions and recommendations.

CONCLUSION 1

Rheumatoid arthritis and systemic lupus erythematosus are very likely to be representative of a large number of chronic diseases that will increasingly come to dominate U.S health care. The study of systems of care for chronic diseases such as RA and SLE demands integrated research and longitudinal studies, despite the inherent limitations imposed by changing health care practices, physician and patient characteristics, population demographics, and limited funds.

Recommendation: The committee recommends that the National Institute of Arthritis and Musculoskeletal and Skin Diseases (NIAMS) seek additional funding to expand its research to include substantial support for high-quality studies that would allow a broad approach more closely linking scientific and technological advances to clinical trials, outcomes research, and health services research more generally. Although some of the required research is of the sort currently funded by the Agency for Health Care Policy and Research (AHCPR), there is much to be said for

bringing fundamental experimental research, clinical trials, and services or outcomes research on rheumatic disease under one roof, so that the benefits of a more coherent and unified approach might be realized. For example, studies might look at the way new technology is assessed and implemented in various types of managed care organizations and the rate of penetration and prevalence of application of medically accepted new technology in various types of managed care organizations.

CONCLUSION 2

Differences in the incidence and severity of chronic diseases such as RA and SLE among individuals are more likely to be due to patient factors such as genetics, age, education, and socioeconomic status than to medical care organization and financing, but outcomes are likely to depend on all of these factors. The committee's review of the literature and the workshop presentation by Davis and Schoen provided convincing evidence that income, age, education, and ethnicity are strongly related to morbidity and mortality from chronic disease in general and rheumatoid arthritis and systemic lupus in particular. The populations of individuals with RA or SLE are far from homogeneous. Just as managed care is not a useful term because it encompasses such a wide variety of care delivery variations, people with RA and SLE vary widely. Disease severity, comorbid conditions, ethnicity, income, age, and education have already been identified as variables that are strongly associated with the course of these diseases and the response to some treatments. It is not unreasonable to suppose that other socioeconomic variables will be discovered to be relevant, and it is almost certain to be the case that each of these variables will render some interventions highly desirable in certain cases and inappropriate in others.

Recommendation: Studies of clinical interventions, health care delivery systems, and clinical course and outcomes should examine clinical, demographic, ethnic, and other subsets of patients with RA and SLE.

CONCLUSION 3

Differences in delivery systems may well impact patient satisfaction and the types and intensity of interventions provided to RA and SLE patients, but to date there has been no clear and compelling demonstration of differential impact on the outcome or course of these diseases. As several speakers pointed out, the continuing evolution of health care delivery has already made simplistic comparisons such as managed care versus fee for service pointless or even misleading. Potentially relevant variables discussed at length at the workshop and often confounded in the existing literature assessing managed care are the method of payment (capitation versus fee for service, for both patient-to-plan and plan-to-provider payments), specialty of the provider (generalist versus subspecialist), and health and socioeconomic background of the enrolled population. Yelin, for example, pointed out that although his study of RA patients controlled for specialty type by drawing all of the subjects from the practices of California rheumatologists, this very consistency may well be the reason the study failed to reveal differences in treatment of patients in FFS and fully capitated HMOs.

Recommendation: Method of payment, medical specialty of the provider, and initial health and socioeconomic background of the patient subjects should be carefully controlled in future studies or, preferably, studied in their own right, and measures of health status and function should be included in addition to simply noting the interventions provided.

CONCLUSION 4

In addition to the pharmacologic and surgical interventions which are important elements of care for RA and SLE patients, several clinical and social interventions that are especially important for patient satisfaction and compliance, particularly strategies emphasizing the role of the patient in managing chronic diseases (i.e., self-management) were identified by our speakers. Holman's address and the associated commentary by Lappin draw together a variety of excellent management practices (subscriber and patient education programs, remote monitoring and support via telephone or visits, and aerobic exercise and strength conditioning programs, for example).

Recommendations: The incorporation of these clinical and social interventions into different health care delivery systems should be another area of research for NIAMS. In fact, the availability of such interventions would have to be considered in any evaluation of quality of care. Other research should focus on how these interventions might be improved and extended. For example, how can poorer, less educated patients and patients from different ethnic or cultural backgrounds be persuaded to take a more active role in the management of their rheumatic disease? Would "patient report cards" or more explicit planned feedback from

provider to patient make RA or SLE patients more effective team members in management of these diseases?

CONCLUSION 5

The elderly, the poor, and the chronically ill may well be differentially and adversely affected by enrollment in prepaid health care plans or plans with stong incentives for providers to limit services. Some of the data presented by Davis and Schoen and the data presented by Tarlov point to a significant interaction between the delivery system and age, income, and health status. Davis and Schoen, for example, reported that respondents to a Commonwealth Fund managed care survey who rated their health as fair or poor or who reported that they or a family member had a serious illness in the past year, rated their plans quite differently depending on the type of plan providing their care. Figure 2 in the paper by Davis and Schoen, for example, shows that patients in managed care systems of all types were more likely to rate their plan fair or poor in providing access to specialists than were unmanaged fee-for-service patients. Tarlov's longitudinal data from the Medical Outcomes Study highlighted precisely this type of interaction among patients with chronic conditions (some patients had a rheumatic disease, but the study entry criteria specified diabetes, hypertension, congestive heart failure, postacute myocardial infarction, or clinical depression). Although a comparison of FFS and HMO coverage using the study's entire sample revealed no differences in self-reported health over the course of the study, comparisons using subsamples of elderly, poor, or initially sicker subjects all yielded significant differences favoring fee-for-service systems. Tarlov suggested that this pattern in the data may be attributable to the relative cost of care for these groups. It may be that excessive medical costs have largely been incurred by a relatively healthy segment of the general population whereas expenditures for the aged, the poor, racial minorities, and those with chronic diseases have been more reflective of actual medical needs. Under such conditions, a general reduction of expenditures for health care would differentially impact these vulnerable subgroups even if care for the relatively healthy majority was not seriously compromised.

Recommendation: Future research should examine interactions of patient factors and system factors, and their effects on costs, clinical course, and outcomes rather than attempt straightforward univariate comparisons of the sort suggested by question 2 above.

CONCLUSION 6

It is generally believed that as many as 40 million Americans may be without health insurance of any kind. The charge to the committee assumes access to a health plan or health insurance by all persons with RA or SLE, but such access may be the most important determinant of care and outcome for all but the most affluent.

Recommendation: Community-based samples that include nonmembers of health plans should be included in longitudinal studies of differential disease course and functional status of RA and SLE patients.

CONCLUSION 7

The potential impact of "carve-outs" on persons with RA or SLE is not yet clear. This term refers to the practice of some health plans of treating a specific group of patients or services with special policies not applicable to the majority of the plan's enrollees. Mental health services, for example, may be provided at a different location, by a different group of providers, and/or at a different premium, fee, or capitation rate. The committee is concerned about access to plans, as well as services for enrolled patients once in a plan, and a potential advantage of the carve-out strategy is that it can remove or diminish the incentive for prepaid plans and fully capitated practices to avoid or discourage enrollment by individuals likely to require far more services than the average enrollee. Plans could, for example, carve enrollees with preexisting RA out of their standard agreement, assign a rheumatologist as their primary care provider, charge a premium more in line with their expected outlay, and provide the rheumatologist witha higher than average capitation payment.

Recommendation: NIAMS should encourage research investigating the possibility of increased access to health care plans by persons with RA and SLE where plans opt for, and states allow, such carve-outs.

CONCLUSION 8

Checklists and health plan report cards developed for purposes of accreditation or consumer education are useful, but still primitive developments and by their nature are unlikely to provide answers to the questions posed to the committee. Quality-of-care measures need further development if delivery models (health care plans) are to be usefully evaluated. The National Committee for Quality Assurance (NCQA) has emerged as the primary source of accreditation for health care plans, in a rough parallel with the Joint Commission on Accreditation of Healthcare Organizations (JCAHO) and hospital accreditation. The NCQA evaluation relies heavily on the Health Plan Employer Data and Information Set (HEDIS), which includes specific quality measures (e.g., immunization rates) as well as data on enrollee access to care, utilization of specific services, and satisfaction, along with financial indicators. The aim of this effort is to provide a standard set of data that will be useful to consumers (especially employers) faced with choosing a health plan. The implicit assumption that potential enrollees are most likely relatively healthy, full-time employees dictates that the measures be generic and/or focused on commonly used services. The current version of HEDIS, for example, has no data to help a person with RA or SLE find a health plan that is especially well equipped for managing these diseases. Future versions of HEDIS may contain an element addressing RA or even SLE, but given the intent of the evaluation it will certainly not contain more than one or two relevent items. Thus, it appears unlikely that report cards on health care plans will provide the type and quantity of data on specific chronic diseases that would allow valid comparisons of individual plans or plan types.

Recommendations: Reliable answers to the sort of generic questions posed by NIAMS will continue to require specific research projects using multivariate disease-specific measures of the sort listed by Matthew Liang in his reaction to Alvin Tarlov's presentation (the Arthritis Impact Measurement Scales, the Functional Status Index, and the SLE-Disease Activity Index, for example). The committee's pessimism about the utility of accreditation data for research purposes does not extend to the very large databases maintained by many health plans. With their defined populations and standardized treatment regimens, managed care plans represent a valuable research resource largely untapped to date. Privacy concerns must be addressed and resolved, but the committee recommends that NIAMS explore means of providing qualified researchers access to some of these databases as well as those associated with the Medicare and Medicaid experiments in managed care, with primary data from randomly selected member-patients to confirm the validity of the secondary data and fill in gaps in knowledge.

CONCLUSION 9

The question of the optimal utilization of subspecialists is still unresolved. A considerable portion of workshop discussion concerned the role of the rheumatologist in the management of RA and SLE, the stimulus being the increasingly common use of a generalist "gatekeeper" by managed care plans to control access to subspecialists. Rheumatologists were the focus of the discussion at the workshop, but it was recognized by all participants that the arguments are by no means unique to rheumatology or even chronic disease. The committee was divided over the utility of further studies comparing treatment and outcomes of RA or SLE patients who have rheumatologists as their sole or primary provider with patients managed primarily by nonrheumatologists. On the one hand it was pointed out that there is already some evidence, including the work reported by Yelin at the workshop, that RA patients may fare somewhat better under rheumatologists, and that the literature as a whole probably supports the conclusion that, all other things being equal, patients of subspecialists generally fare better. The counterargument was that the general literature seems to contain almost as many studies showing no advantage for patients of subspecialists as studies showing an advantage, and perhaps more importantly, in practice the question is not either/or, but when and how a rheumatologist should be involved.

Recommendations: A starting point for research might be an analysis of how specialty referral clinics and affiliated ancillary care providers achieve better outcomes when they do. Is this due to better diagnosis, more appropriate or more timely interventions, or better education and empowerment of patients and their families (to name only a few possibilities)? The committee agreed that some research on the nature of the referral process is certainly merited. Also deserving consideration would be studies investigating the cost-effectiveness of increased clinical training in chronic disease management for general internal medicine, family medicine, pediatrics, and geriatric specialists vis-a-vis continued investment in subspecialist training.

A FINAL NOTE

- Managed care is a powerful and still growing element of U.S. health care, although it is a heterogeneous movement the final form or forms of which are still evolving.
- Chronic disease is responsible for a large and growing proportion of health care utilization in the United States today, but those suffering from

these diseases are also highly heterogeneous.

- The growth of both managed care and chronic disease have cast work force issues into bold relief, demanding reanalysis of the optimal roles of generalists and subspecialists.
- The interaction of managed care and chronic disease is a complex nexus that requires new research paradigms, which should be as integrative as possible.

Appendix A

Biographies of Committee Members and Speakers

Saralynn H. Allaire, Sc.D., R.N., C.R.C., is Assistant Research Professor of Medicine, Boston University Arthritis Center. She holds a doctorate in rehabilitation counseling from Boston University in addition to a masters in nursing. Dr. Allaire's scholarly publications have focused on disability associated with rheumatoid arthritis and rehabilitation programs to overcome it. She is a Trustee of the Massachusetts Chapter of the Arthritis Foundation, and sits on the Education and Services Committee of the National Arthritis Foundation and the Medical and Scientific Advisory Board of Scleroderma Federation, Inc. for which she also writes a health information and exchange column.

William J. Arnold, M.D., F.A.C.P., has been Chairman of the Department of Medicine at Lutheran General Hospital since 1986. He directs the faculty practice plan for the 100 full-time faculty in the Department of Medicine as well as the overall activities of the Department of Medicine at Lutheran General Hospital. Prior to become Chairman, he was Director of the Section of Rheumatology at Lutheran General Hospital from 1977 to 1986. Dr. Arnold remains a practicing Rheumatologist with clinical and research interests in the application of arthroscopy to the management of patients with arthritis. Dr. Arnold practices in an arthritis center with seven other rheumatologists who are members of a 262-physician multispecialty group, the Advocate Medical Group, S.C. Dr. Arnold is a native Chicagoan who received his undergraduate education at the University of Illinois in Champaign-Urbana and went to medical school at the University of Illinois College of Medicine in Chicago. He received his training in Internal Medicine and Rheumatology at Duke

University Medical Center in Durham, North Carolina. Dr. Arnold has been a member of the Board of Governors of the American Board on Internal Medicine and is finishing a six-year term as a representative of the American Board of Internal Medicine on the Residency Review Committee for Internal Medicine. Dr. Arnold has previously been active in the American College of Rheumatology, most recently serving as a member of the Board of Directors. In addition, he serves as a member of the Board of Directors for two large integrated-delivery systems: the Advocate Health Care Network in Oak Brook, Illinois, and the Allina Health System in Minneapolis, Minnesota.

Elizabeth M. Badley, Ph.D., is an epidemiologist and health services researcher, who specializes in the epidemiology of chronic and disabling conditions, particularly musculoskeletal disorders. She is currently the Director of the Arthritis Community Research and Evaluation Unit (ACREU), Toronto, Canada. ACREU receives funding from the Ontario Ministry of Health to carry out research in partnership with The Arthritis Society, Ontario Division. She is a senior staff scientist at the Wellesley Hospital Research Institute. She has an appointment as Associate Professor in the Department of Preventive Medicine and Biostatistics at the University of Toronto, with cross-appointments to the Departments of Physical Therapy, Occupational Therapy and Medicine (Division of Rheumatology), University of Toronto. Prior to moving to Canada in 1989, she was Deputy Director of the Arthritis and Rheumatism Council Epidemiology Research Unit, University of Manchester, Manchester, UK. She has published widely on the epidemiology of rheumatic disorders and their impact in the population including use of health service, and on the assessment of impairments, disabilities and handicaps. Her research includes a major population survey, estimating the impact of musculoskeletal disorders through the analysis of large scale data sets, and applied research directed towards the development and evaluation of services for people with arthritis. She is a consultant to the World Health Organization on the classification of disablement, and has served on a number of international, national and local expert panels and committees concerned with health and welfare service delivery and community-based research.

Teresa J. Brady, Ph.D., is the Director of Chronic Disease Services for the Fairview Health System in Minneapolis. She is the project director for an internally funded demonstration project: Primary Care/Care Coordinator Partnership in Chronic Disease Management. She has 20 years of experience in health care for individuals with chronic diseases in a variety of roles and settings. Dr. Brady is active with the National Chronic Care Consortium. She is also a member of the Fairview Health System's Care Council, and Chronic Care Systems Committee, two internal groups that are developing the models, protocols, and structures necessary to provide effective and appropriate care to individuals with chronic disease in the new health care environment. Dr. Brady has a Ph.D. in Psychology from the University of Minnesota and a B.S. in Occupational Therapy from the University of North Dakota.

Leigh F. Callahan, Ph.D., is Associate Director of Thurston Arthritis Research Center and is a Research Associate in Rheumatology, and adjunct Assistant Professor of Epidemiology. She joined the School of Medicine faculty of the University of North Carolina at Chapel Hill in September, 1995. Prior to joining the Center, she was the Arthritis Epidemiologist in the Aging Studies Branch at the Centers for Disease Control and Prevention (CDC) in Atlanta, Georgia for 2 1/2 years. Dr. Callahan received her Ph.D. in Public Policy in 1992 from Vanderbilt University where she was a Research Associate in the Division of Rheumatology since 1981. She is currently the editor of *Arthritis Care and Research*, the official journal of the Association of Rheumatology Health Professionals (ARHP) and is a former President of the ARHP and sits on several committees for the American College of Rheumatology (ACR). Dr. Callahan presently serves as a of the National Arthritis Foundation and is a member of the Board of Trustees. She has served on numerous National and State committees and boards for the Arthritis Foundation for ten years.

Carolyn Clancy, M.D., is a general internist with research interests in the impact of financial incentives on physicians' decisions, womens' health and physicians' use of preventive services. She attended the University of Massachusetts Medical School (M.D., 1979), did a residency in internal medicine at Worcester Memorial Hospital (Massachusetts), and was a Kaiser Fellow in General Internal Medicine at The University of Pennsylvania from 1982–84. From 1984 through 1990 she was an assistant professor in the Department of Medicine at The Medical College of Virginia in Richmond. In November 1990, she came to the Agency for Health Care Policy and Research (AHCPR) in the Division of Primary Care, and is currently Director of the Center for Primary Care Research, as well as Acting Director of the Center for Outcomes and Effectiveness Research. While at AHCPR, she developed the curriculum for the Public Health Service Primary Care Policy Fellowship, for which she has served as Co-director (1992–94) and principal faculty (1992–present), and has published multiple papers on primary care and the effects of financing on access to care. She holds a clinical appointment in the Department of Health Care Sciences at George Washington University.

Karen Davis, Ph.D., is president of The Commonwealth Fund, a national philanthropy engaged in independent research on health and social policy issues. Ms. Davis assumed the presidency of the fourth oldest private foundation in the country on January 1, 1995. Established by Anna M. Harkness in 1918 with the broad charge to enhance the common good, the Fund seeks ways to help Americans live healthy and productive lives, giving special attention to those groups with serious and neglected problems. Karen Davis is a nationally recognized economist, with a distinguished career in public policy and research. Before joining the Fund, she served as chairman of the Department of Health Policy and Management at the School of Hygiene and Public Health at The Johns Hopkins University, and held an appointment as professor of economics. She served as deputy assistant secretary for health policy in the Department of Health and Human Services from 1977 to 1980, and was the first woman to head a U.S. Public Health Service agency. Prior to her government career, Ms. Davis was a senior fellow at the Brookings Institution in Washington, D.C., a Visiting Lecturer at Harvard University, and an assistant professor of economics at Rice University. A native of Oklahoma, she received her doctoral degree in economics from Rice University, which recognized her achievements with a Distinguished Alumna award in 1991. Ms. Davis has published a number of significant books, monographs, and articles on health and social policy issues, including the landmark books, *Health Care Cost Containment, Medicare Policy, National Health Insurance: Benefits, Costs, and Consequences,* and *Health and the War on Poverty: A Ten-Year Appraisal.* She is the president of the Association of Health Services Research and a member of the National Academy of Sciences Institute of Medicine, the Kaiser Commission on the Future of Medicaid, and the Comptroller General's Health Advisory Committee, General Accounting Office. She serves on the Board of Directors of the Somatix Therapy Corporation and the Mount Sinai Medical Center.

John M. Eisenberg, M.D., M.B.A., is Chairman of the Department of Medicine, Physician-in-Chief, and Anton and Margaret Fuisz Professor of Medicine at Georgetown University Medical Center. Dr. Eisenberg is a graduate of Princeton University (1968) and Washington University School of Medicine, St. Louis (1972). After his residency in Internal Medicine at the Hospital of the University of Pennsylvania, Dr. Eisenberg was a Robert Wood Johnson Foundation Clinical Scholar and earned a Master of Business Administration degree at the Wharton School. He served as Chief of the Division of General Internal Medicine at the University of Pennsylvania from 1978–1992 and was Sol Katz Professor of General Internal Medicine. Dr. Eisenberg was a Commissioner on the Congressional Physician Payment Review Commission from 1986 through 1995 and was Chairman from 1993–1995. He has served in various capacities in the arena of health outcomes and health economics, including: President of the Society for General Internal Medicine, Vice President of the Society of Medical Decision

Making; and the first physician to be elected President of the Association for Health Services Research. He has been elected to a number of honorary societies, including the Institute of Medicine of the National Academy of Sciences, the American Society for Clinical Investigation, and the Association of American Physicians. Since 1992 Dr. Eisenberg has been Program Director of the Robert Wood Johnson Foundation's Generalist Physician Faculty Scholars Program. Dr. Eisenberg is the author of two books and over 200 articles and chapters on topics such as physicians' practices, test use and efficacy, medical education and clinical economics.

Alan M. Fogelman, M.D., is the William S. Adams Professor of Medicine and Executive Chairman, Department of Medicine at the University of California, Los Angeles School of Medicine from which he also graduated. He is also the Director of the UCLA Atherosclerosis Research Unit in the UCLA Division of Cardiology. He has served as a member of the NIH Metabolism Study Section and of the NHLBI Program Project Review Committee. He is the Editor of *Arteriosclerosis, Thrombosis and Vascular Biology* and has served as Editor-in-Chief of the *Journal of Lipid Research.* He has been a member of the editorial committee of the American Society for Clinical Investigation and served as President of the Western Society of Clinical Investigation. He is a member of the Board of Directors of the American Board of Internal Medicine and a member of the Board of Directors of the Association of Professors of Medicine.

Deborah Freund, M.P.H., Ph.D., has served as Vice Chancellor for Academic Affairs at Indiana University Bloomington (IUB) since January, 1994 and Director of The Bowen Research Center since 1990. She received her A.B. in classical languages from Washington University in St. Louis in 1973, plus an M.P.H. in medical care organization in 1975, an M. A. in applied economics in 1975 and a Ph. D. in economics in 1980, all from The University of Michigan. Dr. Freund is the author of two books and over 100 articles and chapters. She has also been the principal investigator or Co-P.I. on $32 million in research grants and has served on many study sections for various agencies and major private foundations. Included was the Patient Outcome Research Team on Knee Arthritis on which she was the principal investigator. She is particularly noted for her research on Medicaid, health care outcomes and pharmaceuticals. She is credited with being one of the founders of the field of pharmacoeconomics. She has been on the editorial board of 9 journals in her fields of health economics and health services research. For her efforts, she has been awarded three research prizes, from the American Public Health Association, The Association of Public Policy Analysis and Management and The Wisconsin Medical Society. Her research has also resulted in the enactment of public policies in the United States and in Australia.

Bradford H. Gray, Ph.D. (Yale University, 1973), is Director of the Institution for Social and Policy Studies and the Program on Non-Profit Organizations at Yale University, and Professor (Adjunct) of Research in Public Health at the Yale School of Medicine. He also holds an appointment in Yale's Department of Sociology. He is author of *The Profit Motive and Patient Care: The Changing Accountability of Doctors and Hospitals* (Harvard University Press, 1991) and *Human Subjects in Medical Experimentation* (NY: Wiley, 1975) and editor of *The New Health Care for Profit* (Washington, National Academy Press, 1983), *For-Profit Enterprise in Health Care* (Washington, National Academy Press, 1986), and (with Marilyn J. Field) *Controlling Costs and Changing Patient Care? The Role of Utilization Management* (Washington, National Academy Press, 1989). He came to Yale in 1989 from the Institute of Medicine, National Academy of Sciences, where he was the director and primary author of six major reports. In Washington, he also served on the staffs of the National Commission for the Protection of Human Subjects of Biomedical and Behavioral Research and the President's Commission for the Study of Ethical Problems in Medicine and Research. He directed national studies of the conduct and regulation of research involving human subjects for both commissions and was also the primary author of reports by both bodies. Prior to going to Washington, he taught at the University of North Carolina at Chapel Hill (1971–1975). He has chaired several committees of the American Sociological Association and the American Public Health Association and serves on the advisory boards of the *Bibliography of Bioethics*, *IRB: A Journal of Human Studies*, and Lyceum Books. He has served as a consultant to several governmental agencies, foundations, trade associations, and the National Academy of Sciences.

Jerome H. Grossman, M.D., F.A.C.P., is the Chairman and CEO of a newly formed corporation, Health Quality, Inc., and of The Lion Gate Foundation. He is also Professor of Medicine at Tufts University School of Medicine. A graduate of the Massachusetts Institute of Technology in 1961, Dr. Grossman received his M.D. from the University of Pennsylvania School of Medicine in 1965. He joined the staff of Massachusetts General Hospital in 1966, where he served in a variety of positions including Director of Ambulatory Care, Associate Physician, and Assistant Professor of Medicine at Harvard Medical School. From 1979 through 1995, Dr. Grossman served at New England Medical Center as President and subsequently Chairman and Chief Executive Officer, and has recently been elected Chairman Emeritus. Dr. Grossman is known for his leadership in the evolving role of the academic health center in American medicine. From 1966 to 1972, he was one of the original staff of the Harvard Community Health Plan Health Maintenance Organizational (HMO), where he developed the world's first automated medical record system, known as COSTAR, to support the HMO's patient care and academic missions. In 1981 he was one of the founders of the Tufts Associated Health Plan, a network based IPA HMO. Dr. Grossman has served as Program Director of the Commonwealth Fund Task Force on Academic Health Centers; as an Administrative Board member of the Association of American Medical Colleges and subsequently as chairman of its Council of Teaching Hospitals; and as Chairman of the Academic Medical Center Consortium, a cooperative of twelve leading Academic Medical Centers that pioneered the use of health services research techniques to develop and implement effective and efficient health care delivery strategies. Dr. Grossman founded The Health Institute of New England Medical Center in 1988 for the purpose of expanding the Medical Center's research capacity to include the social sciences as well as natural sciences. The work of The Center involves research and development programs and practical applications in the areas of medical outcomes, functional health status, the organization and operation of the health care system, and the relationship of health status to other non-biological factors in society at large, such as income and education. In recent years, Dr. Grossman has worked to encourage development of strategies to reform the health care system at both the local and national level. In Massachusetts, he is a founding director of the Health Action Forum of Greater Boston, a member of the Health Care Committee of the Massachusetts Business Roundtable, and he served as Co-Chairman of the Health Care Industry Task Force of the Governor's Council on Economic Growth and Technology. He is spending 1996 as a Scholar-in-Residence at the Institute of Medicine studying public policy and lawmaking at the federal level.

Bevra H. Hahn, M.D., is Professor of Medicine and Chief of the Division of Rheumatology at the School of Medicine, University of California, Los Angeles, a position she has held since 1983. A summa cum laude graduate of Ohio State University, Dr. Hahn received her medical degree from Johns Hopkins and did an internship and residency in medicine in St. Louis at Barnes Hospital, Washington University. She is a Fellow of the American College of Rheumatology, and is currently serving on its Board of Directors for the second time. She was elected Treasurer of that organization for 1994–95, and President of the Central (1981–83) and Western (1994–95) Regions. Among her many awards are the Dunlop-Dottridge Award of the Canadian Rheumatism Association for research in rheumatology, the Joseph Bunim Medal and Prize of the American College of Rheumatology, the Holley Research prize in Rheumatology, the Southern California Arthritis Foundation's Klinenberg Medal for Arthritis Research, the Carol-Nachman

Award for Rheumatology Research, and the Jane Wyman Humanitarian Award for 1996. Dr. Hahn has authored close to 80 peer-reviewed research papers and over 40 book chapters or reviews as well as serving as co-editor of an influential textbook on lupus erythematosus. She is on the editorial boards of both the *Journal of Clinical Investigation* and the *Annals of Internal Medicine*. Her current research on the pathogenesis and treatment of lupus is funded by grants from the National Institutes of Health, Baxter Healthcare Corporation, the Arthritis Foundation (National and Southern California Chapters), and the Lupus Foundation of America, and support from the Bertram Maltz, M.D. Laboratory of Molecular Rheumatology and the Jeramie Dreyfuss Laboratory for Lupus Research at UCLA.

William R. Hazzard, M.D., is Director of the J. Paul Sticht Center on Aging at the Bowman Gray School of Medicine of Wake Forest University and Chairman of the Department of Internal Medicine at that institution. A native of Ann Arbor, Michigan and a product of the Ann Arbor public schools, Dr. Hazzard received his undergraduate education at Cornell University and graduated from its medical school in 1962. His postgraduate medical education included a medical internship at the New York Hospital and residency at the University of Washington Affiliated Hospitals in Seattle, where he also completed a fellowship in Endocrinology and Metabolism prior to joining the faculty at that institution (1969–1982). He then moved to Johns Hopkins University Medical School in Baltimore, where he was Associate Director of the Department of Medicine and charter director of the Center on Aging at that institution (1982–1986) prior to moving to Winston-Salem in 1986. Throughout his professional career his enduring intellectual interest has been in issues related to sexual dimorphism, notably in the sex steroid-mediated gender differential in lipoprotein metabolism and cardiovascular disease and, more recently, the sex differential in longevity and the medical and social problems of older persons, notably women.

Halsted R. Holman, M.D., is Guggenheim Professor of Medicine at the Stanford University School of Medicine. He served as Chairman of the Department of Medicine for more than a decade, and is now Program Director for the Carnegie-Commonwealth and Robert Wood Johnson Foundation Clinical Scholar Training Program as well as Co-Chief of the Division of Family and Community Medicine. Since 1977 Dr. Holman has also served as Program Director for the Stanford Multi-Purpose Arthritis Center. Among the many awards he has received since receiving his medical degree from Yale have been Kaiser awards for Excellence in Clinical Teaching (from Stanford students) and for outstanding innovative contributions to medicine education (from Stanford School of Medicine faculty). He received the Laureate award from the Northern California Chapter of the American College of Physicians, and was selected as Master by the American College of Rheumatology and Fellow by the American Association for the Advancement of Science. Formerly president of the Western Association of Physicians and the American Society for Clinical Investigation, he now serves on the Advisory Committee for the Kaiser Health Plan Project on chronic care coordination.

Debra R. Lappin, Esq., currently serves as Chair of the National Arthritis Foundation. Over the past decade she has worked with the Arthritis Foundation as Senior Vice Chair, Secretary, and Vice Chair of the Board of Trustees, Chair of the Rocky Mountain Chapter, and in numerous committee positions. Her work, which includes frequent public appearances on behalf of the Foundation, is focused in the areas of public policy and advocacy, research and programs especially as they relate to preserving the quality of life for people with arthritis, and access to care for people with arthritis within changing healthcare systems. Ms. Lappin served as a member of the NIAMS Advisory Council from 1991 to 1995. Professionally, Ms. Lappin has served as a partner with the national law firm of Mayer, Brown & Platt, as General Counsel for the U.S. operations of Dome Petroleum Corp., and as an associate with the Denver law firm, Dufford and Brown. Her professional and civic activities have included membership in the American Arbitration Association, the Board of Governors of the Colorado Bar Association, the Board of Advisors of the National Center for preventive Law, and the Colorado Association of Commerce and Industry, Blueprint for Colorado, Health Care Task Force.

Norman G. Levinsky, M.D., is Chairman of the Department of Medicine at Boston University Medical Center and serves as Chief of Medicine both at Boston City Hospital and at the Boston University Medical Center Hospital. A graduate of Harvard College and Harvard Medical School, he received postgraduate training in internal medicine at Beth Israel Hospital. He served as a fellow in renal physiology in the laboratory of Robert W. Berliner at the National Institutes of Health, and as a fellow in nephrology at Boston University Medical Center under Dr. Arnold S. Relman. Dr. Levinsky's initial academic pursuits were in clinical nephrology and renal physiology. He has published research and clinical studies of the regulation of sodium excretion in the kidney, the concentration of the urine, and acute renal failure. In addition, Dr. Levinsky has published numerous book chapters and reviews in these and other scientific and clinical areas. During much of this period in his career, Dr. Levinsky served as Chief of the Renal Section at Boston University Medical Center. In 1968 Dr. Levinsky became Chief of the Boston University Medical Service at Boston City Hospital and in 1972 was appointed Wade Professor and Chairman of the Department of Medicine at Boston University and Chief of Medicine at University Hospital. Under his leadership, the Department of Medicine has greatly expanded in size, has established an outstanding medical residency program, and maintains a vigorous research program which involves specialized research departments both at Boston University Medical Center and Boston City Hospitals. Dr. Levinsky's recent academic interests include medical ethics, rationing, and medical education. He has written numerous articles in these areas and has appeared on regional and national panels and programs discussing these issues. From 1988 to 1990 he served as Chairman of the Institute of Medicine's Committee to Study the Medicare End-Stage Renal Disease Program. He is currently serving as Chair of the Institute of Medicine's Committee on Xenotransplantation: Ethical Issues and Public Policy. Dr. Levinsky is a member of numerous academic societies, including the American Society for Clinical Investigation, the American College of Physicians, and the Association of American Physicians. He has served as secretary-treasurer and president of the Association of Professors of Medicine. He has been awarded a Mastership of the American College of Physicians and in 1992 received its Distinguished Teacher Award. Dr. Levinsky lives in Newton, Massachusetts with his wife. They are the parents of three children.

Matthew H. Liang, M.D., M.P.H., is Professor of Medicine at Harvard Medical School and Professor of Health Policy and Management at the Harvard School of Public Health. He is the Director of the Robert B. Brigham Multipurpose Arthritis and Musculoskeletal Diseases Center at the Brigham and Women's Hospital, a multidisciplinary research group performing studies on outcome, technology assessment, clinical decision making, clinimetrics, and the epidemiology of rheumatic disease disability and modifiable risk factors for high risk populations with rheumatic and musculoskeletal diseases. He is an Attending Physician in the Division of General Medicine and the Division of Rheumatology and Immunology at the Brigham and Women's Hospital, the Medical Director of Rehabilitation Services at Brigham and Women's Hospital, and the Medical Director of the Mariner at Longwood Subacute Rehabilitation Center in Boston. He is one of the principal faculty of the Clinical Effectiveness Program at the Harvard School of Public Health which teaches clinical research methods to clinician scientists and runs the clinical research training program in the Division of Rheumatology and Immunology and has trained over 30 individuals ranging from Instructor to Professor. Dr. Liang has served on a number of national committees for the Arthritis Foundation, the National Institutes of Health, the VA Hospitals, the Canadian Arthritis Society. He is on the Editorial Boards of a number of publications and a member of the Board of the Medical Foundation and the Arthritis Foundation. He directed the development of the guidelines for arthritis and musculoskeletal diseases and served on committees which developed the guidelines on low back pain and whiplash injuries. Dr. Liang is a graduate of Johns Hopkins University, Harvard Medical School, and Harvard School of Public Health. He has authored over 200 publications.

Larry M. Manheim, Ph.D., is Acting Director of the Program in Health Care Financing at the Institute for Health Services Research and Policy Studies, Northwestern University, and Research Scientist at the Veterans Administrations Midwest Center for Health Services and Policy Research. After earning his doctorate in economics at the University of California, Berkeley, Dr. Manheim held positions with Mathematics Policy Research, Inc. with the Civil Aeronautics Board, and with the Interstate Commerce Commission before coming to Northwestern. He has been principal investigator on numerous grants from private and public sources, including a feasibility grant to survey rheumatologists on imports of HMOs on rheumatology practice. His publications include a wide variety of topics related to hospital costs and the organization and delivery of health care.

Michael R. McGarvey, M.D., is Senior Vice President of Health Industry Services for Blue Cross and Blue Shield of New Jersey, Inc., the state's largest health insurer providing coverage for more than 2 million people. As Senior Vice President, Dr. McGarvey is responsible for all aspects of BCBSNJ's managed care operations in New Jersey, as well as market research, product development, provider relations and health care management. Dr. McGarvey has more than 25 years of experience in health care delivery and administration. Before joining BCBSNJ he was Managing Director of Health strategies for Alexander & Alexander Consulting Group, a leading international human resources and benefits consulting organization. Previously, he was an executive with Empire Blue Cross and Blue Shield, New York, first as Vice President of Health Services Management, then as Corporate Vice President of Health Affairs. He is a former Chief Medical Officer and Deputy Director for the New York State Department of Health's Office of Health Systems Management, and a former Vice President for Health Affairs and Professor of Health Sciences at Hunter College of the City University of New York. Dr. McGarvey is a Trustee of the New York Academy of Medicine, and a Director of the New York County Society of Internal Medicine and the American Medical Review Research Center. Dr. McGarvey received his medical degree from the University of Southern California School of Medicine. He is licensed to practice medicine in New York and California.

Robert E. Mechanic, M.B.A., is a Senior Manager at Lewin-VHI where he specializes in health care financing and reimbursement. Mr. Mechanic manages the firm's analytic modeling of hospital capacity, reimbursement and financial performance and has conducted a series of studies on the impact of health care reform and managed care on academic medical centers. He has conducted a wide range of strategic planning studies for health care providers, insurers, government agencies, foundations, and associations. In work with the American College of Rheumatology, Mr. Mechanic prepared a managed care monograph for rheumatologists and a computer model to project future work force supply and demand. He has assisted government agencies and special commissions in the design and analysis of health care reform proposals at the national level and in a variety of states including Utah, North Carolina, Maryland, Delaware and West Virginia. Mr. Mechanic has worked with over a dozen states on Medicaid financing and reimbursement policy and has conducted numerous studies of federal health care programs including the Federal Employees Health Benefits Program (FEHBP) and Medicare's hospital prospective payment system (PPS). Prior to joining Lewin-VHI, Mr. Mechanic was an analyst at the Congressional Budget Office. He holds an M.B.A. in finance from the Wharton School at the University of Pennsylvania and a B.S. in Economics with distinction from the University of Wisconsin.

Robert F. Meenan, M.D., M.P.H., M.B.A., is the Director of the Boston University School of Public Health. He also serves as Chairman of the Department of Socio-Medical Sciences and Community Medicine, Associate Dean for Public Health, and Professor of Medicine and Public Health at Boston University School of Medicine. Dr. Meenan is a graduate of Harvard College, Boston University School of Medicine, the School of Public Health at the University of California, Berkeley (M.P.H. in Health Planning and Administration), and the Graduate School of Management at Boston University (M.B.A. in Health Care Management). He trained in Internal Medicine at Boston City Hospital and in Rheumatology at the University of California, San Francisco. He is a member of the American Society for Clinical Investigation, a past president of the American College of Rheumatology, and a member of the Board of Trustees of the Arthritis Foundation at both the national and state levels. Dr. Meenan's research interests focus on outcome measurement and health economics as they relate to rheumatic diseases.

Robert J. Newcomer, Ph.D., is Professor and Chair of the Medical Sociology program at the School of Nursing, University of California, San Francisco and a faculty member in the Institute for Health & Aging. He earned a masters in city planning from the University of Southern California in 1971 and completed a Ph.D. there in 1975. He joined the research faculty at the University of California, San Francisco in the fall of 1976 where he later directed an extensive study of state, area, and community agency programs on aging. Dr. Newcomer then directed the National Policy Center on Health, a center grant providing technical assistance to the Administration on Aging and the network of state and area agencies. During the past 10 years he has been involved in studies and consultation with managed care systems, both as an evaluator of program performance (including patient surveys, administrative data systems, Medicare claims systems), and in the formulation of delivery models for the high risk plan members. His current work includes the development of a framework for chronic care monitoring and high risk patient identification in managed health plans. As part of this work, he was the principal investigator of the Social Health Maintenance Organization (S/HMO) Demonstration evaluation, a five year evaluation funded by the Health Care Financing Administration that involved a 36-month longitudinal analysis of Medicare Part A and B claims data, collection of primary data on health status, service use, health plan choice, and health care satisfaction, and case study analyses of four project sites. Dr. Newcomer and his team are now collaborating with the University of Minnesota in the design and implementation of the second generation of the S/HMO. Dr. Newcomer has concurrently (1989-1996) directed a five year evaluation and technical assistance project involving Medicare reimbursement for case management and home care benefits to persons with dementia, and he has recently completed a three year project for the Robert Wood Johnson Foundation examining potential indicators and data sources for tracking the service needs, use, and processes of care for those with chronic health conditions. Dr. Newcomer has published more than 60 articles and book chapters and seven books, including *Indicators of Chronic Health Conditions: Monitoring Community-Level Delivery Systems* (with A.E. Benjamin), which will be published by the Johns Hopkins University Press in 1997, and *Managed Care and Quality Assurance: Integrating Acute and Chronic Care* (with Anne Wilkinson),published in 1996 by Springer Publications.

Mark Robbins, M.D., M.P.H., has been practicing rheumatology within the staff model of Harvard Community Health Plan, now the mixed IPA, group, and staff model Harvard Pilgrim Health Care with 1.2 million members. Elected by his 600 physician peers, he serves on the Physician's Council of the HPHC Health Centers Division. During this time he has also been involved in health services research and consulting for a Boston-based public health consulting firm called John Snow, Inc. He has worked for state primary care associations around issues of community and migrant health centers market position and ability to deliver managed care. He is currently working on two Robert Wood Johnson studies of managed care. This first study benchmarks the most innovative practices of large employers and business coalitions in evaluating and purchasing health care services in four distinct health care markets (Boston, San Francisco, Orlando, Minneapolis) and their impact on managed care organizations. The second study for the State of Florida, Agency for Health Care Administration, is an organizational assessment of evolving managed care and alternative integrated delivery systems (PHOs) across the state. He has recently participated in the American College of Rheumatology's ad hoc committee on clinical guidelines for rheumatoid arthritis and the consensus panel on Manpower Planning for Rheumatology through 2010.

Naomi Rothfield, M.D., has been Chief of the Division of Rheumatic Diseases at the University of Connecticut School of Medicine since 1972. She directs a faculty of 12 physicians and basic scientists who carry out basic and clinical research and a busy rheumatology clinical practice with daily outpatient sessions. The Division also is responsible for the teaching of nearly 50 medical and orthopedic residents in addition to providing teaching for medical students. She has been the Director of the NIAMS funded University of Connecticut Arthritis and Musculoskeletal Diseases Center since 1979. Dr. Rothfield graduated from New York University School of Medicine and did her rheumatology fellowship at New York University School of Medicine/Bellevue Hospital under the supervision of Drs. Currier McEwen and Edward S. Franklin and remained there on the faculty until moving to University of Connecticut in 1968. She has published extensively on systemic and cutaneous lupus, and on autoantibodies in various rheumatic diseases. She has served on the Editorial Boards of a number of journals. She has authored more than 200 publications and has served on Study Sections for the NIH, the Arthritis Foundation, and the Veterans Administration. She was selected as a Master by the American College of Rheumatology, and received an Achievement Award from the Afro-American College of Rheumatology . In 1995 she was the recipient of the Solomon A. Berson Alumni Achievement Award in Clinical Science from New York University School of Medicine. She is a member of a number of academic societies including the American Society for Clinical Investigation and the Association of American Physicians. Dr. Rothfield is married to Lawrence Rothfield, M.D., Professor of Microbiology, University of Connecticut School of Medicine. They are the parents of 4 children and have 5 grandchildren.

John W. Rowe, M.D., is President of the Mount Sinai School of Medicine and The Mount Sinai Hospital in New York City, where he also serves as a Professor of Medicine and of Geriatrics. Mount Sinai one of the nation's largest academic health science centers, has the only formal medical school department of geriatrics in the United States. The Mount Sinai Health System, one of the nation's largest regional systems, extends throughout the greater metropolitan area and provides an accessible, high-quality integrated network of care. Before joining Mount Sinai in 1988, Dr. Rowe was a Professor of Medicine and the founding Director of the Division on Aging at Harvard Medical School and Chief of Gerontology at Boston's Beth Israel Hospital.

He has authored over 200 scientific publications, mostly in the physiology of the aging process, and a leading textbook of geriatric medicine. Dr. Rowe has received many honors and awards for his research and health policy efforts regarding care of the elderly including the Allied Signal Award in 1995. Dr. Rowe is Director of the MacArthur Foundation Research Network on Successful Aging. He served on the Board of Governors of the American Board of Internal Medicine and is a member of the Institute of Medicine of the National Academy of Sciences.

Alvin R. Tarlov, M.D., served for 13 years as Chairman of the Department of Medicine at the University of Chicago, later for seven years as President of the Henry J. Kaiser Family Foundation, and from 1990 through December, 1994 he was the Director of the Division of Health Improvement, The Health Institute, New England Medical Center. He holds professorships at two universities, Tufts and Harvard. Dr. Tarlov's research interests have been in health manpower (Chairman and author of the Graduate Medical Education National Advisory Committee Report), and in measuring the effects of medical services. He was the founder in 1983 of The Medical Outcomes Study and continues actively in analysis and interpretation of the results. He is President of the Medical Outcomes Trust, a non-profit public service organization that is a depository and distributor of high quality standardized questionnaires that measure health-related quality of life. In 1994 Dr. Tarlov became Chairman of the Board and President of the Massachusetts Health Data Consortium. In January, 1995 Dr. Tarlov was named Executive Director of The Health Institute at New England Medical Center.

Edward Yelin, Ph.D., is Director of the Education, Epidemiology, and Health Services Research Component of the Multipurpose Arthritis Center at the University of California-San Francisco. He is also a member of the Division of Occupational and Environmental Medicine at UCSF; a member of the faculty of the Institute for Health Policy Studies and the Aging Health Policy Center at UCSF. He received his A.B. in public affairs from the University of Chicago, and his M.C.P. and Ph.D. in City and Regional Planning from the University of California-Berkeley. He is an active member of the Arthritis Foundation, and the American College of Rheumatology.

Appendix B

Workshop Guests

Joyce Dubow
Senior Analyst
Public Policy Institute
American Association of Retired Persons

Robert S. Epstein, M.D., M.S.
Vice President
Merck-Medco

Theodore Fields, M.D.
Director
Rheumatology Faculty Practice Plan
Hospital for Special Surgery
Cornell Medical School

Richard Finkbiner, M.D., Ph.D.
Senior Analyst
The National Committee for Quality Assurance

Claude Earl Fox, M.D., M.P.H.
Deputy Assistant Secretary for Health (Disease Prevention and Health Promotion)
Public Health Service
US Department of Health and Human Services

Julia Freeman, Ph.D
Director, Centers Program
National Institute of Arthritis and Musculoskeletal and Skin Diseases

Steven J. Hausman, Ph.D.
Deputy Director
National Institute of Arthritis and Musculoskeletal and Skin Diseases

John Huber
Executive Director
Lupus Foundation
of America

John K. Iglehart
Editor, Health Affairs Quarterly
National Correspondent
New England Journal of
Medicine

Stanley B. Jones
Director
George Washington University
Health Insurance Reform
Project

Stephen I. Katz, M.D.
Director
National Institute of Arthritis
and Musculoskeletal and Skin
Diseases

Harry R. Kimball, M.D.
President
American Board of Internal
Medicine

C. Ronald MacKenzie, M.D.
Assistant Professor
of Internal Medicine
Hospital for Special Surgery
Cornell Medical School

Laura Robbins, D.S.W.
Director, Education Division
Hospital for Special Surgery
Cornell Medical School

Helen Simon
Director, Office of Program
Planning and Evaluation
National Institute of Arthritis
and Musculoskeletal and Skin
Diseases

Susana Serrate-Sztein, M.D.
Chief, Rheumatic Diseases
Branch
National Institute of Arthritis
and Musculoskeletal and Skin
Diseases